IEG | **WORLD BANK GROUP**
INDEPENDENT EVALUATION GROUP | World Bank • IFC • MIGA

World Bank Group Support to Public-Private Partnerships

LESSONS FROM EXPERIENCE IN CLIENT COUNTRIES, FY02–12

Contents

Figures

Tables

Abbreviations

AAA	analytic and advisory activity
ADB	Asian Development Bank
AfDB	African Development Bank
BOT	build, own, and transfer
C3P	PPP advisory services (IFC)
CAS	Country Assistance Strategy
CSO	civil society organization
DBO	design, build, operate
EBRD	European Bank for Reconstruction and Development
EIB	European Investment Bank
EIU	Economist Intelligence Unit
EU	European Union
FDI	foreign direct investment
GDP	gross domestic product
IBRD	International Bank for Reconstruction and Development
ICR	Implementation Completion and Results Report
IDA	International Development Association
IDB	Inter-American Development Bank
IEG	Independent Evaluation Group
IFC	International Finance Corporation

IICCR	Institutional Investor Country Credit Rating
LIC	low-income country
LMIC	lower-middle-income country
MDB	multilateral development bank
MEI	municipal and environmental infrastructure (EBRD)
MIC	middle-income country
MIGA	Multilateral Investment Guarantee Agency
NSG	non-sovereign guarantee
OECD	Organisation for Economic Co-operation and Development
PCR	Project Completion Report
PER	Project Evaluation Report
PPA	power purchasing agreement
PPI	private participation in infrastructure
PPIAF	Public-Private Infrastructure Advisory Facility
PPP	public-private partnership
PRG	partial risk guarantee
PRI	political risk insurance
UMIC	upper-middle-income country
VfM	value for money
WBI	World Bank Institute
XPSR	Expanded Project Supervision Report (IFC)

Acknowledgments

This evaluation of the World Bank Group's Support to public-private partnerships was prepared by a team from the Independent Evaluation Group led by Stefan Apfalter. It was carried out under the direction of Marvin Taylor-Dormond (Director), Stoyan Tenev (Manager), and Andrew Stone (Head, Macro Evaluation), and the overall guidance of Caroline Heider (Director General, Evaluation).

Team members (in alphabetical order) were Iradj Alikhani, Sotero Arizu, Asita de Silva, Houqi Hong, Takatoshi Kamezawa, Victor Malca, Urvaksh Patel, Maria Elena Pinglo, Sanjivi Rajasingham, Ida Scarpino, and Aurora Siy. Crucial contributions related to risk factors came from Hiroyuki Hatashima, sector-specific knowledge from Michael Latham on education and from Antonia Remenyi on health, and data analysis from Anqing Shi. The report also benefited from contributions from Kelly Andrews Johnson, Beata Lenard, and Raghavan Narayanan on IFC advisory services and investments. Additional guidance was provided by Ade Freeman. Heather Dittbrenner edited the report and Emelda Cudilla provided administrative support and formatted the report.

The peer reviewers were Gary Bond, former Manager, International Finance Corporation/ Infrastructure, and Director, Monitoring and Impact Assessment, European Bank for Reconstruction and Development; Raymond Bordeaux, Lead Infrastructure Specialist; and Rosario Macario, Professor at the Instituto Superior Técnico at the Lisbon Technical University.

Overview

HIGHLIGHTS

Public-private partnerships (PPPs) have seen a rise in the last two decades and are now used in more than 134 developing countries, contributing about 15–20 percent of total infrastructure investment. Nonetheless, most developing countries—and the World Bank Group itself in its latest strategy *A Stronger, Connected Solutions World Bank Group*—continue to see significant potential and need for expanded use of PPPs to help overcome inadequate infrastructure, which constrains economic growth.

Designing, structuring, and implementing PPPs remains a challenging and complex endeavor. Their success depends on the enabling environment they are embedded in. The World Bank Group has supported countries to create an enabling environment for PPPs along with structuring advice and finance. This evaluation finds that:

▶ The World Bank's upstream policy reform and institution building reaches the right countries. Most of the upstream work aims at sector reform, which, however, failed in almost half of the cases because of the complexity and political implications of the reform processes. Advice on how to manage fiscal implications from PPPs is rarely given.

▶ The World Bank Group has made a significant contribution to capacity building for PPPs, but a lack of local skills and resources for the preparation of a PPP pipeline and bankable PPP projects poses a serious limitation across most World Bank-supported countries.

▶ International Finance Corporation (IFC) Advisory Services have achieved important impacts in advising on PPP structuring, despite the fact that only about half of the projects result in the award of a contract, mostly because of volatile government commitment.

▶ IFC also added value when investing in PPPs during due diligence and implementation, but a higher share of its PPP portfolio could be located in countries and markets with less developed PPP frameworks.

▶ The Multilateral Investment Guarantee Agency increased investors' confidence and effectively implemented PPPs in those countries that are about to develop their PPP frameworks.

▶ PPPs supported by the Bank Group are largely successful in achieving their development outcomes, but data are scarce on the effects on the poor.

▶ The three Bank Group institutions deploy their respective comparative advantages well, but their approach should be more strategic and better tailored to countries.

To further improve the World Bank Group's PPP ambitions as spelled out in its latest strategy, the Independent Evaluation Group recommends:

▶ Translate the World Bank Group's strategic PPP intentions into an operational framework.

▶ Better assist governments in (i) making strategic decisions with regard to the level and nature of private sector participation and (ii) assessing fiscal implications.

▶ Identify avenues to increase IFC investments in PPPs located in countries and markets that do not yet have a well-developed enabling environment.

▶ Ensure broad stakeholder consultation and government commitment in IFC's advisory work.

▶ Provide authoritative guidance to staff on how to handle unsolicited PPP proposals.

▶ Define principles for the monitoring of PPPs over the long run to capture all vital performance aspects of PPPs, including—where relevant—user aspects.

Public-Private Partnerships in Development

Public-private partnerships (PPPs), if implemented well, can help overcome inadequate infrastructure that constrains economic growth, particularly in developing countries. Poor infrastructure is often a reflection of constraints that governments face, for example, lack of public funds, poor planning, or weak analysis underpinning project preparation. PPPs can help overcome these constraints by mobilizing private sector finance and helping improve project preparation, execution, and management.

The use of PPPs has increased in the last two decades. PPPs are now used in more than 134 developing countries, contributing about 15–20 percent of total infrastructure investment. During FY 07–11, investments in PPPs accounted for $79 billion annually and are now also being applied outside the traditional infrastructure sectors, including in the health and education sector.

In parallel with this development, the World Bank Group has expanded its support to PPPs through a wide range of instruments and services. During the last 10 years, Bank Group support to PPPs has increased about threefold. Lending, investments, and guarantees have risen both in absolute terms and in relative terms, from $0.9 billion to $2.9 billion and from 4 percent in 2002 to 7 percent in 2012.

More specifically, IFC invested in 176 PPPs with total commitments of $6.2 billion; the Multilateral Investment Guarantee Agency (MIGA) supported 81 PPP projects through political risk insurance (PRI), with a total $5.1 billion gross exposure; and International Finance Corporation (IFC) PPP Advisory Services completed 140 transactions, with a total expenditure of $177 million. On the public sector side, the International Bank for Reconstruction and Development (IBRD)/International Development Association (IDA) approved 353 lending and partial risk guarantee (PRG) projects during FY02–12 with a PPP component totaling $7.6 billion. Of these, 12 are PRG projects. This was complemented by 112 capacity building activities of the World Bank Institute (WBI) and 683 trust fund-supported advisory activities by the Public-Private Infrastructure Advisory Facility (PPIAF), with total expenditures amounting to $134 million.

Countries need to be sufficiently mature to apply the concept of PPPs well. For example, the market structure of a sector must create conditions for the private sector to operate, regulatory bodies should be competent and protect operators from political interferences and ensure adequate tariffs, and public authorities need to have the skills to prepare a pipeline of bankable PPP projects to interest the private sector. Eventually, PPPs also need finance and, at times, protection against political risks. And because private sector operators require at least cost recovery tariffs, the introduction of PPPs may lead to end user cost increases.

Hence the decision of whether to implement PPPs (or not) is closely linked to the decision to adopt policies aimed at absorbing these cost increases, at least for the poor.

The World Bank Group's support for PPPs builds on the rationale of readying client countries for most of these aspects. Its potentially unique value proposition to its client countries rests with the capacity to provide support along the entire PPP cycle, from policy advice to transaction closure. Countries that are about to embark on their PPP agendas and that are in the process of developing their PPP frameworks will appreciate policy and sector reform advice the most. The private sector-oriented arms of the World Bank Group can catalyze a market for PPPs by facilitating the structuring of PPP transactions or providing finance or guarantees. Supporting pioneering transactions early in a country's PPP agenda will have higher additionality than supporting transactions in relatively established markets.

In this evaluation the Independent Evaluation Group (IEG) assesses how effective the World Bank Group has been in supporting countries to use PPPs. The evaluation covers the last 10 years, from 2002 to 2012. For this evaluation, PPPs are "long-term contracts between a private party and a government agency, for providing a public asset or service, in which the private party bears significant risk and management responsibility." This definition appears to be a common denominator across the PPP concepts of the World Bank Group, International Monetary Fund, and the Organisation for Economic Co-operation and Development (WBI 2012; IMF 2004; OECD 2008) and translates into a well-defined spectrum of contractual arrangements. These arrangements have in common that they are long term, usually bundling design, construction, and maintenance and possibly operation, and contain performance-based elements with private capital at stake.

According to its most recent strategy A Stronger, Connected, Solutions World Bank Group (World Bank 2013), the World Bank Group intends to intensify its PPP support. The strategy also lays the framework for many important components of a potentially effective PPP agenda, including a strong emphasis on knowledge products and collaboration across the Bank Group—a precondition to working effectively along the PPP delivery chain. This evaluation is conceived with a view to distilling lessons from the past for the implementation of this new strategy.

Strategic Relevance

PPPs are of high strategic relevance to the World Bank Group. An explicit objective of its strategy is to "increasingly promote public-private partnerships," and PPPs are also envisaged as a Cross-Cutting Solutions Area. In addition, PPPs have been widely reflected in various sector strategies and conceptual notes. However, there is little guidance on how the World Bank Group plans to translate its strategic ambitions into country programs, working across its various entities engaged at corporate and country levels. Furnishing the envisaged PPP Cross-Cutting Solutions Area with sufficient authority that is commensurate with the planned role will be essential, as will be a clear understanding of how the solution area will interact with the Global Practices and the PPP Policy Unit.

Generally speaking, the World Bank Group's PPP support reaches the countries that need it. In particular, the World Bank and PPIAF's policy reform and institutional building projects target countries that are at a "nascent" stage of developing an enabling environment for PPPs or one stage further—so-called "emerging" PPP countries, per a country classification system of the Economist Intelligence Unit. Similarly, MIGA has been able to emphasize those "nascent" and "emerging" countries when issuing guarantees. IFC advisory also has a strong focus on lower-middle-income countries and Sub-Saharan Africa, regions with relatively untested PPP frameworks.

By contrast, IFC investment often reaches "developed" countries, that is, those that already have a track record of implementing PPPs and have relatively well-established frameworks in place. This is, in principle, understandable, as successful PPPs need a sound enabling environment. However, these countries are increasingly served by commercial banks. The prevalence of PPPs in the market, that is, those supported by other investors, suggests that IFC can—and should—shift parts of its PPP business into less developed countries, that is, "emerging" countries.

At the country level, World Bank Group support for PPPs was relevant to client countries inasmuch as it supported clear development priorities. Typically, the Country Partnership and Country Assistance Strategies embedded PPPs in sector reform programs. The most common PPP constraints addressed are governance issues, regulatory failure, and inadequate sector structure. Country strategies, however, tend to address other important PPP constraints less systematically, such as the capability of governments to make a strategic decision on PPPs based on value for money assessments, or to assess fiscal implications associated with PPPs; political economy factors and issues of the government's commitment to the PPP agenda are almost entirely ignored.

Looking at country-level relevance from a "dynamic" perspective over the period evaluated (FY02–12), the World Bank Group was responsive to client countries' needs and changing priorities.

Support to Policy Reform and Institution Building

Most of the Bank Group upstream support on policy and institutional issues was provided by the World Bank, complemented by support from PPIAF and WBI.

World Bank upstream support was delivered through sector reform efforts. Such efforts are usually broad based and complex. They typically aim at increasing the financial viability of the sector, restructuring sector-relevant institutions, increasing sector management capacity, improving the regulatory regime, and creating a space for private sector participation. Sector reform goals were, however, the most difficult to achieve. Despite the World Bank's leverage and country presence, success on sector reform was only evident in 55 percent of World Bank loans—an important finding, given that proper sector reform is often a necessary condition for implementing PPPs successfully. Sector reform efforts were particularly prominent in the water and energy sectors, indicating the heavy reliance of PPPs on reform in these areas. In the same two sectors, reform efforts show the lowest success in achieving their objectives because of their complexity. The choice of lending instrument is another essential factor in advancing the PPP agenda and needs to be made contingent on the country's readiness.

Capacity building for PPPs and building the legal and institutional framework for them were found to be the next most frequently addressed enabling factors. These relatively narrow interventions—for example, World Bank efforts to build institutions for PPPs—worked the best. Similarly, building up consensus or regulatory commissions succeeded more often than complex sector reform efforts.

Whether a dedicated "PPP unit" at the country level is needed remains to be seen; identifying a "PPP champion," however, may facilitate interministerial coordination in any case.

Contingent liabilities for governments that emerge from PPPs are rarely fully quantified at the project level, although World Bank Group projects tend to give attention to ensuring adequate risk sharing at the project structuring stage. Efforts to systematize and introduce a framework are under way.

Strong government commitment and the availability of a government champion to promote the PPP agenda were the most important drivers of success for upstream work. Frequent stakeholder consultation and active involvement of local staff likewise contributed to the success of policy reform.

The design of PPP component(s), if and how they are embedded in a larger World Bank lending operation, and if and how related knowledge products are conceived and delivered matters. The current involvement of PPIAF suggests that engaging PPIAF further upstream in defining PPP aspects of country engagement strategies would use its resources more strategically.

On the side of the countries' governments, a lack of skills and resources for the preparation of a PPP pipeline and bankable PPP projects is a serious limitation across all World Bank-supported countries. For subnational PPPs to be successful, capacity, regulations, and incentives need to be in place and embedded in a clear accountability system.

Did PPPs Deliver?

PPPs are largely successful in achieving their development outcomes. According to the development outcome rating of project evaluations, more than two-thirds of PPPs are successful.

The 176 IFC-supported PPPs show very high development outcome ratings, with 83 percent rated satisfactory or better. This high rate of success should not, however, lead to the conclusion that all other national or local PPPs necessarily perform well. IFC is selective with regard to where it invests; that is, it concentrates on countries that have more proven frameworks to handle PPPs. Its due diligence screens out sponsors of lower quality and mitigates project risks through smart structuring. IFC also plays an active role in supervising its investments. These success factors may not be present in cases without IFC engagement; hence PPPs are likely exposed to more potential pitfalls and risks.

To shed more light on important aspects of public service delivery—for instance, access, pro-poor aspects, and quality of service delivery—PPPs need to be measured in a more multifaceted manner. But such data are rare. The existing monitoring and evaluation systems primarily build on a PPP's business performance. Project-level evaluations, IFC's Development Goals, and its Development Outcome Tracking System measure mainly the operational aspects of a PPP that are relevant to cash flow, such as the number of people that obtained access to infrastructure. Therefore, for only about half of projects are data available for one dimension. There is not a single project with data available for all the above-mentioned dimensions.

The fewest data are available on pro-poor and fiscal effects; access has the most data available. In view of the Bank Group's central goal of fighting poverty—reaffirmed by the 2013 strategy's dual goal of ending extreme poverty and promoting shared prosperity—and in light of the intent to increasingly pursue PPPs, there is an urgent need to introduce a more systematic way of monitoring PPPs. Such a system should not only better capture the end-user aspects of PPPs, but should also monitor PPP performance beyond the early years of operational maturity. Existing systems, such as the IFC Development Goals or the

Development Outcome Tracking System, would have to be strengthened, and an IFC advisory post-implementation monitoring system fully rolled out—and possibly expanded to the World Bank—to better assess the breadth of PPP effects.

Improving access was generally achieved. When data were available, financial, efficiency, and quality improvements could be confirmed for the majority of cases, but data on efficiency and quality were scarce. A statistically nonrepresentative but in-depth assessment of 22 PPPs conducted as part of IEG's 9 country case studies indicates good results along all dimensions, except for efficiency, where results were mixed.

It cannot, however, be assessed how far PPPs benefited the poor, as large data gaps exist. Confirmation that access did improve for the poor was recorded in only about 10 percent of cases. Beyond reaching the poor through improved access to infrastructure, a review of broader benefits showed that such effects—for example, employment effects—occurred in 42 percent of World Bank PPPs, in 39 percent of IFC investments, and in 20 percent of MIGA's guarantees.

Country readiness drives PPP success. Development outcome ratings of PPP projects tend to be better in countries with a higher level of readiness in handling PPPs, that is, those countries with better established frameworks for preparing and approving PPPs and a longer track record of executing actual transactions. As a general rule, the presence of a strong regulatory framework was necessary for projects to succeed in the water and power sectors; in the transport sector (ports, airports, and roads) project-level parameters on pricing and oversight, along with the legal framework governing PPPs, seemed adequate. In addition to country maturity, PPPs need a sound business case and a competent sponsor to be successful.

Cross-sector approaches as envisaged by the World Bank Group 2013 strategy appear an appealing solution for supporting countries in improving their "PPP maturity," for example, through upstream policy support and downstream transaction finance. But given the high importance of progress in the individual sector, such cross-sectoral approaches need to be well synchronized with and built on sector reform efforts.

IFC investment added value to PPPs during due diligence and implementation, in addition to providing finance and catalyzing other financiers. IFC-supported PPPs tend to be less risky than other infrastructure investments, because of the thorough due diligence. This thoroughness is also reflected in the high work quality ratings for IFC investments in PPPs. As a consequence, IFC-supported PPPs exhibit consistently higher development outcome ratings than other infrastructure investments—and significantly higher ratings than the rest of the portfolio.

Risk is also adequately priced into IFC's PPP deals—resulting in an even higher-than-average business success and investment outcome. IFC-supported PPPs are often located in countries with already well-established enabling environments, and less in emerging or nascent countries. Supporting more PPPs in emerging countries will not decrease their success rate: in fact, 86 and 88 percent of PPPs are successful in developed and emerging PPP countries, respectively. Even increasing IFC's—currently very small—investment portfolio in nascent countries is likely to maintain the overall high success rate (83 percent satisfactory) at a still very reasonable level.

IFC could afford taking more "smart risk," as envisaged by the 2013 Bank Group strategy. This could help support more PPPs in countries that need IFC's support the most, that is, those that are building up their PPP frameworks and have a limited track record of implementing PPPs. Such investments would set an important demonstration effect and show that private participation is possible even in less tested regulatory regimes—increasing IFC additionality and developmental footprint.

The focus of IFC Advisory Services is to bring PPP transactions to commercial and financial closure. Although almost all transaction cases reviewed (97 percent) delivered the specific advice for the first phase of the process (up to the decision to open a bidding process), about half resulted in an award of a contract, a prerequisite for creating a successful PPP. Among projects that led to contract closure, the largest success factors are government commitment and IFC's role.

IFC advisory's value added is also demonstrated by its ability to adjust and balance government objectives with the needs of a bankable transaction, which would interest the private sector. Lacking somewhat the long-term and close relations, in-depth policy dialogue, and financial leverage that the World Bank would normally have with governments may also explain why only half of its projects reach contract closure; so can the fact that IFC advisory operates a lot in lower-middle-income countries and Sub-Saharan Africa, where one could expect relatively untested PPP frameworks. IFC advisory's experience in these countries could therefore inform IFC investments on the country's and market's readiness and help leading their investment more into emerging—and even nascent—countries. More upfront work should be undertaken, including more proactive dialogue with civil society stakeholders. A Bank Group-wide systematic country diagnostic for PPPs may be helpful in determining the entry point of such upfront work.

MIGA guarantees helped effectively increase investors' confidence and improve their capacity to raise capital, lower their financing costs, and mediate disputes with governments. MIGA's effectiveness and underwriting quality for PPP projects is on a par with the quality of underwriting of other MIGA projects. Similar to all World Bank Group PPP transactions, regulatory failure and political economy factors were drivers of success and failure.

MIGA's PRI offered cover for specific risks and was effective in helping establishing a track record of PPPs in countries that need support the most, that is, those that are in the process of building up their PPP frameworks. MIGA-supported PPPs have been more strategically relevant than MIGA's other infrastructure projects, corroborating their important role in nascent and emerging PPP countries. Strengthening MIGA's role in World Bank Group-wide efforts and benefiting from its role appears to be the way forward when bringing PPPs to more nascent and emerging countries.

Sixty-two percent of World Bank–supported PPP downstream transactions were successful. This means that, measured by their overall development outcomes, PPPs are quite successful—but significantly less successful than IFC's investments. But the World Bank takes on significantly more country risk. Countries in which the World Bank engages tend to have worse Institutional Investor Country Credit Ratings—and a higher share of these are nascent countries (19 percent, compared to 6 percent for IFC investments). Furthermore, PPP projects are markedly more difficult to implement than normal infrastructure projects. They are often restructured, delayed, or flagged for procurement issues. This stems from the rather complex nature of PPP projects, half of which combine upstream policy work and downstream transaction support.

Leading factors of failure are overly complex project design and an initial unrealistic timeframe—that is, a timeframe that forces reform measures into a World Bank project cycle, instead of acknowledging the complexity and political nature of such processes. As with IFC and MIGA, government commitment plays an important role. Adhering to environmental and social safeguards has also contributed to slow implementation, to the extent that it sometimes "clouded" the positive perception of project benefits. But implementing these safeguards was important and delivered public benefits.

Staying engaged beyond financial closure of a PPP is a strategic necessity for the entire Bank Group. The current practice to stop monitoring PPPs once the contract is awarded or a few months into their life span is insufficient. If the World Bank Group plans to intensify its PPP support, arrangements are needed to monitor the performance of PPPs throughout major parts of their lifespan, as currently envisaged by IFC advisory's post-implementation monitoring system. This may also help identify if World Bank Group support is called for during the implementation of a PPP contract, for example, should a need for renegotiations arise.

Bank Group–supported transactions often created a market for PPPs through their demonstration effects and, at times, helped shape the regulatory environment. Demonstration and replication effects of individual PPPs may be as important as the actual transaction.

Frequently, Bank Group–supported PPP transactions also helped shape the regulatory environment, often facilitated by close Bank Group-wide collaboration and stakeholder involvement.

Working as One World Bank Group

The World Bank Group's support to PPPs addresses issues along the entire delivery chain, from upstream support for the enabling environment and pipeline development to downstream transactions and execution. It touches on about 20 different entities of the World Bank Group. Collaboration across these entities is crucial for proper sequencing and leveraging of the relative comparative advantage each institution holds.

Leveraging the comparative advantages of the various World Bank Group institutions works quite well. In about half of the countries IEG reviewed, the World Bank Group institutions effectively coordinate and collaborate across policy reform aspects and PPP transactions; in a few cases all three institutions were involved. There is also evidence for proper sequencing of instruments across upstream and downstream support. Among its peer organizations, the World Bank Group has been acknowledged as offering the most comprehensive PPP solution package. However, there were also a few missed opportunities.

Going forward, working as "one World Bank Group" will become central. The Bank Group's intention to explore mechanisms to promote a stronger pipeline of joint infrastructure projects and the envisaged review of World Bank Group advisory services to governments are essential for the PPP agenda. But most importantly, incentives must be in place for individual task managers and investment officers to collaborate. They only collaborate if such collaboration adds value and allows them to achieve better results or at least the same results faster. Introducing metrics to measure collaborative behavior, as suggested by the latest Bank Group strategy, is likely perceived as artificially imposed and will not necessarily increase collaboration. Aligning practice areas through a "delivery lens" and integrating currently separate units may be more effective.

Improving the focus of country programs through a systematic country diagnostic will be particularly important for the PPP agenda. As any diagnostic is resource intensive, it should be applied mainly to countries in which at least a minimum prospect exists that a bankable pipeline of projects will emerge. A PPP country diagnostic would have to consider country, sector, and project parameters as part of a phased approach and could represent a platform for sharing knowledge as well as clarify Bank Group-wide collaboration. Advocacy and stakeholder consultation have thus far received too little attention and should therefore be emphasized. Such a diagnostic would help (i) ensure that the Bank Group institutions leverage their respective comparative advantages, (ii) tailor upstream support to country-level constraints, and (iii) determine who should take the lead in advancing the country's PPP agenda.

A concerted one World Bank Group approach is needed to close the upstream deal gap—one of the major challenges for the future. Lack of funding and capacity causes a gap of bankable PPP projects across client countries. To close this upstream deal gap, a dedicated PPP pipeline and project development facility is needed that works in close collaboration with all World Bank Group institutions.

Working as one World Bank Group also requires watching out for conflicts of interest. Going forward, as the change management process develops concepts for organizational adjustments, management is well advised to give high priority to this issue to ensure that changes to processes and organizational structures enable an effective and efficient management of the risks from potential conflicts of interest. Finally, given their importance, there is a need for a Bank Group-wide policy on how to best handle unsolicited bids. Unsolicited proposals often play a role in countries with an upstream deal gap. To benefit from the upside of unsolicited proposals—that is, funding of project preparation and innovation—countries need to have a framework in place to deal with them. Guidance to Bank Group staff engaged in both upstream and downstream work will be crucial going forward.

Experience of Other Multilateral Development Banks with PPPs

For most multilateral development banks (MDBs) PPPs are of great relevance, and several feature PPPs explicitly either in stand-alone strategy documents or as an integral part of sectoral/corporate strategies. In implementing these strategic plans, some MDBs have come up with specific roadmaps and matrix management structures. In particular, the Asian Development Bank undertook an evaluation of PPPs that has triggered a rethinking of the institution's approach to PPPs and has moved to make the process more strategic and less opportunistic. Its operational plan for PPPs turns strategy into implementation more readily. The four pillars of its operational plan also help define the PPP instruments that it will offer. Similarly, the African Development Bank set up an operational framework for PPPs in conjunction with its private sector development strategy, where PPPs figure prominently.

Across the MDBs, three (the Asian Development Bank, the African Development Bank, and the Inter-American Development Bank) have PPP approaches that recognize the importance of upstream as well as downstream support. Compared to its peers, the World Bank Group likely offers the widest and deepest set of services and products, a conclusion corroborated by IEG's nine country missions.

Recommendations

The following recommendations are intended to strengthen the implementation of the PPP-relevant aspects of the latest Bank Group strategy. They seek to ensure that PPP interventions have the maximum value for client countries and private sector partners, to make the PPP agenda of the Bank Group build on better country diagnostics and pursued in a more strategic manner, and to leverage the comparative advantages of all Bank Group institutions and trust funds involved in the PPP response. The recommendations are clustered into two groups: (i) strategic and organizational and (ii) operational recommendations.

STRATEGIC AND ORGANIZATIONAL RECOMMENDATIONS

Recommendation 1: IFC investment services should identify avenues that would allow IFC to invest increasingly in PPPs located in countries and markets that do not yet have a well-developed enabling environment, while keeping its mandate of achieving high development outcomes and remaining financially self-sustaining.

Recommendation 2: IFC PPP Advisory Services should rethink its client engagement management with a view to ensuring broad stakeholder consultation up front and maintaining or even improving government commitment to PPP transactions, in collaboration with relevant World Bank Group staff.

OPERATIONAL RECOMMENDATIONS

Recommendation 3: Once the new PPP Cross-Cutting Solution Area has been established, it should translate the World Bank Group's strategic intentions with regard to PPPs into an operational framework, covering aspects of organization and processes, resources, knowledge management, and monitoring and evaluation. This framework should (i) define the role of the PPP Cross-Cutting Solution Area and its interactions with other relevant Bank Group stakeholders, (ii) facilitate the identification of country-tailored solutions based on country diagnostics, and (iii) foresee a Bank Group-wide PPP knowledge management platform.

Recommendation 4: The World Bank Group should systematically integrate efforts to assist governments in (i) making strategic decisions with regard to the level and nature of private sector participation in infrastructure and social service provision and (ii) assessing fiscal implications, including any fiscal liabilities associated with PPPs.

Recommendation 5: The World Bank Group should provide authoritative guidance to its staff on how to handle unsolicited PPP proposals, both in its upstream and downstream work. Given the importance of unsolicited bids, in particular in countries with an upstream deal gap, there is a need for a Bank Group-wide policy on how to handle them best, so that countries can benefit from the upside of unsolicited proposals—that is, funding of project preparation and innovation—while at the same time safeguarding public interests and integrity.

Recommendation 6: The World Bank Group should define principles for the monitoring of PPPs over the long run, that is, beyond operational maturity (IFC/MIGA) and projects closure (World Bank), to capture all vital performance aspects of PPPs, including—where relevant—user aspects.

References

IMF (International Monetary Fund). 2004. *Public-Private Partnerships*. Washington, DC: IMF.

OECD (Organisation for Economic Co-operation and Development). 2008. *Public-Private Partnerships: In Pursuit of Risk Sharing and Value for Money*. Paris: OECD.

World Bank. 2013. *A Stronger, Connected Solutions World Bank Group*. Washington, DC: World Bank.

WBI (World Bank Institute). 2012. *Public-Private Partnerships Reference Guide*, Version 1.0. Washington, DC: World Bank Institute and Public Private Infrastructure Advisory Facility.

Management Response

Introduction

The World Bank Group commends the Independent Evaluation Group's (IEG) evaluation of the Group's support to public-private partnerships (PPP). The timing of this evaluation is pertinent, given that PPPs have been identified as a Cross Cutting Solution Area (CCSA) that will be developed under the revised structure of the World Bank Group. Understanding how the World Bank Group can prepare governments to deliver PPPs, advise governments on specific transactions, and improve internal coordination will be central to realizing the mandate for the CCSA and stepping up the leveraging of private sector skills, technologies, and resources in basic service delivery.

Under its new strategy, the World Bank Group intends to work with the public and private sectors to end extreme poverty and promote shared prosperity and seeks to increase synergies across the Bank Group. Client countries are increasingly interested in PPP arrangements to provide badly needed public services, and PPPs are, by their nature, a prime area for close World Bank Group collaboration.

Overall, management concurs with the findings and conclusions in the report. Management believes that IEG has presented a balanced account of World Bank Group support to its client countries during the period of FY02–12. Management is in general agreement with the report's recommendations. The Management Action Record (p. xxxv) presents management's response to individual recommendations.

World Bank Group Comments

Importance of PPP for development and strategic relevance for the World Bank Group. Management agrees with IEG's statement that PPPs, if implemented well, can help overcome inadequate infrastructure that constrains economic growth. The World Bank Group is uniquely positioned to help overcome these constraints by mobilizing private sector participation, helping improve the enabling environment for investment, and strengthening project preparation, execution, and management. As the report recognizes, Bank Group support to PPPs addresses issues along the entire delivery chain, from upstream support for the enabling environment and pipeline development to downstream transactions and execution.

Alignment with country needs. The report concludes that the World Bank Group's deployment of its PPP interventions is well synchronized with client country needs and that, over the period evaluated (FY02–12), the World Bank Group was responsive to client countries' needs and changing priorities. The report articulates well the unique and complementary roles of the World Bank Group entities in the PPP delivery chain and captures their specific contributions. World Bank Group institutions each play distinct and complementary roles when they support upstream and downstream work in client countries. In particular, the report shows that the International Finance Corporation (IFC) and the Multilateral Investment Guarantee Agency (MIGA)-supported projects do not happen in a policy vacuum, but in response to deliberate policy reforms. The analysis also confirms that coordination across the World Bank Group institutions is critical for maximizing the development effectiveness of Bank Group operations in the sector.

World Bank Group coordination. Management is encouraged by IEG's conclusion that leveraging the comparative advantages of the various Bank Group institutions works quite well with adequate sequencing of instruments across upstream and downstream support. In addition, IEG finds that among the World Bank Group's peer organizations, the Bank Group has been acknowledged as offering the most comprehensive PPP solution package. While the Bank Group's efforts have been well targeted to client needs, management appreciates IEG's recommendation that the World Bank Group support to PPPs could be more strategic and better coordinated. The ongoing reorganization of the Bank Group includes the creation of a CCSA for PPPs. This unit will create an institutional locus for the PPP agenda within the Bank Group, as well as for the sectoral and infrastructure economics and advisory work that underpins the solutions the World Bank Group delivers to client countries. The PPP CCSA is a bold initiative that is expected to deliver the strategic and operational direction called for by the report.

Potential conflicts of interest are managed appropriately through current business practices. The discussion on the potential of conflicts of interest among the various World Bank Group institutions concludes that the existing mechanism to manage the "actual, potential and/or perceived" conflict of interest is functioning well. As the reorganization of the World Bank Group moves ahead, management will continue to manage this process transparently in order to ensure that the interests of both its public and private sector clients are balanced and drive the work program, rather than any actual, or perceived, institutional interests.

Monitoring PPPs impact on various dimensions of public service delivery.
Management concurs with the IEG's finding that the World Bank Group can further improve its monitoring of PPPs. In particular, management agrees that a "multifaceted" approach to identifying and monitoring the effects of PPPs on end users is required and that the various monitoring systems within the Bank Group should be harmonized to the extent that there is interoperability in PPP data. The World Bank Group needs to move past the current state of "data scarcity" on the effects of PPPs on the poor in order to fully appreciate the effect PPPs play in realizing the World Bank Group's twin goals of reducing extreme poverty and boosting shared prosperity in a sustainable manner.

Overcoming the "upstream deal gap." IEG's report describes the specific constraints in client countries that create an "upstream deal gap" (that is, an insufficient number of bankable PPP projects). This represents a bottleneck for PPPs, as countries across the income distribution are constrained by weak capacity for project preparation and/or financing gaps. As part of a concerted response to this challenge management is exploring, together with the World Bank Group's clients and partners, the possibility of developing a Global Infrastructure Facility, a new project preparation and financing vehicle to increase the Bank Group's ability to support its client countries' PPP ambitions in infrastructure.

World Bank–Specific Comments

Upstream work through sector reforms should be analyzed as a composite of several interventions, rather than as an independent variable in its own right. Management agrees that there is significant room for improving the effectiveness of World Bank upstream support to client countries' PPPs delivered through sector reform operations. However, while IEG correctly notes that several World Bank Group upstream objectives are pursued within broader sector reforms, IEG does not disaggregate the particular success rate for each of these dimensions when it compares sector reforms to more narrowly defined PPP upstream interventions. In this context, IEG's figure of "55 percent success rate for sector reforms" can be misleading. IEG missed an opportunity to delve deeper into the challenges faced by the World Bank's sector reform efforts. Consequently, it may overstate the evaluation's findings by claiming that the Bank's sector reform work "failed in almost half of the cases" when it comes to PPP upstream objectives.

Overcoming constraints to pipeline identification and project preparation. Bank management concurs with IEG's finding in relation to the "upstream deal gap." The World Bank has become one of the leading voices within global fora working to familiarize clients and donor countries with the sector policies, project structures, and institutional arrangements required to attract private finance to public infrastructure investments. Moreover, through its operations, management strives to bring development solutions that allow decision makers to prioritize investments in a fiscally informed and prudent manner. For instance, a recent Reimbursable Advisory Service agreement with the government of Vietnam will develop a tool that will allow the Ministry of Planning and Investment to prioritize a pipeline of infrastructure investments, including public and PPP projects.

Concerted effort to consider fiscal impacts of PPPs. The IEG report advises the World Bank Group to systematically assist governments to assess the fiscal implications of PPPs, including current or contingent liabilities associated with PPPs. Management concurs that government transfers, guarantees, backstopping, concessional finance, and future obligations should be viewed in concert with the projected effect the instrument or mechanism will have on the government's fiscal situation, either today or in the future.

Unsolicited bids are covered within many guidance notes and toolkits, but management recognizes the need to systematize guidance to staff. As the evaluation rightly mentions, unsolicited bids frequently occur within countries that require additional technical support to fully vet such bids. The World Bank has developed a number of Guidance Notes and toolkits on the subject, directed to internal and external audiences. Management agrees that the existing knowledge could be codified into an "authoritative" literature set that World Bank Group staff can refer to. However, a one-size-fits-all approach is not recommended in the face of the highly segmented client base of the World Bank Group. Management will actively advise governments to ensure that unsolicited bids are within the strategic, fiduciary, and fiscal priorities of the state, but with a degree of flexibility to treat each client engagement with unsolicited bids on the merits.

IEG's definition of PPPs excludes the types of risk-sharing mechanism most commonly used within fragile and conflict-affected states. Management recognizes fragile and conflict-affected states (FCS) as an urgent development priority and following the publication of the World Development Report 2011 has further increased PPPs emphasis on FCS. However, IEG's definition of PPPs does not consider lease, management contracts, or hybrid schemes, which are generally the mechanisms used to introduce private sector participation into FCS. Management appreciates the argument presented by IEG that these mechanisms do not induce the level of risk sharing common to the other PPPs analyzed within this evaluation. Nonetheless, FCS are critical clients for the Bank, and by excluding the mechanisms mentioned previously, IEG has excluded many of the Bank's innovative attempts to improve access to basic services to some of the world's poorest citizens with private sector participation.

International Finance Corporation–Specific Comments

Management welcomes IEG's evaluation of the World Bank Group's support for PPPs. The report provides a valuable assessment of IFC's development results in a key intervention area for both Investment Services and Advisory Services. Support for PPPs will remain an important IFC contribution to a "Solutions World Bank Group" to improve the sustainability of private sector engagement in service delivery, particularly in infrastructure, health, and education.

Management welcomes the report's recognition of the strong additionality and development impact of IFC interventions in PPPs. In Advisory Services, IFC successfully balances the public good objectives of the government and the needs of the private sector for a bankable transaction. The report correctly recognizes the political and economic risks that are often the main obstacle to contract closure. The nine case studies illustrate well the innovative nature of many of the Advisory Services PPP projects, which help explain successful award of contract.

In Investment Services, the report underscores the consistently higher development outcome success rate of PPP investments relative to both other infrastructure investments and the rest of the portfolio. IFC achieved these impressive results through solid screening, appraisal, and structuring. Selectivity played a key role. This led to IFC supporting projects in environments that are reasonably ready for PPP investments, where it has a strong additionality, where expected development results are significant, and where financial sustainability risk is acceptable.

IFC agrees with the assessment that demonstration and replication effects may be as important as the actual transaction. In fact, IFC has already conducted two separate studies on IFC demonstration effects in the past two years: one of them focuses specifically on PPPs in Africa, while the other has a broader scope for all IFC projects.

IFC recognizes that sufficient and reliable public services, including infrastructure, are intrinsic to sustainable economic growth and poverty reduction. In order to better leverage private sector resources and expertise in developing infrastructure and public services, IFC emphasizes a programmatic approach to PPP engagements and focuses both on the core transaction advisory services for governments as well as on pipeline generation and upstream support for clients. IFC partners across the World Bank Group, including through the new PPP CCSA, will identify and address skill gaps and build capacity of implementing agencies. To improve its own operations, IFC will continue to proactively leverage expertise within the World Bank Group through joint activities at the country level, for instance, through World Bank Group Systematic Country Diagnostics, Country Partnership Frameworks, and Joint Implementation Plans. Additionally, at the project level, it will work through joint business development and appraisals.

Multilateral Investment Guarantee Agency–Specific Comments

Overall, MIGA finds the evaluation useful and important. This report has made a serious effort to analyze and understand MIGA contributions to PPPs, despite the limited sample of projects with completed Project Evaluation Reports validated by IEG. MIGA hopes that the approach adopted by IEG in the PPP evaluation will serve as a good example for other IEG evaluation reports.

MIGA's role in World Bank Group support for PPPs. The report makes the case for strengthening MIGA's role in Bank Group-wide efforts in PPPs, as well as benefitting from its role in bringing PPPs to more nascent and emerging markets, in terms of PPP readiness. MIGA agrees with this assessment and notes that the suggestion bodes well in the context of the increased emphasis on "One World Bank Group" as an integrated solutions provider for client countries.

Focus of MIGA-supported PPPs on middle-income countries. The report states that MIGA Guarantee Operations were focused on middle-income countries. The report also states that this pattern reflects the flow of foreign direct investment for PPPs, which have been focused on middle-income countries in the past 10 years and indicates the demand-driven nature of MIGA operations. MIGA notes from the analysis in the report that juxtaposes country income levels and PPP readiness that PPPs are concentrated in middle-income countries. Further, most of the PPPs located in nascent and emerging markets also turn out to be in middle-income countries (only a small percentage of PPPs located in nascent and emerging markets belongs to low-income countries). MIGA notes that its PPP focus on middle-income countries was indeed driven by the flow of foreign direct investment for PPPs but also other factors such as selectivity, risk return, and client demand. MIGA also notes that MIGA has been collaborating with the rest of the Bank Group to expand PPPs to low-income countries and fragile countries, especially in Sub-Saharan Africa.

Broader assessment of PPPs. The report states the need for assessing PPP results beyond development outcome success rates by seeking more information on the quality and efficiency of public service delivery, effects on the poor, and fiscal sustainability, among other areas. MIGA agrees with this assessment and notes these are important aspects in assessing the results of PPPs. However, some of the information is already captured in the project-level evaluations. MIGA also finds the discussion in the report outlining the key components of an monitoring and evaluation system for PPPs as useful, but notes that it may be better to integrate these components into existing results frameworks, rather than formulate a new one for PPPs.

Country risks and MIGA-supported PPPs. The report states that MIGA's political risk insurance did not necessarily allow PPPs to get structured in higher-risk environments, with MIGA-supported PPPs located in countries with Institutional Investor Country Credit Risk rating scores (35–50, that is, medium and low risk). MIGA notes that this finding is consistent with the fact that PPPs are mostly concentrated in middle-income countries, as previously discussed, with most of the MIGA-supported projects located in nascent and emerging markets from a PPP-readiness standpoint. MIGA also notes its recent efforts to support PPPs in more high-risk countries and low-income countries, especially in Sub-Saharan Africa, as part of the broader World Bank Group efforts.

Demonstration and replication effects. The report states that at times demonstration and replication effects may be as important as the actual transaction. MIGA agrees with this assessment and notes that demonstration and replication effects are fundamental to the private sector development process that has been well documented in previous IEG reports (IEG 2010), as part of the effort to understand better the "how" of the private sector development process. MIGA also notes several examples from the report regarding the demonstration and replication effects of MIGA-supported projects that contributed to significant development impacts.

Reference

IEG (Independent Evaluation Group). 2010. *Results and Performance of the World Bank Group 2010.* Washington, DC: World Bank.

Management Action Record

Focus on Markets without Well-Developed Enabling Environments

IEG FINDINGS AND CONCLUSIONS

Support to PPP transaction through IFC's investments emphasizes countries with already quite well established PPP frameworks, that is, those rated "developed" by the Economist Intelligence Unit (EIU) global ranking. Five percent of IFC investment business is located in nascent countries, where arguably the deal flow can be expected to be less reliable. However, this is about half of what the market generates, with 9 percent of all PPPs occurring in these countries. In "emerging" countries, about 38 percent of IFC investments take place, whereas 49 percent of all PPP are structured there. Hence, IFC's investment activity clearly lags behind the rate at which the market itself generates PPPs. By contrast, IFC invests more in developed PPP countries than the market does: Fully 56 percent of IFC's investments are directed to developed countries—compared to 42 percent of all PPPs being structured there. In addition, IFC-supported PPPs tend to be less risky than other infrastructure investments, because of the thorough due diligence. This thoroughness is also reflected in the high work quality ratings for IFC investments in PPPs. As a consequence, IFC-supported PPPs exhibit consistently higher development outcome ratings than other infrastructure investments—and significantly higher ratings than the rest of the portfolio. Risk is also adequately priced into IFC's PPP deals—resulting in an even higher-than-average business success and investment outcome.

Supporting more PPPs in emerging countries need not decrease their success rate: in fact, 86 percent of PPPs are successful in developed countries and 88 percent in emerging PPP countries, respectively. Even nascent countries exhibit a success rate of 50 percent.

Note: The EIU rating scheme captures 83 percent of IFC investments, hence is representative of IFC's investment portfolio in PPPs. Looking at the 17 percent of IFC investments that are not covered by the EIU ratings, full 90 percent of these are concentrated in only 10 countries.

Recommendation 1: IFC investment services should identify avenues that would allow IFC to invest increasingly in PPPs located in countries and markets that do not yet have a well-developed enabling environment, while keeping its mandate of achieving high development outcomes and remaining financially self-sustaining.

ACCEPTANCE BY MANAGEMENT

IFC agrees

MANAGEMENT RESPONSE

IFC plays a convening role in Investment Services, helping bring together different players to support a project developed by the sponsor. In the majority of investment projects that IFC supports, it comes in after the sponsor has already chosen the location and prepared a project. The demand-driven and demand-contingent offering is difficult to execute in less developed (from PPP perspective) markets. With the exception of few cases where IFC can influence project development, it will continue to be a financier of already developed project proposals, and one cannot realistically expect too much of a move toward the PPP frontier. However, there are recent efforts in this direction such as an increased focus on FCS countries. The report is also sanguine about the ability of IFC Investment Services to continue achieving high development outcomes in more risky environments. IFC has to proceed with caution, given that it is possible that the high overall development outcome success rate in Investment Services may not be sustained as it grows its PPP Investment Services portfolio in difficult countries.

Ensure Broad Stakeholder Engagement Up Front
IEG FINDINGS AND CONCLUSIONS

Although almost all IFC advisory services for PPPs transaction cases (97 percent) delivered specific advice for phase 1, about half resulted in an award of a contract. Among projects that failed to reach contract closure, the top drivers of failure were political and economic risk factors and lack of government commitment. Collectively the two factors contributed to the failure in 75 percent of these projects. Of projects where government capacity was weak, over half of them reached contract closure, which indicates that IFC advisory can step in with its capacity to handle the process. An important lesson is that more upfront work should be undertaken to better assess client commitment and to determine the areas of potential support and opposition to a project within the client government. Such work could occur before signing the Financial Advisory Services Agreement. For projects that involve commitments from multiple stakeholders, IFC should engage in a pre-mandate assignment to identify and map stakeholders and engage in discussions with them to determine their support for the projects. It is also important to ensure that the client has real decision-making authority and is not a source of technical expertise/oversight who still needs to go elsewhere for decisions on project implementation. This is likely to require more field presence of senior staff who can technically engage in such business development activities with key policy makers. Efforts to increase awareness about the circumstances under which PPPs can present a solution for infrastructure constraints and how PPPs work, would be important components of such upfront work.

IEG RECOMMENDATIONS

Recommendation 2: IFC PPP Advisory Services should rethink its client engagement management with a view to ensuring broad stakeholder consultation up front and maintaining or even improving government commitment to PPP transactions, in collaboration with relevant World Bank Group staff.

ACCEPTANCE BY MANAGEMENT

IFC agrees

MANAGEMENT RESPONSE

The recommendation is consistent with IFC's understanding of the critical nature of ensuring client commitment. It is also in harmony with IFC's due diligence process and current efforts to integrate World Bank Group colleagues in the project approval and implementation. IFC PPP Advisory Services already have a process of mapping out the key stakeholders at project approval and will continue to strengthen the practice.

IFC PPP Advisory Services will continue to work on improving government commitment by building capacity of government counterparts through workshops. The workshops are intended to enhance the government understanding of the process and requirements for a successful transaction.

Incorporate Strategic Intentions into an Operational Framework
IEG FINDINGS AND CONCLUSIONS

PPPs are high on the World Bank Group's strategic agenda. The recently adopted World Bank Group's strategy expresses the firm intention to "increasingly promote public-private partnerships." PPP are also widely reflected in other conceptual and strategic notes. However, the Bank Group does not provide coherent direction on how these various strategic intentions would be translated into operations. Currently there is no explicit managerial framework that could provide guidance to staff and management on issues, such as roles and responsibilities and processes in implementing the PPP agenda, resource allocation, knowledge management, or monitoring and evaluation. In view of the various entities engaged in PPPs at the corporate and country levels across the PPP delivery chain and the currently envisaged PPP Cross-Cutting Solutions Area (CCSA), a minimum of guidance appears essential to facilitate translating the strategic intent into a country-tailored solution. The evaluation also finds that the World Bank Group would benefit from applying PPP country diagnostics that assess a country's readiness and help to tailor the Bank Group-wide PPP response.

IEG RECOMMENDATIONS

Recommendation 3: Once the new PPP CCSA has been established, it should translate the World Bank Group's strategic intentions with regard to PPPs into an operational framework, covering aspects of organization and processes, resources, knowledge management, monitoring and evaluation. This framework should (i) define the role of the PPP CCSA and its interactions with other relevant Bank Group stakeholders, (ii) facilitate the identification of country-tailored solutions based on country diagnostics, and (iii) foresee a Bank Group-wide PPP knowledge management platform.

ACCEPTANCE BY MANAGEMENT

World Bank Group agrees

MANAGEMENT RESPONSE

Management broadly agrees with the recommendation. The formation of a PPP-CCSA is aimed at harmonizing the PPP agenda across the World Bank Group.

Management will work to articulate a strategic direction for the PPP-CCSA and to develop a consistent operational framework for engaging with PPPs.

Through the PPP-CCSA, management will work with counterparts in regional units and the Global Practices to identify the most appropriate means for supporting operations with sound PPP diagnostics.

Integrate Efforts to Help Governments Assess Strategy and Implications

IEG's analysis of the country strategies of 45 countries did not reveal much evidence that the Bank Group had provided advice on whether private sector involvement (in the form of a PPP) was the best option, given the relevant country-level circumstances. The nine country cases indicate that the World Bank Group's approach to PPPs has been based on the assumption that involving the private sector is a good thing. Although careful analysis of a transaction's economics, feasibility, and sustainability is of course encouraged, public sector comparators—systematically comparing PPP's against the public sector for value for money to justify private sector involvement—were not a part of the World Bank Group activities.

Systematic approaches to the client government's capacity to assess the fiscal implications of PPPs were rarely found during FY02–12. IEG's portfolio review indicates that although World Bank Group projects tend to give attention to ensuring adequate risk sharing, downstream contingent liabilities are rarely fully quantified at the project level. Recent efforts to systematize and introduce a framework for assessing fiscal implications of PPPs are a valuable contribution, but it is unclear how they would be implemented Bank Group-wide.

IEG RECOMMENDATIONS

Recommendation 4: The World Bank Group should systematically integrate efforts to assist governments in (i) making strategic decisions with regard to the level and nature of private sector participation in infrastructure and social service provision and (ii) assessing fiscal implications, including any fiscal liabilities associated with PPPs.

ACCEPTANCE BY MANAGEMENT

World Bank Group agrees

MANAGEMENT RESPONSE

As the evaluation mentions in the overview, the World Bank Group is already increasing efforts to assist countries to develop PPP project pipelines. These efforts include the development of systematic tools capable of integrating various pieces of data into a comprehensive tool for decision makers. Moreover, these tools consider the fiscal space available for infrastructure investments.

The future PPP-CCSA is expected to provide analysis, guidance and tools to strengthen the groups' capacity to support client countries decision making about partnering with the private sector, including assessing potential fiscal liabilities associated with PPPs.

In addition, if the Bank Group is to set up a Global Infrastructure Facility or Platform focused on PPPs, the Facility will be managed from the PPP-CCSA, which will work to establish criteria for project selection and technical support from the Bank, upstream, in project preparation and for financial arranging of investments.

Guide Staff on Unsolicited PPP Proposals

IEG FINDINGS AND RECOMMENDATIONS

To date the Bank Group has not adopted a policy on how to address unsolicited proposals. In 2013, IFC advisory services issued guidelines on how to handle negotiated contracts for its PPP business line, expanding its product offerings; however, there is no Bank Group-wide practice yet. Ongoing Bank Group practice ranges from advising countries to reject unsolicited bids and solely rely on PPPs tendered out; to advising countries to design a suitable framework for managing them. Given their importance and the 2013 Bank Group strategy's emphasis on PPPs, there is a need to provide guidance on this issue to Bank Group staff engaged in both upstream and downstream work. The expanded product offering and resulting experience from IFC advisory services may offer useful learning for the rest of the World Bank Group.

IEC RECOMMENDATIONS

Recommendation 5: The World Bank Group should provide authoritative guidance to its staff on how to handle unsolicited PPP proposals, both in its upstream and downstream work. Given the importance of unsolicited bids, in particular in countries with an upstream deal gap, there is a need for a Bank Group-wide policy on how to handle them best, so that countries can benefit from the upside of unsolicited proposals, that is, funding of project preparation and innovation, while at the same time safeguarding public interests and integrity.

ACCEPTANCE BY MANAGEMENT

World Bank Group partially agrees

Management agrees that this is a pressing issue that warrants authoritative guidance to staff across the World Bank Group. Management, however, does not agree that a new Bank Group-wide policy needs to be introduced.

Determining the most appropriate means for addressing unsolicited PPP bids will require consolidating the knowledge generated within the World Bank Group as well as external organizations.

The PPP-CCSA will perform the vital function of managing and collating PPP-related knowledge. Accordingly, it will develop a comprehensive understanding of the various methods for managing and responding to unsolicited PPP bids that can be used to create a literature set on the topic of unsolicited bids.

Define Principles for Monitoring PPPs

IEG FINDINGS AND CONCLUSIONS

IEG found that evaluation reports that shed light on important aspects of public service delivery are rare, for instance, on access, pro-poor aspects, and quality of service delivery. The existing monitoring and evaluation systems (Expanded Project Supervision Reports, Implementation Completion and Results Reports, Project Evaluation Reports, and so forth), IFC's Development Goals and Development Outcome Tracking System do not record these data systemically. In light of the Bank Group's central goal of fighting poverty—reaffirmed by the new 2013 strategy's twin goals of ending extreme poverty and promoting shared prosperity—and in light of the intent to increasingly pursue PPPs, there is an urgent need to introduce a more systematic way of monitoring PPPs. Such a system should not only better capture the end-user aspects of PPPs (when relevant), but should also monitor PPP performance beyond the early years of operational maturity.

As monitoring and evaluation systems are resource intensive and need to be embedded in corporate reporting systems—which should in any case collect the relevant outcome data on a regular basis—and national statistics services.

IEG RECOMMENDATIONS

Recommendation 6: The World Bank Group should define principles for the monitoring of PPPs over the long run, that is, beyond operational maturity (IFC/ MIGA) and projects closure (World Bank), to capture all vital performance aspects of PPPs, including—where relevant—user aspects.

World Bank Group agrees

MANAGEMENT RESPONSE

The World Bank Group is focused on decreasing the incidence of absolute poverty and boosting shared prosperity. Access to basic services remains far from universal across the developing world, which lowers quality of life and can constrain productive activities. Accordingly, the Bank Group has identified PPPs as an important delivery mechanism to maximize the reach of public resources, while improving the efficiency and quality of the basic services reaching citizens.

Management agrees with IEG that monitoring the effects of World Bank Group PPP operations is vital. Together with IFC and MIGA, the World Bank will identify a process through which a suite of principles can be created to guide and inform task teams seeking to monitor the performance of PPP operations. Additional work on impact evaluation placing PPPs against other models of service delivery may have to be explored for a fuller understanding of potential impacts.

Chairperson's Summary: Committee on Development Effectiveness

The Committee on Development Effectiveness met to consider the Independent Evaluation Group's (IEG) *World Bank Group Support to Public-Private Partnerships—Lessons from Experience in Client Countries, FY02–12* and World Bank Group draft Management Response.

The committee welcomed the report and appreciated management's broad concurrence with the findings and recommendations. They commended IEG and management for the constructive dialogue and encouraged them to continue working to achieve better results. Members acknowledged that public-private partnerships (PPPs) are crucial for closing the infrastructure gap in developing countries.

Members emphasized the importance of using the new Systematic Country Diagnostic and Country Partnership Framework to assist governments in making strategic choices regarding PPP infrastructure development. They supported incorporating PPPs into the World Bank Group's operational framework in new country engagements and stressed the importance of early analytical work and early government engagement to identify the need for PPPs in each country context. Noting the timeliness of the evaluation with the establishment of the Global Practices and Cross Cutting Solution Areas (CCSA), members were pleased to learn that leads on PPPs will be identified in each Global Practice to ensure the PPP agenda moves forward. Members noted they expected strengthened multilateral Investment Guarantee Agency (MIGA) support and close coordination between the International Finance Corporation (IFC), MIGA, the Global Practices, CCSAs, and the operational group, and looked forward to more information on how an integrated approach and strategic alignment among the different entities will be effectively achieved.

Members emphasized that IFC should apply a pro-poor lens to measure PPP impact. They underscored the importance of improving the World Bank Group's monitoring and evaluation systems to better systematically record data about the impact of PPPs on poverty reduction, and to ensure such monitoring and evaluation work feeds back into future PPP project design and implementation. They welcomed that IFC will work with the Poverty Global Practice and results measurement experts in the World Bank Group in order to come up with adequate indicators and were encouraged to learn that client feedback on results measurement will be extended to all Global Practices to measure progress and ensure adequate service is being provided.

Members encouraged IFC to use a well-balanced risk-based approach and to strengthen its engagement in frontier, nascent, and emerging markets, particularly those with weak PPP-enabling environments, where IFC's additionality is strongest. They agreed that coordination with MIGA would be crucial. Members agreed with the need for more ex ante fiscal analysis and a deepening of political economy expertise by IFC. The committee stressed the importance of clearer communications about PPPs' benefits and transaction costs. They called for a stronger focus on assisting governments manage PPP fiscal implications and local resources; spreading knowledge and best practices; assisting clients in making strategic decisions on the level and nature of private sector participation in infrastructure; and addressing client countries' resource and capacity limitations to operationalize PPP pipelines.

Juan José Bravo
CHAIRPERSON

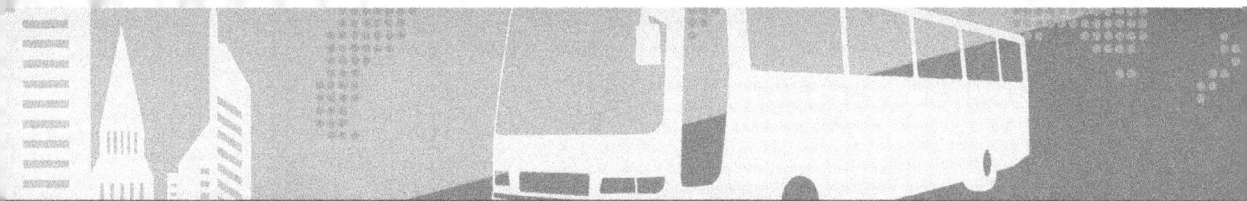

1 Introduction to Public-Private Partnerships

HIGHLIGHTS

- Public-private partnerships (PPPs), if implemented well, can help overcome inadequate infrastructure that constrains economic growth, particularly in developing countries.

- PPPs have seen a rise in the last two decades and are now used in more than 134 developing countries, contributing about 15–20 percent of total infrastructure investment.

- Conceptually, PPPs are an instrument to respond to market failures while minimizing the risk of government failure.

- The World Bank Group has deployed a wide range of instruments and services targeting PPPs during FY02–12—and in increasing numbers. In its support, International Finance Corporation Investment Services and the Multilateral Investment Guarantee Agency focused on middle-income countries, whereas the World Bank and IFC Advisory Services tend to support lower-income countries.

- This evaluation assesses how well the World Bank Group has supported countries in applying PPPs from 2002 to 2012, both "upstream" in preparing the enabling policy and regulatory environment, as well as "downstream" with transaction support and finance.

- The assessment focuses on the core types of PPP arrangements that have a similar level of risk sharing between the public and private sides.

- Beyond broader economic effects, PPPs can benefit the poor through several channels, including by creating jobs or improving service provision in a targeted manner.

Public-private partnerships (PPPs), if implemented well, can help overcome inadequate infrastructure that constrains economic growth, particularly in developing countries. Infrastructure investments are known to accelerate much-needed growth in developing countries and reduce income disparities.[1] But poor infrastructure is often a reflection of several constraints governments face, for example, insufficient public funds, poor planning, weak analysis underpinning project selection, or corruption. Infrastructure assets are also often poorly maintained (WBI 2012).

PPPs can help overcome some of these challenges by mobilizing private sector sources, helping improve project selection and on-time and on-budget implementation, and ensuring adequate maintenance. Although initially restricted to public infrastructure in the form of roads, railways, power generation, or water and waste treatment facilities, PPPs have increasingly moved into the provision of so-called "social infrastructure," such as schools, hospitals, and health services.

PPPs have become more common not only in the aftermath of the 2008 financial crisis, as governments are eager to leverage scarce public funds, but have seen a rise in developing countries over the last two decades. More than 134 developing countries apply PPPs, contributing about 15–20 percent of total infrastructure investment.[2] Widely utilized because of their purported advantages in off-budget funding, anticipated efficiency gains, and improved service quality, PPPs are a mechanism that governments regularly turn to in fulfilling their responsibilities regarding public infrastructure and service—a phenomenon increasingly taking hold in developing countries (Colverson and Perera 2011).

In parallel, in its effort to spur growth and fight poverty, the World Bank Group has expanded its assistance to developing countries in improving access to infrastructure and basic services through PPPs. The Bank Group's portfolio addressing PPPs grew during FY02–12, with 20 units currently contributing to the PPP agenda—from *upstream* policy advice to *downstream* transaction support—comprising a multi-billion-dollar lending, investment, and guarantee portfolio and several hundred capacity building and analytical and advisory activities (AAA).

This evaluation analyzes World Bank Group support to PPPs in a strategic context. The Bank Group's most recent strategy, *A Stronger, Connected, Solutions World Bank Group*, adopted by the Board in October 2013, features PPPs prominently; it intends to "increasingly promote public-private partnerships," given its ability to work with both public and private sector clients (World Bank 2013). In the ongoing change management process, PPPs are also considered a specific cross-cutting solutions area. In this evaluation the Independent Evaluation Group (IEG) reviews World Bank Group historic experience with PPPs with a view to distilling useful lessons for its future endeavors, as laid out in *A Stronger, Connected, Solutions World Bank Group*.

What Are PPPs?

There is no universally accepted definition of PPPs—nor has the World Bank Group adapted an explicit definition. There is a wide variety of definitions of PPPs (see Box 1.1). PPPs may refer to informal and short-term engagements of nongovernmental organizations, the private sector, and/or government agencies that join forces for a shared objective; to more formal, but still short-term private sector engagements for the provision of specific services, for example, annual outsourcing arrangements for janitorial services for a school or operations of the school cafeteria; to more complex contractual arrangements, such as build, operate,

---

BOX 1.1 Selected PPP Definitions

International Monetary Fund – An arrangement where the private sector supplies assets and *services that traditionally have been provided by the government*. In addition to private execution and financing of public investment, PPPs have two other important characteristics: there is an emphasis on service provision, as well as investment, by the private sector; and *significant risk is transferred* from the government to the private sector.

Organization for Economic Co-operation and Development – An agreement between the government and one or more private partners (which may include operators and financiers) according to which the private partners deliver a service so the *service delivery objectives of the government are aligned* with the profit objective of the private partners and the effectiveness of the alignment depends on a *sufficient transfer of risk to the private partners*.

Canada – A cooperative venture between the public and private sector, built on the expertise of each partner that *best meets clearly defined public needs* through the *appropriate allocation of resources, risks, and rewards*.

Australia – Partnerships between the public sector and the private sector for the purpose of designing, planning, financing, constructing, and/or operating projects that would traditionally be regarded as *falling within the remit of the public sector*.

Standard and Poor's – Any medium- to long-term relationship between the public and private sectors, involving the *sharing of risks and rewards* of multisector skills, expertise, and finance to deliver desired policy outcomes.

McKinsey – Differentiates four archetypes of PPPs that all share a common vision, shared goals, investment from all partners, and a formalized structure with shared decision-making coordination, funding, product development, and delivery.

SOURCES: IMF 2004; OECD 2008; McKinsey 2009.

transfer regimes, where the private sector takes on considerable risk and remains engaged long term; or to full privatizations.

In this evaluation, IEG looks at the core types of PPP arrangements that have in common a similar level of risk sharing between public and private entities. This evaluation adopts the definition of the World Bank Institute, according to which PPPs are "long-term contracts between a private party and a government agency, for providing a public asset or service, in which the private party bears significant risk and management responsibility" (WBI 2012, p. 36). This definition appears to be a good common denominator also across the PPP concepts of the International Monetary Fund and the Organisation for Economic Co-operation and Development (OECD) (WBI 2012; IMF 2004; OECD 2008) and translates into a well-defined spectrum of contractual arrangements. These have in common that they are long term, usually bundling design, construction, and maintenance and possibly operation, and contain performance-based elements with private capital at stake. Figure 1.1 illustrates these core types of PPP along a risk sharing dimension. Other forms of private sector involvement, located on the left side of the risk sharing spectrum—for example, short-term outsourcing arrangements without incentives or private capital at stake—would not fall under this evaluation; nor would construction (design-build) contracts for a new road. On the right side of the spectrum, fully privately owned licensed/regulated businesses would not meet this definition of core PPP arrangements either.[3]

Conceptually, PPPs can be seen as an instrument to respond to market failures while minimizing the risk of government failure. As a general rule, private ownership is preferred where competitive market prices can be established (Ter-Minassian 2004). Under such circumstances, the private sector is driven by competition to sell goods and services at a price consumers are willing to pay and by the discipline of the capital market to make profits. However, various market failures (natural monopoly or externalities, and so forth) can justify government ownership, for example, in roads or water distribution. At times, government ownership may also be a policy choice, in particular, in the case of merit goods; these goods, for example, education, would be underconsumed as the average consumer makes decisions based on an individualistic assessment of benefits and within a short-term horizon. But governments—which deliver these services because of market failure or positive externalities in the first place—may subsequently struggle, as they may have difficulties operating efficiently or containing the costs, or may lack the capability to achieve a desired quality standard, or both. In other words, government failure can simply substitute—or may follow—market failure. These arguments can be used to motivate PPPs as an instrument that combines the relative strength of government and private provision in a way that responds to market failure but minimizes the risk of government failure.

FIGURE 1.1 The Spectrum of PPP Arrangements

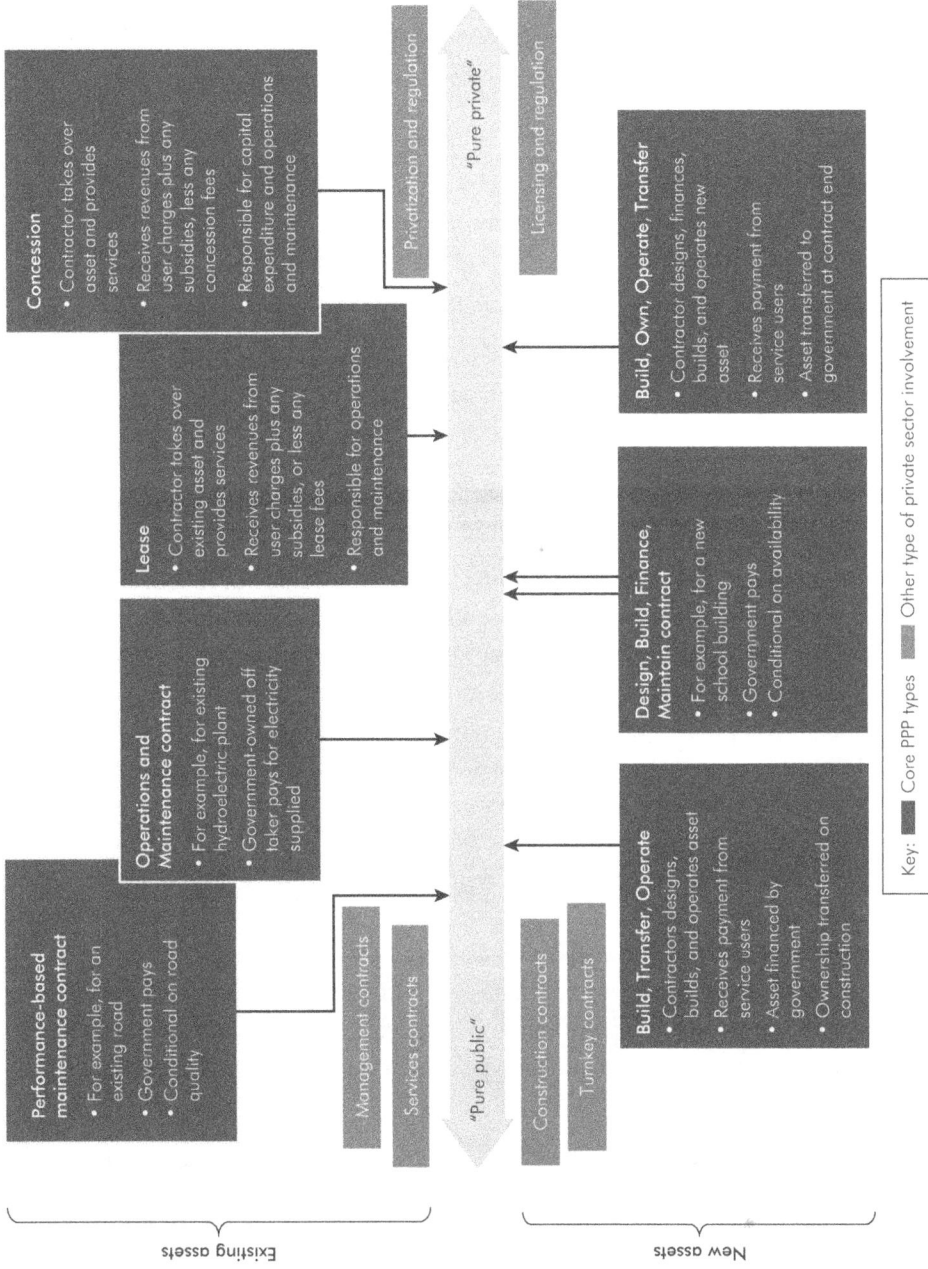

Existing assets

Performance-based maintenance contract
- For example, for an existing road
- Government pays
- Conditional on road quality

Management contracts

Services contracts

Operations and Maintenance contract
- For example, for existing hydroelectric plant
- Government-owned off taker pays for electricity supplied

Lease
- Contractor takes over existing asset and provides services
- Receives revenues from user charges plus any subsidies, or less any lease fees
- Responsible for operations and maintenance

Concession
- Contractor takes over asset and provides services
- Receives revenues from user charges plus any subsidies, less any concession fees
- Responsible for capital expenditure and operations and maintenance

Privatization and regulation

Licensing and regulation

"Pure public"

"Pure private"

New assets

Construction contracts

Turnkey contracts

Build, Transfer, Operate
- Contractors designs, builds, and operates asset
- Receives payment from service users
- Asset financed by government
- Ownership transferred on construction

Design, Build, Finance, Maintain contract
- For example, for a new school building
- Government pays
- Conditional on availability

Build, Own, Operate, Transfer
- Contractor designs, finances, builds, and operates new asset
- Receives payment from service users
- Asset transferred to government at contract end

Key: ▉ Core PPP types ▉ Other type of private sector involvement

SOURCES: WBI 2012; World Bank Institute and Public Private Infrastructure Advisory Facility 2012 (http://www.ppiaf.org/sites/ppiaf.org/files/documents/Note-One-PPP-Basics-and-Principles-of-a-PPP-Framework.pdf).

Private sector actors in PPPs can use their management skills and capacity for innovation to improve efficiency and quality standards. Efficiency gains play an important role in increasing value for money through PPPs. Governments pay a fee to the private partner for the services provided (for example, in terms of usage fees and availability payments), which the private sector uses to pay operating costs and interest charges and to repay debt and return on equity.

In cases where efficiency increases offset the higher financing costs of the private sector, the PPP may have a higher value for money and hence be the preferred option for the government.[4] Such efficiency effects may include improved analysis during project selection, better planning, on-time and on-budget implementation, improved construction expertise, and adequate maintenance (WBI 2012). If implemented well, PPPs can therefore help overcome inadequate infrastructure, which constrains economic growth, particularly in developing countries. Details on the effects of PPPs from a public finance perspective are set out in Box 1.2.

BOX 1.2 The Public Sector Finance Perspective of PPPs

Contrary to intuition, PPPs generally do not provide additional resources for the public sector. Governments can finance their public infrastructure investments just as well as private firms. Only when governments are credit constrained and thus cannot borrow may private finance be superior. When governments do not have credit constraints, the primary effect of private finance in PPP arrangements is that the investment becomes more affordable within annual authority budgets and better matches user benefits, allowing governments to realize infrastructure investments earlier. PPPs mobilize private sector resources to cover the capital expenditure costs up front (or at least most of it) and make the public sector pay during delivery of the services, either through availability payments or usage payments (shadow toll) or a combination thereof (see figure on p. 7). Only if PPPs introduce fees for actual end users do they effectively increase total government revenues and funding. Hence the primary advantage PPPs may offer over traditional public procurement is potential efficiency gains that privately led construction and maintenance may bring, partly offset, however, by higher capital costs of the private investor.

The assessment of public sector liabilities triggered by a PPP project is hence of utmost importance. These can amount to substantial direct liabilities, for example, up-front viability gap funding to make projects more commercially viable and the referred usage payment, or contingent liabilities, such as guarantees on particular risk variables, for example, to buffer the traffic demand risk for the private party, compensation payments for uninsurable force majeure, or termination payments.

Traditional government procurement

Costs / expenditures

Capital and operating costs are paid for by the public sector, which also takes the risk of cost overruns and late delivery

Cost overruns

Estimated capital costs

Running costs overruns

Estimated running costs

5   10   15   20
YEARS

Construction   Operation and maintenance phase

PPP procurement

Costs / expenditures

- Public sector pays over the long term as services are delivered
- Has to cover increased preparation costs and, at times, part of capital costs to make PPP project bankable
- Takes on contingent liabilities

Contingent liabilities

Payment based on usage

Upfront VGP Preparation

Payment based on availability

5   10   15   20
YEARS

Construction   Operation and maintenance phase

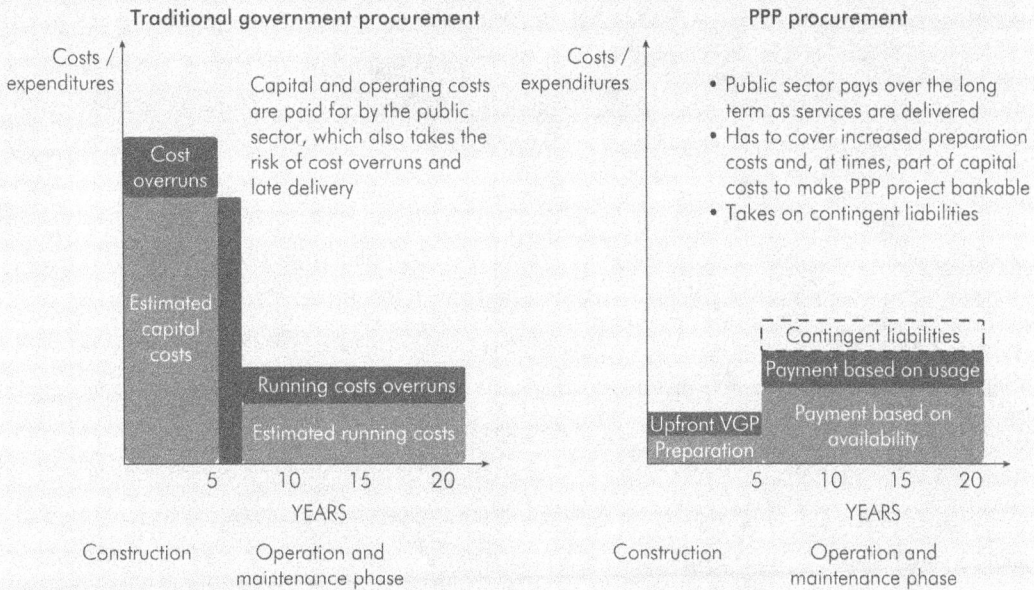

SOURCES: PricewaterhouseCoopers Advisory Services 2005; World Bank 2012; Klein 2012.
NOTE: VGP = viability gap funding.

Rationale for Supporting PPPs

The rationale for the World Bank Group's support to PPPs is based on the claim that PPPs have the potential to close the infrastructure gap by leveraging scarce public funding and introducing private sector technology and innovation to provide better quality public services through improved operational efficiency. Improving the provision of infrastructure and social services through better efficiency and quality contributes directly to growth and poverty reduction. This rationale motives the World Bank Group's engagement in PPPs in its most recent infrastructure strategy update, as well as in the most recent World Bank Group strategy.[5] It also aligns well with the intervention logic of a recently conducted systematic review (Ministry of Foreign Affairs of the Netherlands 2013).

However, countries and markets need to be sufficiently mature to apply the concept of PPPs wisely. Success in PPPs is contingent on certain arrangements: (i) clear and stable market rules; (ii) sound and predictable legal and regulatory environments; and (iii) well-designed projects, including appropriate risk allocation. This implies that government authorities need to be sophisticated enough to develop sector reform policies, assess fiscal risks associated with PPPs, base their decision of public procurement versus PPP on comprehensive value for money assessments, and have impartial transaction advisory at hand to make PPP deals bankable and sustainable. In contrast, markets also need to be sufficiently liquid, that is, having enough potential investors with adequate regional experience in bidding for PPPs in an economy with available long-term capital. The World Bank Group, with its private and public sector arms, can potentially play a crucial role in "readying" countries to use PPPs and in assisting in specific PPP transactions.

The Bank Group's potentially unique value proposition to its client countries rests with the capacity to provide support along the entire PPP cycle, complemented by analytical work— often donor or grant funded—that can help countries establish their PPP frameworks and create PPP pipelines. Countries that are about to embark on their PPP agendas and are in the process of developing their PPP frameworks will appreciate such support the most. The private sector-oriented arms of the World Bank Group can play a catalyzing role in creating a PPP market by facilitating the structuring of PPP transactions or providing finance or guarantees. Supporting transactions that have a pioneering character, that is, those that are structured within yet untested PPP frameworks (in a particular sector, country, or region within a country) will have higher additionality than supporting transactions in relatively established markets.

PPPs and the Poor

PPPs need to be looked at through a "poverty lens" as well, in view of the Bank Group's central goal of fighting poverty—reaffirmed by the 2013 strategy's dual goal of ending extreme poverty and promoting shared prosperity. The underlying rationale for PPP interventions is that PPPs can help improve infrastructure, spurring economic growth that eventually reaches the poor ("trickle down" effect). The majority of PPP interventions followed that logic, as they were positioned with the growth pillar of country assistance strategies (Chapter 2).[6] In addition, through leveraging infrastructure investments through private sector funds, PPPs can free resources that the government would have used to fund its public investment program and can now use for other priorities. PPPs can also advance important investments and hence contribute to economic growth earlier. But the link from growth to poverty reduction is not automatic (DFID 2008). Deliberate action is often required to ensure that project outcomes and transmission channels focus on the poor. Such a proactive position is particularly important for institutions such as the World Bank Group, which aim to achieve poverty-reduction objectives.

The distribution of the benefits of PPP projects to the poor can occur through several channels. Beyond the trickle-down effect, PPPs can improve the livelihood of the poor by either (i) explicitly focusing on the poor (for example, by creating jobs for the poor) or (ii) targeting the poor, based on geographic or household criteria. For example, PPPs can increase basic service coverage in poor areas. This could be a PPP specifically servicing a poor area, possibly using an innovative (alternative) approach developed by a private provider. It could also happen by having a private provider service a poor area in exchange for the right to service a wealthier area. A PPP can raise the service quality in a poor area through efficiencies of a private provider (the same money buys better services) and setting service standards. These pro-poor channels can be reflected in the project design, either as an explicit or implicit objective or project implementation may track poverty and social outcomes.

Improving access and quality for the poor needs to be balanced with affordability. The private sector requires cost recovery tariffs in general, which may have repercussion effects on tariff levels. Involving the private sector in the design, construction, operations, and/or maintenance of a service provision introduces market forces into a scheme that—in many cases—has been public before. As tariffs are in most cases the major source of the cash flow with which the private operator services its debt and equity, tariffs need to recover at least costs.

This stands in sharp contrast to the frequently encountered "soft budget constraints" to state-owned enterprises and publicly owned utilities, where hidden subsidy schemes often squeeze the financial performance of the utility, eventually putting the entire sector in financial stress. In fact, hopes were high that PPP schemes would turn around many of these poorly performing public utilities through increased commercial orientation, tariff transparency, and cost recovery. As a consequence, tariff setting (preferably independent) needs to factor in input prices—for example, oil price developments—and pass them on to the consumer. This, however, may make services unaffordable for the poor and vulnerable, unless the cost increases are buffered by a targeted subsidy scheme.

Hence the decision as to whether to introduce PPPs (or not) is closely linked to policies that aim at protecting the poor from sudden tariff increases (see Box 1.3). Given the various ways PPPs can impact the poor, IEG therefore looked at the effect of PPPs on the poor and how far the World Bank Group has considered pro-poor aspects in the design, implementation, and monitoring of PPPs.

PPP Trends Globally and the World Bank Group's Engagement

The last 10 years have seen a rise of PPPs in developing countries. Looking at the broader picture of private sector investments in developing countries, private capital has contributed between 15 and 20 percent of total investment in infrastructure during the last 10 years.[7] Looking more specifically at PPPs, after experiencing a slowdown from 1997 to 2004 as a result of the Asian financial crisis, PPPs are back on the rise in the aftermath of the 2008 global financial crisis. PPP investments peaked in 1997 at $60 billion, then accounted for only $30 billion *per year* on average during FY02–06; they subsequently increased to

Most poorly performing public utilities in developing countries have tariffs that are well below cost-recovery levels, and raising them is often a necessary component of reform toward financial sustainability. In practice, the potential impact of a PPP on the tariff depends on two things: how far the initial tariff level is from the cost-recovery level and the extent of efficiency gains that can be made by the private operator—two factors that move in opposite directions and can be of very large magnitude in developing countries.

The evolution of tariff levels in a number of PPP projects was analyzed through various studies, reviewed by Marin (2009). In most cases, tariffs rose over time, but the underlying reasons for them, as well as whether those increases were justified, could not be assessed. Analyzing the impact of PPPs on tariffs can be misleading, because that impact is heavily dependent on prevailing tariff policies. Tariff increases are not necessarily a bad thing for customers when they translate into wider access to better services. In many developing countries, low water tariffs mostly benefit the connected middle class and work against the interests of the unconnected urban poor, who need to access water from often unsafe and/or more expensive sources. It is likely that many of the poor households that gained access to piped water under PPP projects ended up paying a lower price for water than when they were not connected to the network. In a few recorded cases, private operators made large enough efficiency gains to allow for significant tariff reductions in real terms after a few years.

The evidence from the literature on the impact of PPPs on tariffs is largely inconclusive. Costs are greatly affected by local factors, such as water availability, and comparing tariff levels between private and public utilities can be misleading because of differences in the legal, administrative, and financial frameworks in which the two sets of utilities operate. One study using a large sample to control for the many exogenous factors found no statistically significant difference in water tariffs between comparable public and private utilities.

SOURCES: Marin 2009; Gassner, Popov, and Pushak 2009.

$79 billion *per year* on average during FY07–11. PPPs have now spread across the globe: 134 developing countries implemented new PPP projects in infrastructure alone between 2002 and 2011.[8] Although initially restricted to infrastructure, PPPs have increasingly moved into the provision of "social infrastructure," such as schools, hospitals, and health services.[9] Much of the growth of PPPs has been captured by middle-income countries (MICs) and in two regions, Latin America and the Caribbean and East Asia and Pacific.[10]

The World Bank Group has deployed a wide range of instruments and services targeting PPPs during FY02 alone 12—and in increasing numbers.[11] The International Finance

Corporation (IFC) invested in 176 PPPs with total commitments of $6.2 billion; the Multilateral Investment Guarantee Agency (MIGA) supported 81 PPP projects through political risk insurance (PRI), with a total $5.1 billion gross exposure; and IFC PPP Advisory Services completed 140 transactions, with a total expenditure of $177 million. On the public sector side, the International Bank for Reconstruction and Development (IBRD)/ International Development Association (IDA) approved 353 lending and partial risk guarantee (PRG) projects during FY02–12 with a PPP component totaling $7.6 billion.[12] Of these, 12 are PRG projects; that is complemented by 112 capacity building activities of the World Bank Institute (WBI) and 683 trust fund-supported advisory activities by the Public-Private Infrastructure Advisory Facility (PPIAF), with total expenditures amounting to $134 million.[13] During the last 10 years, World Bank Group support to PPPs has increased threefold. Lending, investments, and guarantees have risen from 2002 to 2012 both in absolute and relative terms, from $0.9 billion to $ 2.9 billion and from 4 percent to 7 percent (Figure 1.2).

In its support, IFC Investment Services and MIGA focused on MICs, whereas World Bank and IFC Advisory Services tend to support more lower-income countries (LICs).[14] IFC investments and MIGA guarantees tend to benefit mostly projects in MICs or upper-middle-income

FIGURE 1.2 World Bank Group Lending, Investments, and Guarantees Targeting PPPs—Volume and Share of Volume per Institution, FY02–12

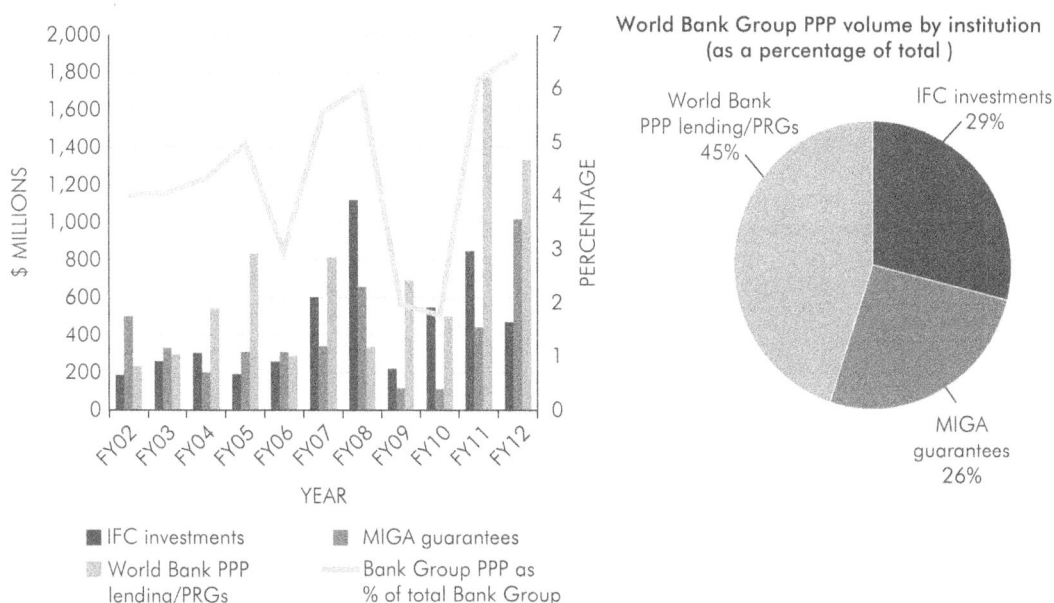

SOURCES: IFC extract data as of June 31, 2012; MIGA database; World Bank lending data.
NOTE: Volume = sum of World Bank lending (commitments), IFC investments (commitments), and MIGA guarantees (gross exposure issued); PRG = partial risk guarantee.

countries (UMIC), with 65 percent and 72 percent in MICs and UMICs, respectively. This reflects the flow of foreign direct investment (FDI) for PPPs, which also has been directed toward MICs in the last 10 years and indicates the demand-driven nature of IFC's investments and MIGA guarantees.

By contrast, World Bank and IFC Advisory Services target a higher share of LICs and lower-middle-income countries (LMICs), 17 and 51 percent and 19 and 48 percent, respectively. Their engagements tend to be inherently of a different risk profile, as the interaction with client countries does not foresee a "positive selection bias;" that is, that World Bank and IFC Advisory Services do not have much freedom to choose what to engage in, but are more bound to follow the country's strategic development priorities.

Globally, the World Bank Group has assisted 134 **countries** with PPP-targeted interventions, that is, with at least one intervention; 103 countries have received multiple PPP-targeted interventions. Looking at how "deep" the PPP-related interactions were between the Bank Group and its client countries reveals that particularly strong support was given to a few countries: Brazil, China, and India. Figure 1.3 depicts the distribution by total number of targeted interventions per country ("depth").

FIGURE 1.3 Depth of World Bank Group Support Targeted to PPPs, per Country

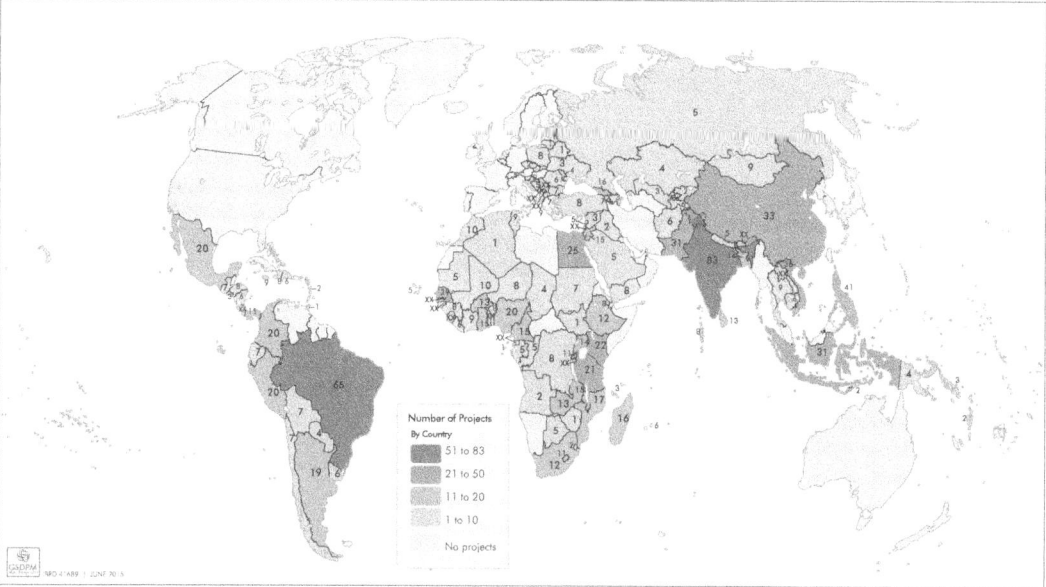

SOURCE: IEG.

NOTE: Each country received one point for each project in each of the following categories: IFC Investment, IFC Advisory Services, World Bank lending and partial risk guarantees, MIGA guarantees, PPIAF, WBI.

Evaluation Design

In this evaluation IEG assesses how well the World Bank Group has supported countries in applying PPPs from 2002 to 2012. It covers all sectors and focuses on "targeted interventions," referring to activities aimed at either improving the enabling environment specifically for PPPs—as opposed to broad-based macroeconomic or investment climate interventions—and or facilitating specific PPP transactions (Figure 1.4).[15]

The evaluation covers IFC Investment and Advisory Services, MIGA guarantees, World Bank guarantees, lending and in principle also nonlending (AAA, including nonlending technical assistance, economic and sector work, and reimbursable technical assistance),[16] World Bank Group-managed trust funds with a focus on PPPs—that is, PPIAF—as well as activities of the World Bank Institute (WBI) that target PPPs. For World Bank projects, this evaluation focuses primarily on projects where PPPs were the *major theme*. This was necessary, as a significant number of World Bank projects had only an ancillary PPP reference. The evaluation covers projects that were "active" during FY02–12.[17] In terms of types of PPPs, this evaluation focuses on the core PPP types defined in Figure 1.1.

IEG assessed results along a specific "results chain." The World Bank Group deploys its instruments upstream, ranging from lending to non-lending technical assistance to AAA to put in place sector reforms and to improve the enabling environment, for example, regulatory

FIGURE 1.4 PPP Framework

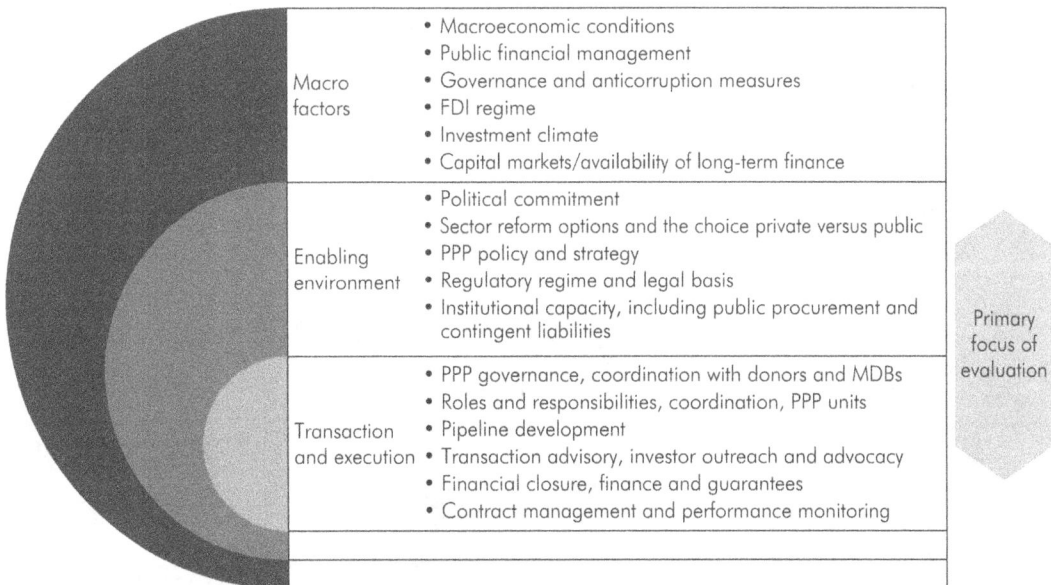

Macro factors	• Macroeconomic conditions • Public financial management • Governance and anticorruption measures • FDI regime • Investment climate • Capital markets/availability of long-term finance	
Enabling environment	• Political commitment • Sector reform options and the choice private versus public • PPP policy and strategy • Regulatory regime and legal basis • Institutional capacity, including public procurement and contingent liabilities	Primary focus of evaluation
Transaction and execution	• PPP governance, coordination with donors and MDBs • Roles and responsibilities, coordination, PPP units • Pipeline development • Transaction advisory, investor outreach and advocacy • Financial closure, finance and guarantees • Contract management and performance monitoring	

SOURCE: IEG, based on 33 interviews with World Bank Group managers.
NOTE: FDI = foreign direct investment; MDB = multilateral development bank.

and legal frameworks and institutional capacity to better plan and assess PPP options and their fiscal implications. The World Bank guarantee program (PRGs), IFC investments, and MIGA guarantees complement this effort by providing finance and political risk coverage, thus enabling specific PPP transactions to reach financial closure—potentially setting demonstration effects. Such PPPs may then contribute to improving access to infrastructure and social services, which drives economic growth and poverty reduction. Figure 1.5 summarizes this results chain.[18]

IEG evaluated evidence at all three stages of this results chain. At the activity level, this evaluation presents an assessment of the strategic relevance of World Bank Group PPP-targeted activities and their complementary nature. This assessment focuses on the country level, as the most crucial question is whether the support was relevant. IEG presents evidence for 45 client countries in which the World Bank Group has had at least five PPP targeted activities during FY02–12. At the output level, IEG assesses how far activities that aimed to create an enabling environment actually achieved that objective, for example, if regulatory regimes are functioning and fulfilling their duty. IEG also collected evidence on effects of these activities on subsequent PPP transactions. For activities that aimed at

FIGURE 1.5 Evaluation Results Chain

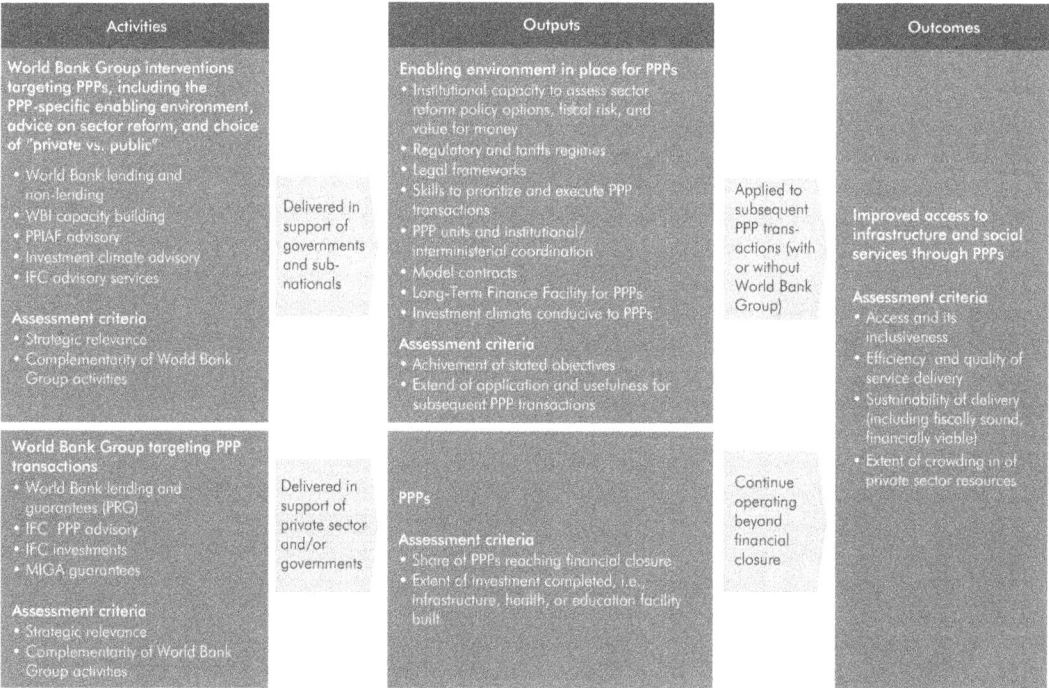

Activities	Outputs	Outcomes
World Bank Group interventions targeting PPPs, including the PPP-specific enabling environment, advice on sector reform, and choice of "private vs. public": • World Bank lending and non-lending • WBI capacity building • PPIAF advisory • Investment climate advisory • IFC advisory services Assessment criteria • Strategic relevance • Complementarity of World Bank Group activities	*Delivered in support of governments and sub-nationals* — Enabling environment in place for PPPs • Institutional capacity to assess sector reform policy options, fiscal risk, and value for money • Regulatory and tariffs regimes • Legal frameworks • Skills to prioritize and execute PPP transactions • PPP units and institutional/interministerial coordination • Model contracts • Long-Term Finance Facility for PPPs • Investment climate conducive to PPPs Assessment criteria • Achievement of stated objectives • Extent of application and usefulness for subsequent PPP transactions	*Applied to subsequent PPP transactions (with or without World Bank Group)* — Improved access to infrastructure and social services through PPPs Assessment criteria • Access and its inclusiveness • Efficiency and quality of service delivery • Sustainability of delivery (including fiscally sound, financially viable) • Extent of crowding in of private sector resources
World Bank Group targeting PPP transactions • World Bank lending and guarantees (PRG) • IFC PPP advisory • IFC investments • MIGA guarantees Assessment criteria • Strategic relevance • Complementarity of World Bank Group activities	*Delivered in support of private sector and/or governments* — PPPs Assessment criteria • Share of PPPs reaching financial closure • Extent of investment completed, i.e., infrastructure, health, or education facility built	*Continue operating beyond financial closure*

Assumptions: Demand for PPPs based on country priorities and infrastructure gap, political commitment, macro economic stability, competition, demographic changes, natural disasters, and other external factors

SOURCE: IEG.

NOTE: PPIAF = Public-Private Infrastructure Advisory Facility; WBI = World Bank Institute.

PPP transactions, this level of assessment focuses on evidence of reaching financial closure and financial leveraging. Finally, IEG presents evidence on outcomes, that is, on improved access to infrastructure and social services to PPPs.

The overarching question that this evaluation seeks to answer is: "How effective has the World Bank Group been in assisting the private and public sector in client countries in improving access to infrastructure and social services through PPPs?" This overarching question will be addressed with a view to gaining an understanding how successful PPPs can be replicated in different country contexts. The supporting questions are as follows:

- *Relevance:* Has the World Bank Group's support for PPPs been relevant to client countries?

- *Effectiveness upstream:* Has the World Bank Group been effective in its *upstream work*, that is, in creating an enabling environment so that countries can engage in PPPs? Has the Bank Group's upstream support helped countries improve access to infrastructure and social services through subsequent PPPs, regardless of Bank Group involvement in the actual transaction?

- *Effectiveness downstream:* Have PPPs that benefited from World Bank Group *downstream* support in the form of IFC investments, advisory services, MIGA guarantees, and/or World Bank lending and guarantees contributed to improved access to infrastructure and social services?

- *Working as one World Bank Group:* To what extent do the World Bank Group's organizational structures, processes, and incentives enable a coordinated and effective delivery of PPP targeted activities?

IEG used a combination of the following methodologies: (i) a comprehensive portfolio review of all World Bank Group projects and activities targeting PPPs; (ii) a systematic analysis of a statistically representative sample of project-level evaluations of individual PPP projects; (iii) nine in-depth country case studies, including field missions; (iv) desk reviews of 45 countries' Country Assistance Strategy Completion Reports; and (v) a review of policy and strategy documents at country and corporation levels. The approach combines qualitative and quantitative methods and draws on the experience of other multilateral development banks (MDBs). Identification of PPP-targeted projects was carried out in close cooperation with World Bank Group management (Appendix A).

IEG's analysis focused on country-level results, in addition to covering a statistically representative sample of lending, investment, and guarantee projects. The starting point for the selection of PPP projects to be evaluated in detail was a sample of countries that had a minimum of World Bank Group–supported PPP activities. Forty-five countries were identified using a minimum threshold of at least five PPP targeting activities by any of the World Bank Group entities FY02–12.[19] The assessment of strategic relevance (Chapter 2) builds on these countries.

Relevance of PPP-targeted activities was assessed on the basis of development priorities spelled out in County Assistance/Partnership Strategies and their implementation reports. In addition, IEG collected evidence at the strategic level that may indicate the advancement of the PPP agenda at country and sector levels that went beyond the individual intervention. For the portfolio analysis the sample size was further expanded to include a statistically representative sample size, at least for the major products, that is, World Bank loans, IFC investments, IFC Advisory Services, and MIGA guarantees.[20] Using this approach, of the total 1,545 PPP targeted activities, 811 were reviewed in detail. These were categorized by their main features, lending and investment volumes, objectives, and components of the activities and analyzed their development results. The portfolio analysis relied primarily on available micro evaluation data, that is, on results achievement at project closure for World Bank lending projects and at the point of operational maturity for IFC and MIGA projects.[21] Table 1.1 provides an overview of the total number of PPP interventions, classified by upstream and downstream support.

The study was complemented by interviews with beneficiaries, stakeholders, other donors and World Bank Group staff. The IEG team interviewed relevant Bank Group staff and

TABLE 1.1 World Bank Group Activities Targeting PPPs, by Number, Operationally Matured/ Exited FY02–12

	PPIAF	World Bank	World Bank	IFC AS	IFC IS	MIGA	Total
Upstream	194	33	126	10	n.a.	n.a.	366
Up- and downstream	14	n.a.	65	20	4	n.a.	100
Downstream	2	n.a.	63	75	143	62	345
Total reviewed	210	33	254	105	147	62	811
Total PPP	683	112	353	140	176	81	1,545

SOURCE: IEG.
NOTE: This may include projects approved since 1997. AS = Advisory Services; IS = Investment Services; MIGA = Multilateral Investment Guarantee Agency; n.a. = not applicable; PPIAF = Public-Private Infrastructure Advisory Facility; WBI = World Bank Institute.

management in headquarters and in each field visit. IEG gathered opinions and insights from clients, beneficiaries, and other major stakeholders in field visit countries, including other donors and MDBs, private sector investors and business associations, government counterparts, civil society organizations, think tanks and academia, and other interested parties. In addition, IEG conducted discussions and outreach to interested stakeholders through social media.

Nine country case studies identified drivers of success, assessed non-lending and advisory work, and addressed issues of complementarity and synergies. Country case studies were elected on a purposive basis[22] with the goal of generating three sets of case studies in Latin America and the Caribbean and East Asia and Pacific, the two most active regions in applying PPPs, and Sub-Saharan Africa, with one of the lowest PPP activity levels and high cancellation rates. Each set contained one country where the World Bank Group provided mainly upstream support, one country where the World Bank was active only downstream, and one country where the World Bank was active both upstream and downstream, to study the added value of continuous engagement and the effects of direct support to PPPs. This design allowed drawing lessons within and across these regions, in particular across these "horizontal" cases to yield more valid and robust lessons.[23] The list of countries reviewed and the detailed country-level assessment methodology are in Appendix C.

The study design has also limitations. The assessment did not cover developmental effects beyond improved access to infrastructure, that is, potential impacts on economic growth or poverty eradication. The extent to which PPPs deliver their services over the long term—that is, their sustainability—could only be assessed for IFC investments, where monitoring data are available beyond operational maturity, and for other PPP projects in the context of the nine country cases.

The World Bank's non-lending (economic and sector work, non-lending technical assistance, and reimbursable technical assistance) is not yet integrated in an overall results framework; hence evaluation benchmarks, that is, "objectives" against which these activities could be assessed, do not exist. IEG had to adapt a pragmatic approach for the evaluation, that is, make reasonable assumptions about what non-lending work was trying to influence. Because of limited availability of records in this area, only the major pieces were assessed in the context of the country case studies. The scant availability of project-level data on actual PPP performance also posed limitations to the statistical significance of findings, primarily for World Bank non-lending activities, IFC Advisory Services, and MIGA projects.[24]

This report is structured to allow understanding the World Bank Group-wide engagement for PPPs. Instead of presenting findings in isolated chapters per World Bank Group entity, this report follows the logic of the PPP delivery model. First, for a PPP intervention to be useful to a country, it must be relevant given the country's development priorities. Hence, this report starts with a discussion of the relevance of Bank Group's PPP support. Typically, a minimum of an enabling environment must be available for PPPs to materialize; hence the report then assesses the World Bank Group's effectiveness in assisting countries to build up the needed environment, across all institutions engaged in the World Bank Group upstream—that is, policy reform—response.

Then actual results of PPPs and the effectiveness of World Bank Group's downstream support to actual PPP transactions are discussed in the chapter "Did PPPs Deliver?" Again, all transaction-focused operations across the Bank Group will be assessed in that chapter. The report concludes with a chapter on World Bank Group-wide coordination and management.

Notes

[1] A 10 percent increase in infrastructure development contributes to 1 percent growth in the long term (see Röller and Waverman 2001; Calderon and Serven 2010; and Calderon and others 2011).

[2] World Bank Private Participation in Infrastructure project database.

[3] Note that the literature treats the right side of the risk sharing spectrum sometimes as a continuum rather than a clear cut-off line with regard to what is considered a PPP and what is not. This is particularly true in cases where a privately owned network operator functions as a natural monopoly within a licensed, regulated space. IEG covered such arrangements in the nine country case studies to enable the assessment of a broad PPP spectrum.

[4] The net present value of capital expenditure and usage fees combined may be lower for PPPs than for the public procurement option (OECD 2008).

[5] Based on World Bank (2012) and 33 preliminary IEG interviews with World Bank Group managers.

[6] This is also corroborated for IFC's portfolio by the IEG evaluation *Assessing IFC's Poverty Focus and Results* (IEG 2011). This evaluation found that the majority of IFC projects are designed to contribute to growth. Of the 211 nonfinancial sector projects analyzed in that study, 86 percent reported economic rate of return estimates of more than 15 percent. Given a benchmark rate of return of 10, this shows that the majority of projects are expected to generate net positive returns in the economies in which they are being implemented.

[7] This percentage is indicative of *total* global investment in infrastructure, not of World Bank Group investment or lending specifically. The figure is intended to serve as a proxy for the importance of PPPs, as the concept of private sector investments in infrastructure is broader than mere PPP-related investments (World Bank Private Participation in Infrastructure project database in Delmon and others 2010).

[8] According to the World Bank Private Participation in Infrastructure project database, using the definition of this evaluation.

[9] However, an assessment of trends for social infrastructure is not possible, as a global database for private sector engagement in these areas does not exist.

[10] MICs saw a growth of PPPs over the last 10 years by more than 100 percent, from $147 billion of investments during FY02–06 to $384 billion in FY07–12. With these investment volumes in PPPs, MICs have not only had a stronger PPP growth, but they also have attracted far more funding for PPPs in absolute terms than LICs. LICs attracted PPP investments

of $6 billion during FY02–06 and $9 billion during FY07–12, representing only 4 and 2 percent of what MICs had attracted, respectively. PPPs were also concentrated regionally during FY02–12. Latin America and the Caribbean showed the highest PPP concentration, with 37 percent of investment volume, followed by East Asia and Pacific with 25 percent during FY02–12—even though East Asia and Pacific saw a slowdown recently in absolute terms from 33 percent initially to 13 percent during FY07–12. In contrast, South Asia experienced significant growth, mostly because of investments in India. The Middle East and North Africa Region and Sub-Saharan Africa rank last, each with only four percent of total PPP investment volume. The concentration of PPP investment is also quite pronounced at the country level: the top five countries—Brazil, India, China, Mexico, and Malaysia—combined represent 60 percent of all PPP investments over the period 2002–11.

[11] The term "targeted interventions" refers to activities aimed at either building or improving the enabling environment specifically for PPPs—as opposed to broad-based macroeconomic or investment climate interventions—regardless of whether an actual PPP transaction followed or at facilitating specific PPP transactions, including green as well as brown field operations. For a World Bank Group activity to be captured by this portfolio analysis as "targeting" PPPs, it must have at least one component addressing such PPP issues. The lending amount presented for the World Bank indicates the entire lending amount of projects that contain such PPP components. As many World Bank projects contain multiple components, the lending volume includes also volume targeting other components of these projects. As current information systems are unable to produce PPP-specific reports, only the detailed portfolio analysis of the evaluation will attempt to disaggregate lending volume with the goal to presenting a PPP-specific lending volume. The same applies to World Bank guarantee projects.

[12] Excluding development policy loans (DPLs), as it is not possible to identify loan volumes that target PPPs in DPLs.

[13] The World Bank delivered 1,443 non-lending activities (AAA) in infrastructure, health, and education. PPP-targeted AAA will only be identified during country case studies, as AAA work is generally poorly documented and not captured in an adequately coded database.

[14] Looking at sectors, however, there is no significant difference.

[15] Covers also support to rehabilitation or expansion to existing PPPs.

[16] PPP-targeted AAA activities of the World Bank will be assessed in country case studies only.

[17] That includes projects that were "closed" (for World Bank) or that reached "operational maturity" (for IFC and MIGA) during FY02–12, hence including projects that were approved *prior* to FY02; and "ongoing" projects, that is, those approved in FY02–12, that have not yet reached closure/operational maturity. The purpose of including the cohort of ongoing or not yet operationally mature projects is to answer questions of design and general trends.

[18] The ultimate impact that sound PPP arrangements are expected to deliver—through improved access to infrastructure—is economic growth and poverty eradication; these impacts are not explicitly visualized in the figure.

[19] World Bank, IFC Advisory Services, IFC Investment Services, MIGA, PPIAF, and WBI.

[20] For the World Bank the sample is statistically representative at 99 percent confidence level and a confidence interval of +/−5 percent; for IFC Investment Services and Advisory Services and MIGA the samples are statistically representative at 95–99 percent confidence level and a confidence interval of +/−5 percent.

[21] For World Bank projects, ICRs and their IEG reviews were the primary source of results information, complemented by Project Performance Assessment Reports. For IFC Investment Services and MIGA, this evaluation relied on Extended Project Supervision Reports, Project Evaluation Summaries, and Project Evaluation Reports conducted at operational maturity, about two years after financial closure. Available monitoring data for IFC's investments beyond project maturity were used to extend the assessment of sustainability beyond maturity. Project Completion Reports, the 11 Post-Implementation Monitoring reports, and the 2 evaluation reports of IFC's PPP Advisory Services were the primary source of output and results information for these types of interventions.

[22] A statistically significant sample of the 110 developing countries using PPPs would require 86 countries to be covered.

[23] Given the above regional focus, further selection criteria for case studies countries were population over 1 million; at least one World Bank/IFC/MIGA/WBI/PPIAF activity closed (World Bank) or operationally matured (IFC/MIGA) intervention; and representation of a balanced mix of small and large countries.

[24] World Bank lending operations and IFC investments are subject to a systematic ex post evaluation system. MIGA is mainstreaming its evaluation and self-evaluation systems; as a result, 11 of 96 PPP guarantee projects have been subject to evaluation or IEG validation. For these three products, ex post evaluation report may contain some performance data (see Chapter 4 for actual availability in these documents) on the World Bank's non-lending, trust-funded upstream activities by PPIAF, and the World Bank Institute's activities are generally not subject to ex post assessments, hence can only be assessed for their outcomes in country case studies. IFC advisory services are subject to Project Completion Reports, which assess the success of the mandate up to the point of contract award. They usually cannot be expected to contain actual PPP performance data, as those would not become operational at the time the report is drafted.

References

Calderon, Cesar, and Luis Serven. 2010. "Infrastructure and Economic Development in Sub-Saharan Africa." *Journal of African Economies*, 19 (Suppl 1): 113–87.

Calderon, Cesar, and others. 2011. "Is Infrastructure Capital Productive? A Dynamic Heterogeneous Approach." Policy Research Working Paper, World Bank, Washington, DC.

Colverson, Samuel, and Oshani Perera. 2011. "Sustainable Development: Is There a Role for Public-Private Partnerships?" Summary of IISD Preliminary Investigation. International Institute for Sustainable Development, Winnipeg, Canada.

Delmon, Gassner, Kacaniku, and Baghat. 2010. "Overview of Public Private Partnerships (PPPs) in Infrastructure in Developing Countries." Background Note for the G20 Seoul Meeting.

DFID (Department for International Development). 2008. *Private Sector Development Strategy Prosperity for All: Making Markets Work.* London: DFID.

Gassner, Katharina, Alexander Popov, and Nataliya Pushak. 2009. "Does Private Sector Participation Improve Performance in Electricity and Water Distribution?" *Trends and Policy Options*, 6.

IEG (Independent Evaluation Group). 2011. *Assessing IFC's Poverty Focus and Results.* Washington, DC: World Bank.

IMF (International Monetary Fund). 2004. *Public-Private Partnerships.* Washington, DC: IMF.

Klein, Michael. 2012. "Infrastructure Policy—Basic Design Options." Policy Research Working Paper 6274, World Bank, Washington, DC.

Marin, Philippe. 2009. "Public-Private Partnerships for Urban Water Utilities: A Review of Experience in Developing Countries." *Trends and Policy Options*, 8.

McKinsey. 2009. "Public-Private Partnerships—Harnessing the Private Sector's Unique Ability to Enhance Social Impact." Working Paper, https://mckinseyonsociety.com.

Ministry of Foreign Affairs of the Netherlands. 2013. "Public-Private Partnerships in Developing Countries—A Systematic Literature Review." The Hague: Ministry of Foreign Affairs.

OECD (Organisation for Economic Co-operation and Development). 2008. *Public-Private Partnerships: In Pursuit of Risk Sharing and Value for Money.* Paris: OECD.

PricewaterhouseCoopers Advisory Services. 2005. *Delivering the PPP Promise: A Review of PPP Issues and Activity.* Washington, DC: PricewaterhouseCooper.

Röller, Lars-Hendrik, and Leonard Waverman. 2001. "Telecommunications Infrastructure and Economic Development: A Simultaneous Approach." *American Economic Review,* 91 (4): 909–23.

Ter-Minassian, Teresa. 2004. *Public-Private Partnerships.* Washington, DC: International Monetary Fund.

WBI (World Bank Institute). 2012. *Public-Private Partnerships Reference Guide,* Version 1.0. Washington, DC: World Bank Institute and Public Private Infrastructure Advisory Facility.

WBI and Public Private Infrastructure Advisory Facility. 2012. PPP Basics and Principles of a PPP Framework. http://www.ppiaf.org/sites/ppiaf.org/ files/documents/Note-One-PPP-Basics-and-Principles-of-a-PPP-Framework.pdf.

World Bank. 2012. "PPP Strategy for the FDP Network." Presentation, Washington, DC.

World Bank. 2013. *A Stronger, Connected Solutions World Bank Group.* Washington, DC: World Bank.

2

Relevance of World Bank Group Support

HIGHLIGHTS

- With the intention to increase PPP support in the most recent World Bank Group strategy, PPPs are high on the corporate agenda. Although PPPs are included in many strategies and individual conceptual notes, there is no World Bank Group-wide guidance to implement PPPs as "cross-cutting solutions areas" and to translate the Bank Group's strategic intentions into an operational plan.

- Overall, the World Bank Group's strategic resources allocation for PPP support is synchronized with country needs and their stage of "maturity" of handling PPPs. In particular, the World Bank's and PPIAF upstream policy support truly targets those countries that are most in need of its support, that is, countries with the least developed enabling environments.

- IFC's investments often support countries that already have a well-developed enabling environment and a track record of handling PPPs. IFC seems to push its business less systematically into "emerging" countries (or markets), that is, into countries with a less tested enabling environment.

- MIGA's support is well in sync with countries' needs, as it emphasizes more countries with nascent or at least less-tested environments.

- At the country level, World Bank Group support for PPPs was relevant to client countries inasmuch as it supported clear development priorities.

- The most common constraints the World Bank Group's country strategies address are inadequate sector structure, regulatory failure, and governance issues, such as corruption linked to PPPs.

- Country strategies tend to less systematically address other important PPP constrains, such as government capability to make strategic decisions on PPPs based on value for money assessments, or to assess fiscal implications associated with PPPs; political economy factors, and issues of the government's commitment to the PPP agenda are almost entirely ignored.

- At the country level, the World Bank Group's operation responds well to the PPP constraints identified for that country. The World Bank Group was also responsive over time, that is, to client countries' needs and changing priorities in the respective PPP agenda.

This chapter analyzes to what extent the World Bank Group's support for PPPs has been relevant in the context of Bank Group's strategic framework and country-level priorities. The intervention logic for PPPs builds on their potential to close an infrastructure gap, including in social infrastructure. However, local circumstances vary. Fiscal space that often motivates the use of PPPs—but also at times limits it—may differ across countries. Each country may have its own high-priority sector where deficiencies prevail; and across sectors, reform progress may be uneven. In other words, each country faces particular constraints and developmental challenges requiring a tailor-made PPP solution.

This chapter presents evidence on (i) how PPPs fit into the overall strategic framework of the World Bank Group; (ii) how strategically the Bank Group deployed its resources; and (iii) how the Bank Group addressed development priorities in client countries and identified constraints to the countries' PPP agenda.[1]

The World Bank Group's Strategic Framework for PPPs

The 2002 Private Sector Development Strategy elevated private participation in infrastructure (PPI)—and with it PPPs—to the strategic level for the first time, after the Asian crisis of 1997–98 revealed the underlying weaknesses of many PPI projects. Governments had pursued PPP models to avoid fiscal burdens but had often been politically unwilling or unable to introduce cost-covering retail tariffs; this led to private investors asking for government payment guarantees and, eventually, taxpayers paying anyway. Such schemes resulted in expensive off-balance sheet borrowing by governments and pointed to the importance of sound policy reform *before* the introduction of any PPI (Klein 1999). After a phase of reliance on the private sector in the 1990s, the Infrastructure Action Plan 2003–08 shifted the Bank Group's focus from transfer of infrastructure assets from the public to the private to a more flexible range of PPPs. The subsequent infrastructure strategy, the Sustainable Infrastructure Action Plan 2009–11, focused on strengthening the enabling environment for PPPs and scaling up PPPs.

Both the 2013 World Bank Group Strategy and the previous infrastructure strategy update feature PPPs prominently. The infrastructure strategy update reiterates a PPP scale-up but recognizes at the same time both the lack of incentives for World Bank staff to pursue risky and time-intensive PPP projects and the challenge posed by more than 20 different units contributing across the World Bank Group to the PPP agenda. In October 2013, the latest World Bank Group strategy expressed the intention to "increasingly promote public-private partnerships," given its ability to work with both public and private sector client (World Bank 2013). PPPs are currently also considered as cross-cutting solutions areas in the World Bank Group strategy. This strategy hence sets the stage for potentially increased collaborative work across the World Bank Group from which PPPs in particular can benefit, as their success relies heavily on policy support, as this study shows. With the World Bank and PPIAF engaging upstream, its other more transaction-oriented private sector arms (IFC and MIGA) can then help the first transaction get off the ground—a potentially promising business model.

PPPs are also widely reflected in other conceptual and strategic notes. Various corporate strategies—for example, IFC's Strategic Directions and Road Maps 2002–2015—broadly reflect the PPP emphasis of the infrastructure strategy updates, expanding the PPP concept to health, education, and the food supply chain. It is noteworthy that PPPs have not been subject to a World Bank Group-wide stand-alone policy or strategy, but are rather addressed in the context of sectoral, regional, or corporate strategies. PPPs figure prominently in the public sector development and infrastructure strategies from 2002 through 2015 and are the subject of regional strategies (for example, draft Africa PPP Strategy, Latin America and the Caribbean Region strategy, country-level strategies, and recent economic development in infrastructure reports).

Recently, the World Bank also prepared a PPP strategy for its Financial and Private Sector Development Network. In addition, there are numerous assessments of PPP performance with a sectoral focus (urban water utilities, electricity, water distribution, and so forth). However, the Bank Group does not provide any coherent directions on how these various strategic intentions would be implemented.

There is little operational guidance on how to implement the Bank Group's strategic PPP intentions. Currently there is no explicit managerial framework that could provide guidance to staff and management on issues, such as roles and responsibilities and processes in implementing the PPP agenda, resource allocation, knowledge management, or monitoring and evaluation. In view of the various entities engaged in PPPs at the corporate and country levels across the PPP delivery chain (see Chapter 5) and the currently envisaged PPP Cross-Cutting Solution Area, a minimum of guidance appears essential to facilitate translating the strategic intent into a country-tailored solution.

The World Bank Group's Strategic Resources Deployment on PPPs

One way of assessing the strategic relevance of resources deployment is to see if the World Bank Group support reaches the countries that need it most. The World Bank Group supports PPP projects in 134 countries. Each of these countries has reached a specific level of maturity with regard to managing PPPs. Those "nascent" countries that are about to embark on their respective PPP agenda will need fundamentally different support than those countries already having a certain track record of implementing PPP projects. The first group of countries will appreciate advice on strategic issues and how to make use of PPPs in the context of their national public investment planning and ongoing sector reform programs; they subsequently will have to create a minimum of an enabling environment. The World Bank, WBI and PPIAF are equipped to deliver these services with their public sector-focused operations.

The latter group of "emerging" or "developed" countries will appreciate assistance in creating and deepening the PPP market, which IFC and MIGA guarantees can assist with. The elements of an enabling environment for PPPs are outlined in Box 2.1, starting out with the

---

BOX 2.1 Elements of an Enabling Environment for PPPs

Progress in Sector Reform and the Level of Private Participation

The level of private sector participation—and hence also of PPPs—in infrastructure and social services is a result of the choice of market structure, including the type and level of competition allowed, market entry rules, and the resulting tariff regulations. Lack of adequate market structure impairs economic efficiency and prevents market entry by private players. To decide about sector reform policy options in a smart fashion, and based on the local circumstances, policy makers need to understand the architecture options for infrastructure policies and the various building blocks and how they can fit together (Klein 2012; Ministry of Foreign Affairs of the Netherlands 2013).

Sufficient Government Commitment and Mastering the Political Economy

Ultimately, political will and continued government commitment are needed to support the reform process. Often such changes to a sector are challenged by public sentiment, particularly when the end users are affected through tariffs and quality. At times sector adjustments may also lead to changes in the power relationships within the prevailing political and sector systems: utilities may have to be corporatized and/or restructured (which may entail staffing adjustments), independent regulators established, and governments often contained to policy and planning, as opposed to managing the sector directly. These factors have likely effects on the perception of political parties by voters. Politics hence impacts economy in the end (Ministry of Foreign Affairs of the Netherlands 2013; WBI 2012).

Public Financial Management to Manage Fiscal Risks

PPPs are more common where governments suffer from heavy debt burdens, according to the IMF. Yet PPPs do not provide additional fiscal space, but rather align public spending with benefit consumption.[a] Often government commitments through up-front investment, explicit guarantees, usage, and availability payments are vital ingredients to making a PPP investable for the private sector. They represent direct and contingent liabilities for the public sector but play an important role from the private sector perspective, as they help mitigate risks and can alter the financial viability of a PPP

continued on page 28

business case. Countries hence need sound fiscal management with a clear strategy for assessing fiscal risks up front and for managing fiscal risk during implementation.

Likewise, the decision on public procurement versus PPPs needs to be made on the basis of a comprehensive value for money assessment. In contrast, private investors need to be aware of the sovereign risk they are exposed to as the actual payment of such guarantees depends on the creditworthiness of the issuing municipality, state, or country (Hammami, Ruhashyankiko, and Yehoue 2006; Irwin 2007; Sadka 2006; World Bank 1998).

Access to Long-Term Finance

PPPs require long-term finance, but domestic funding is often constrained. For example, Africa's infrastructure needs are equivalent to total government revenues. Access to *local* capital markets can help mitigate the foreign exchange risks for PPP, depending on cash flows denominated in local currencies, for example, water or electricity utilities (World Bank 2012; World Bank 2009).

Good Governance and the Fight against Corruption

A transparent procurement framework with supporting anticorruption measures needs to contain corruption and market distortion and enable a fair competition. A fair and higher level of competition will also contribute to improved risk sharing between the private and public sides involved (Ministry of Foreign Affairs of the Netherlands 2013; WBI 2012).

PPP-Specific Institutions, Legal Framework, and Capacity

Institutional quality and capacity, an adequate legal framework, the rule of law, and the existence of a regulatory framework are proven drivers for PPPs. They create the business opportunities for private sector investors, as they (i) determine the quality and speed of the transaction process of PPPs; (ii) set prices – ultimately deciding on cost recovery and financial return; and (iii) provide legal certainty on the contractual arrangements and enforcement of the rule of law. The PPP delivery process, from up-front fiscal assessment to transaction execution, demands a high level of public sector capacity. Capacity is essential so the public interests are safeguarded when structuring the PPP as well as when performance is being monitored. An institutional set-up with clear roles and responsibilities across the various ministerial and inter-ministerial coordination councils and implementing agencies is required (EIU and the Economist Group 2010; Hammami, Ruhashyankiko, and Yehoue 2006; OECD 2008; WBI 2012).

SOURCES: EIU and the Economist Group 2010; Hammami, Ruhashyankiko, and Yehoue 2006; OECD 2008; Irwin 2007; Klein 2012; Ministry of Foreign Affairs of the Netherlands 2013; Sadka 2006; World Bank 2012; WBI 2012; and World Bank 1998.

a. Except for the cases where PPPs actually advance the service delivery compared to the public sector comparator and allow the government to benefit earlier from economic growth enabled through these services and associated fiscal revenues.

more general factors, for example, sector reform progress and public finance management, but also including PPP-specific factors related to institutions, processes, and capacity.

The Economist Intelligence Unit (EIU) analyzes countries with regard to PPP maturity according to a standardized procedure, taking into account institutional, regulatory, and legal factors along with factors of operational maturity, investment climate, and financial facilities. Subsequently, countries obtain scores,[2] which are regularly published.[3] "Nascent" countries are those with the least developed enabling environment; "emerging" are those where the enabling environment is under construction and less tested; and "developed" PPP countries are those that already have a quite well-established enabling environment.

These scores cover the regions with the highest PPP activity, that is, Latin America and the Caribbean, Asia and Pacific, and Eastern Europe and Central Asia. Developed countries are largely high- (60 percent) or upper-middle-income countries (30 percent), whereas emerging countries are mainly composed of upper-middle-income (48 percent), followed by lower-middle-income (26 percent) and high-income (23 percent) countries. Nascent countries are mainly made up by lower-middle-income (50 percent) and upper-middle-income countries (UMIC) (43 percent) and 7 percent low income. None of the rated countries is currently a fragile or conflict-affected country.[4]

The EIU country classification covers the portfolios of World Bank, IFC investments and MIGA—allowing for valid conclusions with regard to their strategic relevance. For the World Bank, the countries covered by the EIU rating represent 89 percent of the entire portfolio and 93 percent of its upstream portfolio. For IFC investment, the countries covered by the EIU rating represent 83 percent of its PPP portfolio, and for MIGA 74 percent.[5] For these World Bank Group institutions, the EIU country rating was used to assess to what extent their respective portfolios reach the countries that needed their support the most. For IFC advisory, only 53 percent of the PPP portfolio is covered; hence the analysis was not applied to this service line in greater detail.

Overall, the World Bank Group's deployment of its PPP interventions is synchronized with client country needs. Figure 2.1 maps the World Bank Group's relative deployment of PPP interventions against the level of preparedness of countries per EIU classification. Generally speaking, the World Bank Group has allocated a relative smaller share of its resources to nascent countries, while allotting more toward emerging countries and, to a lesser extent, developed countries.

When weighting the countries' significance by their gross domestic product (GDP), it becomes evident that the World Bank's and PPIAF's resources focus strongly on those countries that need it the most: Both of these institutions devote about 20 percent of their efforts (by number)

FIGURE 2.1 World Bank Group–Wide Deployment of PPP Interventions to Countries According to Their Maturity to Manage PPPs, FY02–12

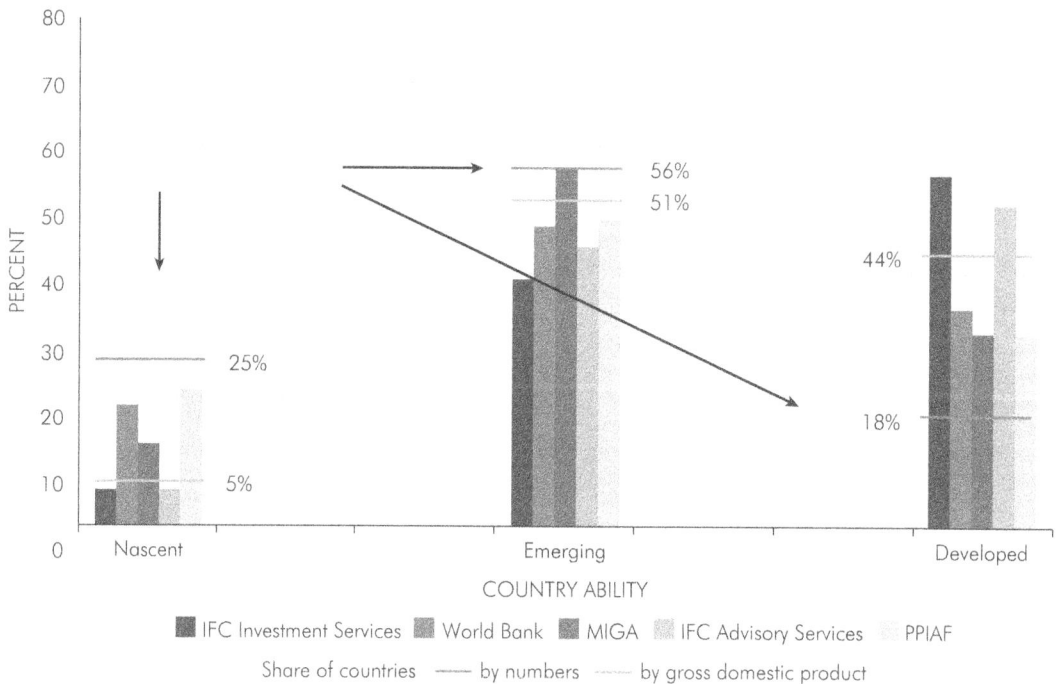

SOURCES: IEG, Economist Intelligence Unit Infrascope scores.
NOTE: For IFC Advisory Services the graph is not representative of its overall portfolio. PPIAF = Public-Private Infrastructure Advisory Facility.

to countries with a low level of maturity (nascent countries), even though their collective GDP only accounts for 5 percent of all countries. Transaction support through finance (IFC investments) reaches these countries to an extent commensurate with their GDP, about 5 percent. Emerging PPP countries are largely served according to the importance in terms of GDP, with relatively more support from MIGA, the World Bank, and PPIAF. Developed PPP countries benefit more from transaction support. IFC investments service these countries to a higher extant than their GDP would suggest.

More specifically, World Bank upstream policy reform work strongly focuses on nascent countries, that is, those that need it the most. Almost 80 percent of World Bank PPP projects either focus exclusively on upstream policy reform or have at least an upstream component. When these upstream-centered projects are analyzed, the focus on nascent countries is pronounced. Thirty-eight percent of the World Bank's upstream work supports nascent countries, although they represent 25 percent of all countries and only 5 percent of GDP collectively—overall an indication that it is targeting the right countries (Figure 2.2).[6]

FIGURE 2.2 Deployment of World Bank Upstream Work to Countries According to Their Maturity to Manage PPPs, FY02–12

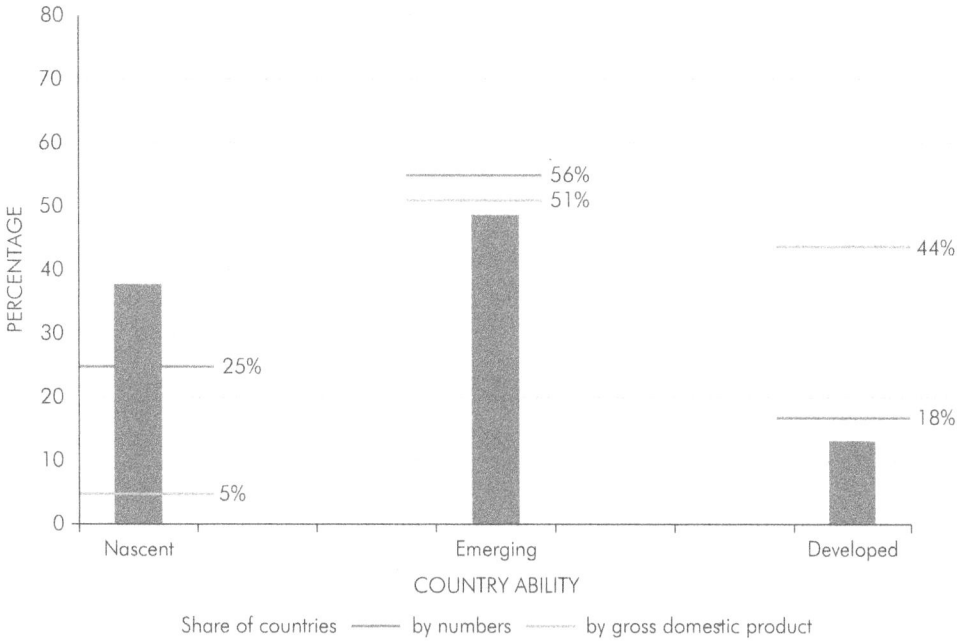

SOURCES: IEG, EIU Infrascope.

Support to financing PPPs is best measured by the market's rate of producing PPPs. The private sector-oriented arms of the World Bank Group, that is, IFC Investment and MIGA, are operated in a demand-driven fashion and as such barely can initiate PPPs—they rather follow the deal flow. Hence, a better measure to examine their resources allocation is the rate at which the market creates PPPs, that is, the natural rate of PPP prevalence. Thus, if IFC investment and MIGA were simply to follow the market trend in PPPs, the allocation of IFC investments and MIGA guarantees would correspond to the prevalence or relative share of PPPs. For example, if the market creates 50 percent of PPPs in "emerging" countries and IFC simply follows these trends, about 50 percent of its PPP investments would be in "emerging" countries. And with IFC's ambitions to support pioneering transactions, one could expect that they would even overweigh countries with not yet fully developed PPP frameworks, that is, "emerging" or even "nascent" countries. However, none of this comes true.

Support to PPP transaction through IFC's investments emphasizes "developed" PPP countries. Five percent of IFC investment business is located in nascent countries, where the deal flow can be expected to be less reliable. However, this is about half of what the market generates, with 9 percent of all PPPs occurring in these countries.[7]

In "emerging" countries, about 38 percent of IFC investments take place, whereas 49 percent of all PPPs are structured there. Hence, IFC's investment activity clearly lags behind the rate at which the market itself generates PPPs. By contrast, IFC invests more in developed PPP countries than the market does: fully 56 percent of IFC's investments are directed to developed countries—compared to 42 percent of all PPPs being structured there (Figure 2.3).

It is generally understandable that PPP transactions are supported in countries where the enabling environment is in good shape to increase the likelihood of these transactions being successful. However, the extent to which developed countries are served by IFC is higher than what the market forces would suggest, that is, higher than the PPP prevalence in developed countries. Shifting some of IFC's PPP investments from already

FIGURE 2.3 Deployment of Downstream Work by IFC Investment and MIGA According to Country Ability to Manage PPPs, FY02–12

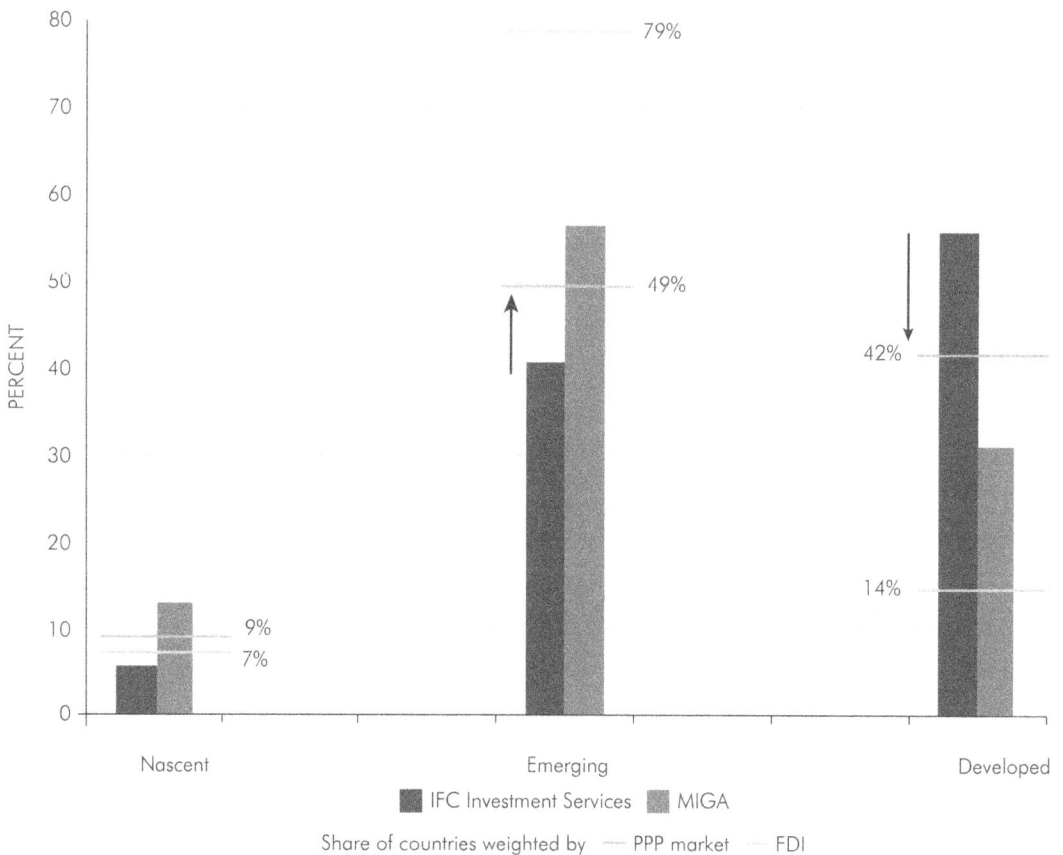

SOURCES: IEG, EIU Infrascope.
NOTE: FDI = foreign direct investment; MIGA = Multilateral Investment Guarantee Agency.

developed countries to emerging countries, appears warranted—and would increase IFC's additionality.

It is important to note that those 16 IFC investments that are located in emerging countries are at least as successful as those in developed countries with 88 percent of PPPs in emerging countries rated satisfactory or better on their development outcome versus 86 percent in developed countries. This suggests that doing more business in emerging PPP countries will not compromise success.[8]

This analysis, based on the EIU scores, is fairly representative of IFC's portfolio. The EIU published scores for country-level readiness for PPPs for three regions—that is, Latin America and the Caribbean, East Asia and Pacific, and Eastern Europe and Central Asia—in 66 countries. The EIU rating scheme captures 83 percent of IFC investments, and hence is fairly representative. Those PPP projects that do fall outside the EIU scheme are concentrated in a few countries. Looking at the 17 percent of IFC investments that are not covered by the EIU ratings, a full 90 percent of these are concentrated in only 10 countries.[9] This indicates that the analysis based on the EIU score is a good proxy for the overall portfolio behavior.

For MIGA, the strategic resources allocated focuses more on nascent and emerging countries. MIGA originates 13 percent in in nascent countries, which is a significant emphasis compared to 9 percent PPP prevalence. Most MIGA projects take place in emerging PPP countries, that is, 56 percent versus 49 percent PPP prevalence. Less emphasis is placed on developed countries, where 30 percent of MIGA's projects are located, compared to 42 percent of PPP prevalence. This indicates that MIGA tends to venture out more into untested territory and introduce PPPs to countries with less of a track record of handling PPPs.

Similarly, IFC Advisory Services tend to be mostly allocated in countries with yet untested PPP frameworks; that is, they support countries that most need it. PPPs supported by IFC Advisory Services are found mainly in LMICs and are concentrated in Sub-Saharan Africa. More than 59 percent of the projects (50 percent by volume) are in LMICs; by region, about one-third of IFC advisory services in PPPs support Sub-Saharan Africa (27 percent by funding and 21 percent by numbers). This reflects the strategic ambitions of IFC advisory to focus strongly on poorer countries.[10] Almost two-thirds of countries where IFC provides advice fall outside the EIU classification scheme; hence these ratings cannot be used for the purpose of IEG's analysis. However, with a strong focus on LMICs and Sub-Saharan Africa, one can safely assume that many of these countries are in early stages of developing PPP frameworks and therefore that IFC's advisory work is relevant to them.

Addressing Countries' Development Priorities and PPP Constraints

World Bank Group support for PPPs was relevant to countries inasmuch as it supported clear development priorities. In all 45 countries reviewed in detail, the World Bank Group's support to PPPs has been relevant to respective developmental priorities, either directly or indirectly. In more than two-thirds of these cases (71 percent), the Bank Group's PPP intervention directly addressed a development priority. These are cases where the intervention logic allowed for a direct link of the PPP and the country specific deficiency—mostly related to shortcomings in infrastructure access, addressed by sector reform measures with a PPP element or a stand-alone investment in a PPP (for IFC and MIGA).

Typically, these country strategies embedded PPPs in sector reform programs. Private sector participation in the form of PPPs is mostly positioned as a mid- to long-term goal to be pursued once reform measures have reached a certain level, for example, a minimum level of financial viability. However, the strategies provide few analytics for assessing how much private sector participation was the best choice; instead, they assume it would be good (see also Chapter 4). In the other third of countries, PPP-related interventions were at least indirectly relevant to development priorities; these usually included support to increase private sector participation, which in turn was envisaged to improve service provision and hence address a development priority indirectly.

Case studies confirmed the relevance of Bank Group PPP interventions at the country level. In Colombia, Ghana, Guatemala, and Senegal, critical factors constraining growth (weak governance and corruption, fiscal capacity, and, in some cases, violence and security) as well as helping build a robust regulatory framework (Brazil) were addressed. In some countries, the approach to harnessing the private sector was broad-based, and in others priorities were assigned more strategically on the basis of factors important to the government.

In Ghana, efficiency gains though private sector involvement were considered substantial in the electricity sector (AICD 2010), which became the priority sector for PPPs. In Senegal significant resources were devoted to developing a toll highway, given the urgent need to expand economic activity out of the Dakar peninsula. The Filipino Electric Power Crisis Act, prompted by brownouts, triggered an avalanche of power BOTs (build, own, and transfer operations) and led the way to a broader use of PPPs in the economy.

PPIAF played a large role in most countries, along with technical assistance from IBRD/IDA. The WBI's presence was slight, and it was hard to judge its effectiveness because of the limited availability of data on outcomes. In one case (Colombia), IFC assisted in attempting to build local capital markets.

Country-specific constraints may impede the implementation of a country's PPP agenda. Based on the factors that constitute a sound enabling environment (Box 2.1), IEG reviewed 45 countries to identify what constraints their respective PPP agendas and to assess if the Bank Group provided the targeted support to resolve those constraints.

The most common PPP constraints identified by the Bank Group's country strategies are governance issues, regulatory failure, and inadequate sector structure. Most country strategies identify governance and corruption-related issues (76 percent), followed by regulatory failure (73 percent) together with an inadequateness of sector structure (64 percent) as constraints to the country's PPP agenda (Figure 2.4). In those countries where these constraints were identified, subsequent World Bank Group interventions largely addressed them—indicating that operational response corresponded to the country's needs. How effective the Bank Group's response was is discussed in Chapter 3.

FIGURE 2.4 PPP Constraints in Country Strategies

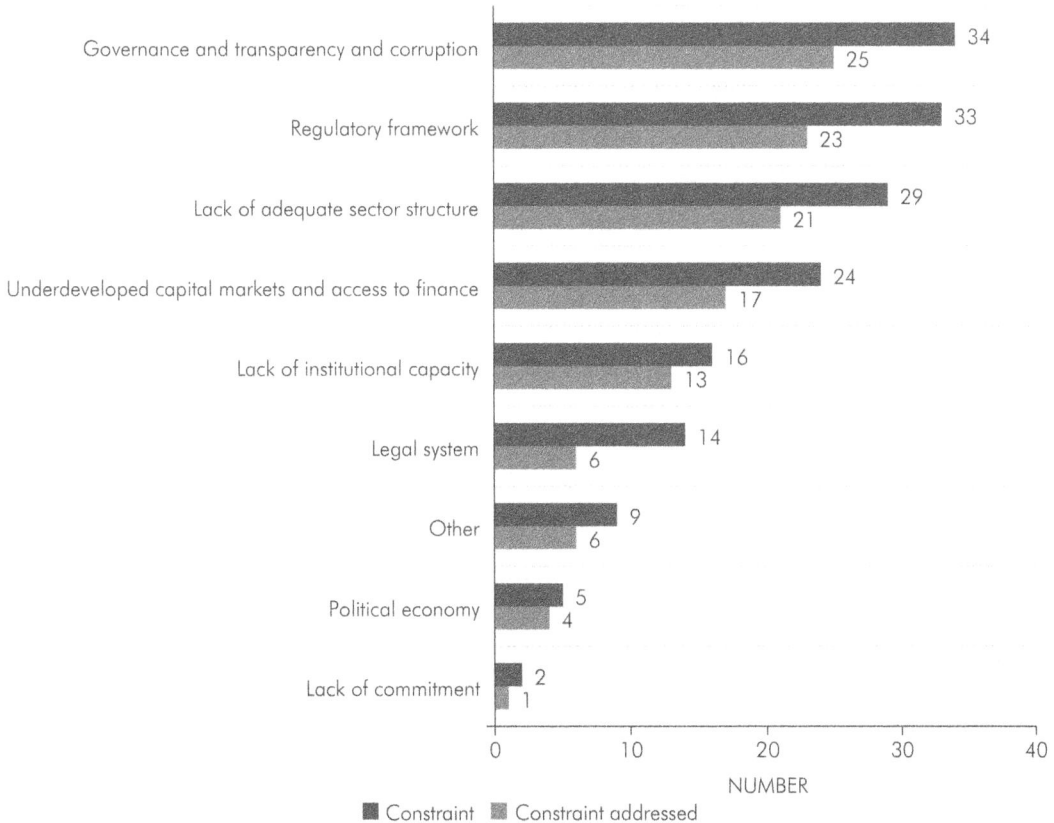

SOURCES: World Bank data, IEG portfolio analysis.
NOTE: 45 countries reviewed.

Other important country-level constraints have, however, been addressed less systematically. Access to long-term capital was addressed somewhat less (53 percent). Insufficient institutional capacity was addressed in about half of the countries reviewed (53 percent), despite its being one of the major limiting factors. Legal framework aspects, political economy factors, and lack of government commitment are addressed the least (31 percent, 11 percent, and 4 percent, respectively). The latter two emerged as a necessary prerequisite from the nine in-depth country cases, and the failure to address these constraints in the case study countries was related to slow progress on the PPP agenda (see Chapter 3). In those cases where these constraints were flagged by the Country Assistance Strategy (CAS) the operational response also addressed them; the only exception was for deficiencies in the legal system for PPPs, which in the 45 countries reviewed was identified as a constraint 14 times and was responded to through six interventions.

There are few cases where the Bank Group has provided strategic advice on private versus public investment and the type of PPPs. IEG's analysis of the country strategies of 45 countries did not reveal much evidence that the Bank Group had provided advice on whether private sector involvement (in the form of a PPP) was the best option, given the respective country-level circumstances. The nine country cases indicate that the World Bank Group's approach to PPPs has been based on the assumption that involving the private sector is a good thing. Although careful analysis of a transaction's economics, feasibility, and sustainability is of course encouraged, public sector comparators—systematically comparing PPPs against the public sector for value for money to justify private sector involvement—were not a part of the World Bank Group support in any of the country cases. However, some countries, for example, Colombia, have independently instituted such checks.

In countries that are facing large infrastructure deficits and that are consequently looking for financial support from the private sector, public sector versus private sector value for money analyses may be pointless, as the public sector option may unaffordable in any event. It would be more relevant in such cases to focus on ensuring a level playing field for bidding and regulation, affordability, sustainability, transparency, and extent of financial leverage achieved—which is generally the thrust of the Bank Group's approach (and is exemplified in the Ghana PPP Adaptable Program Loan).

Looking at country-level relevance from a "dynamic" perspective over the period evaluated (FY02–12), the World Bank Group was responsive to client countries' needs and changing priorities. The in-depth country case studies revealed that country-level strategies showed "flexibility" and signs of responding to development priorities and changes in macro conditions and individual paces of reform. In several countries, PPP support was phased, focusing on private sector development, addressing weaknesses and constraints (fiscal constraints, weak governance, a poor regulatory framework, and in some cases violence and lack of security), and gradually moving to a greater focus on transactions (Brazil, Colombia, Ghana, Guatemala, and Vietnam).

In other cases, the Bank Group shifted gears in response to the situation and had a greater focus on upstream activities as the climate for transactions weakened because of poor governance (the Philippines), or focused on IFC activities as the reform effort slowed (Vietnam). After an initial exploration phase of the Chinese authorities to assess whether PPPs are the right tool, the Bank Group relied on IFC to catalyze PPPs using a bottom-up approach. Although sectoral work was prescribed in the CAS, activities were nonetheless also influenced by local factors and in several instances were also buttressed by "just in time studies" from PPIAF, which were helpful to build momentum on particular issues.

Countries have particularly relied on the World Bank Group in the context of challenging situations that had particular developmental value because of innovation and regulatory and/or transactional issues that set examples for other interventions. For example, after a failed attempt by another agency, the Philippines government asked IFC Advisory Services for assistance with the privatization of a secondary city distribution system. IFC's approach ensured full involvement of the regulator and developing innovative financing. IFC also advised on challenging privatizations of small off-grid generators, after the most attractive ones had already been taken up.

In China, in the face of limited resources from local banks, IFC involvement in a waste treatment project set the stage for mobilizing long-term finance and resulted in an exemplary project that would otherwise have failed. In Brazil, the IBRD demonstrated the use of performance-based contracting in highways projects and helped set up the first Metro after the PPP laws passed in 2004; that set the stage for several more projects in the transport sector.

The other side of the coin, however, is that as PPPs become more accepted and countries gain experience, the need for the Bank Group in standard projects seems to drop off (toll roads and power generation in the Philippines). But new frontiers await, for example, electricity distribution, water supply in rural areas and secondary cities in the Philippines.

Conclusion

Undoubtedly, PPPs are of high strategic relevance to the World Bank Group. The recently adopted World Bank Group strategy expresses the firm intention to "increasingly promote public-private partnerships." However, there is little guidance on how the Bank Group plans to implement its PPP agenda—or more recently, how to institute PPPs as a Cross-Cutting Solutions Area and how this solution area is meant to interact with the global practices. An operational plan may be useful to turn corporate ambitions into country tailored programs.

Overall strategic resource deployment is synchronized with country needs and their respective maturity level in managing PPPs. Upstream policy reform work clearly is directed toward countries that need it most, that is, those that have a nascent enabling environment or those that are in the process of building it up. However, IFC investments largely support already "developed" countries. This is understandable, as a sound enabling environment increases the likelihood of a PPP being successful. But the extent to which "developed" countries are serviced suggests that some of the support could be shifted to "emerging" countries, that is, countries with less established PPP frameworks or a more limited track record of handling PPPs. Results suggest that such a shift of support would not be detrimental to development outcomes, but rather would enhance IFC investment's additionality.

At the country level, Bank Group support for PPPs was relevant to client countries inasmuch as it supported clear development priorities, as evidenced in the 45 countries reviewed in detail. Typically, these CASs embedded PPPs in sector reform programs. The most common PPP constraints addressed by the Bank Group's country strategies are governance issues, regulatory failure, and inadequate sector structure.

Country strategies, however, tend to address other important PPP constraints less systematically: the World Bank Group barely assists in developing the capability of governments to make strategic decisions on PPPs based on value for money assessments; fiscal implications associated with PPPs have received too little attention, even though very recent efforts in this area are promising; and political economy factors and issues of the government's commitment to the PPP agenda are almost entirely ignored. Looking at country-level relevance from a "dynamic" perspective over the time period evaluated, the World Bank Group was responsive to client countries' needs and changing priorities.

Notes

[1] Evidence for questions (ii) and (iii) comes from 45 countries where at least five PPP-targeted interventions occurred during FY02–12. Countries with fewer interventions usually had no mention of a PPP agenda in their CAS, or any specific reference to PPP constraints.

[2] Legend: 0–30 (nascent), 30–60 (emerging), 60–80 (developed), and 80–100 (mature). Mature countries are typically not World Bank group client countries.

[3] EIU has not yet published indices for Africa.

[4] The distribution of income level and lending type according to the EIU category is given in the following table.

Country Percentage Distribution According to EIU Category by Country Income Group and Lending Type

	Nascent	Emerging	Developed	Mature
Income group				
Low	7	3	0	0
Lower middle	50	26	10	0

Upper middle	43	48	30	0
High	0	23	60	100
% total	100	100	100	100
Lending type				
Non-IDA	50	81	86	
Blend	36	7	14	
IDA	14	11	0	
% total	100	100	100	

[5] Although for MIGA the relative coverage was the lowest, a detailed analysis of the portfolio outside of the EIU rating scheme allowed confirming the finding presented in this report, that is, that MIGA shows considerable activity in nascent and emerging countries.

[6] Unfortunately, this detailed analysis, based on actual countries' needs, excludes Africa as EIU scores are not yet available for these countries; however, the World Bank's upstream work has traditionally focused on Sub-Saharan Africa, as evidenced in the portfolio analysis.

[7] Private Participation in Infrastructure database, World Bank.

[8] Success ratings for the few projects in nascent countries were 50 percent rated successful or better, that is, were considerably lower than in emerging or developed countries. Hence it appears more feasible for IFC Investment Services to allocate a portion of its PPP portfolio from developed to emerging countries. To the extent there are also opportunities in nascent countries, these should be seized as this may still yield an overall success rate of well above 65 percent satisfactory or better, given that most PPPs will be in emerging countries and few in nascent.

[9] These countries are Senegal (5 PPPs), Kenya (4), Arab Republic of Egypt (3), Czech Republic (2), Jordan (2), Cameroon (2), Togo (2), Tunisia (2), Sri Lanka (2), and Uganda (2), that is, one OECD country, six MICs, and three LICs.

[10] IFC's strategic goals target IDA countries (ranging from 45 to 54 percent in recent years) and fragile and conflict-affected countries.

References

AICD. 2010 Ghana's Infrastructure: A Continental Perspective, Africa Infrastructure Country Diagnostic. Washington, DC: World Bank.

EIU (Economist Intelligence Unit), The Economist Group. 2010. Evaluating the Environment for Public-Private Partnerships in Latin America and the Caribbean: The 2010 Infrascope. A Guide to the Index and Methodology. London: Economist Intelligence Unit Limited.

Hammami, Mona, Jean-Francois Ruhashyankiko, and Etienne B. Yehoue. 2006. "Determinants of Public-Private Partnerships in Infrastructure." IMF Working Paper, WP/06/99, Washington, DC.

Irwin, Timothy C. 2007. Government Guarantees: Allocating and Valuing Risk in Privately Financed Infrastructure Projects. Washington, DC: World Bank.

Klein, Michael. 1999. *The Asian Crisis and Structural Change in Energy Markets*. Washington, DC: World Bank.

——— . 2012. "Infrastructure Policy—Basic Design Options." Policy Research Working Paper 6274, World Bank, Washington, DC.

Ministry of Foreign Affairs of the Netherlands. 2013. "Public-Private Partnerships in Developing Countries—A Systematic Literature Review." The Hague: Ministry of Foreign Affairs.

OECD (Organisation for Economic Co-operation and Development). 2008. *Public-Private Partnerships: In Pursuit of Risk Sharing and Value for Money*. Paris: OECD.

Sadka, Efriam. 2006. "Public-Private Partnerships: A Public Economics Perspective." IMF Working Paper WP/06/77. IMF, Washington, DC.

WBI (World Bank Institute). 2012. *Public-Private Partnerships Reference Guide*, Version 1.0. Washington, DC: World Bank Institute and Public Private Infrastructure Advisory Facility.

World Bank. 1998. "Contingent Liabilities—A Threat to Fiscal Stability." PREM Notes, Economic Policy, No. 9, Washington, DC.

——— . 2009. *Attracting Investors to African Public-Private Partnerships: A Project Preparation Guide*. Washington, DC: World Bank.

——— . 2012. "PPIAF Assistance in Senegal." Project Appraisal Document for Water and Sanitation Millennium Project.

——— . 2013. *A Stronger, Connected Solutions World Bank Group*. Washington, DC: World Bank.

3

Paving the Way for PPPs through Policy Reform and Institution Building

HIGHLIGHTS

- Of the Bank Group institutions, mainly the World Bank, supported by PPIAF and WBI, was active in creating an enabling environment in upstream work. Most of their support targeted LICs and Africa, using a wide range of instruments.

- World Bank upstream support to client countries' PPP agendas was mostly delivered through sector reform. Few efforts aimed to improve fiscal management or address issues of PPP awareness and commitment.

- Although sector reform plays such an important role in upstream work, it was difficult to achieve because of its complexity and the political nature of the reform process.

- More narrowly targeted upstream support—for example, building institutions for PPPs or installing a regulatory commission—worked the best.

- Key drivers of success were ensuring political commitment, raising public awareness, securing stakeholder support, and identifying PPP champions.

- The design of PPP component(s)—if and how they are embedded in a larger World Bank lending operation and if and how related knowledge products are conceived and delivered—matters, which suggests that PPIAF resources should be used more strategically.

- A lack of skills and resources for the preparation of a PPP pipeline and bankable PPP projects is a serious limitation across all World Bank-supported countries.

PPPs require their own infrastructure for development. Government authorities need to be capable of developing sector reform policies and assessing fiscal risks associated with PPPs; they should base their decisions about public procurement versus PPP on comprehensive value for money assessments and have impartial transaction advisory at hand to make PPP deals bankable and sustainable. PPPs require a fairly developed enabling environment or, as the G-20 High Level Panel put it: "PPPs require their own infrastructure" (High Level Panel on Infrastructure 2011; CEE Bankwatch Network 2008; Hammami, Ruhashyankiko, and Yehoue 2006; Irwin 2007; Sadka 2006; Ter Minassian 2004; World Bank 1998).

This chapter assesses how well the World Bank Group has assisted client countries in creating an enabling environment so that these countries can engage in PPPs. The chapter first describes the World Bank Group portfolio as deployed to prepare countries for PPPs, that is, "upstream work," then assesses how far these objectives were met and presents evidence on effects of this upstream work on subsequent PPP transactions.

Upstream work is defined as support activities that have as an objective the improvement of the country's condition and enabling environment for PPPs. Box 2.1 in Chapter 2 summarized what constitutes an enabling environment, including more general factors, for example, sector reform progress but also PPP-specific factors related to institutions, processes, and capacity. Based on this, upstream work was categorized into (i) building consensus for PPPs, (ii) implementing sector reform (with PPP reference),[1] (iii) introducing the needed regulatory regime and legal framework for PPPs, (iv) building up institutions to manage the PPPs' process, (v) building capacity, (vi) improving fiscal management, (vii) improving governance and anticorruption measures for PPPs, and (ix) increasing access to long-term finance through domestic financial markets.

World Bank Group Interventions to Improve the PPP Enabling Environment

Upstream support for PPPs is provided by three World Bank Group entities. The World Bank, PPIAF, and WBI were active upstream. IFC advisory, IFC investment,[2] and MIGA focused on downstream support (with the exception of few IFC Advisory Services that did engage upstream—see Chapter 4). Table 1.1 summarized all PPP interventions, grouped by their up- and downstream focus. In total, 353 World Bank projects supported PPPs during FY02–12. Of these, a statistically significant sample of 254 projects was reviewed in detail. More than two-thirds of these (75 percent or 191 projects) had an upstream component. In about one-third of cases (26 percent), upstream components were found together with a downstream element (Figure 3.1).

FIGURE 3.1 Share of World Bank Loans with Upstream and Downstream Components

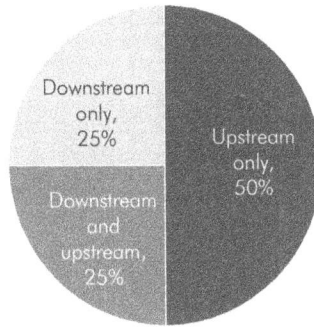

SOURCES: World Bank database; IEG portfolio analysis.
NOTE: n = 254 World Bank loan/partial risk guarantees reviewed.

PPIAF is a multidonor trust fund, managed by the World Bank and working in partnership with the World Bank Group, its donors, and other development organizations. Of the total 683 PPIAF activities, 210 were reviewed in detail, 208 of which supported upstream interventions. PPIAF support to PPPs increased from $9 million in FY02 to $16 million in FY09 and since has slowed down significantly to $9 million in FY12. For more details on PPIAF, see Box 3.1.

In addition, WBI supported the upstream agenda in 112 projects; of these, 33 were reviewed. Most of the support was through building consensus (42 percent) and capacity building (39 percent) on a variety of issues (contract management, PPP procurement, value for money and project development among others). In addition, WBI worked on collaborative governance and issues of disclosure of information and transparency of PPPs. Of the 105 reviewed IFC advisory projects, 10 had only upstream focus, whereas 20 had some upstream components contained in support of a specific PPP transaction.

Most of the World Bank Group's upstream work supported LICs, LMICs, and Africa. Of PPIAF's 683 projects, most can be found in LICs (46 percent, by numbers) and LMICs (41 percent), with the relatively most important share concentrated in Sub-Saharan Africa, accounting for 36 percent of total portfolio volume. In contrast with other World Bank Group support, multisectoral projects dominate, accounting for 40 percent of total PPP funding (by total funding), followed by support to specific sectors, that is, energy and water, with each accounting for about 19 percent of total funding.

Similarly, the WBI capacity building support was mostly focused in LICs (38 percent) and LMICs (35 percent) by numbers and on Africa (32 percent). The 191 World Bank and 13 IFC advisory with upstream components focused mostly in LMICs (49 and 63 percent, respectively) and Sub-Saharan Africa (48 percent and 28 percent, respectively). Looking at

PPIAF is a World Bank-managed multidonor trust fund, aimed at helping governments in developing countries improve the quality of their infrastructure through private sector involvement. Most of PPIAF activities are carried out in support of World Bank Group projects, for example, technical advisory services during the preparation of or in support of the implementation of a World Bank loan for IFC advisory services. PPIAF funds country specific or multicountry advisory and related activities focusing on upstream work, including on building institutions to enable PPPs to take place; exceptionally, PPIAF gets involved in other parts of the PPP project cycle to support pioneering transactions. PPIAF can support upstream work by other World Bank Group institutions or can also be a stand-alone intervention.

PPIAF activities provide assistance mainly through capacity building, consensus building, and sector reform, typically through workshops, seminars, advice, or studies. PPIAF provides capacity at all stages of the PPP project cycle on contract management, pipeline development and support to those involved in oversight of PPPs (for example, audit agencies and PPP units). Consensus building activities are generally done through training activities to build PPP awareness and stakeholder consultation to enhance political commitment.

SOURCES: IEG; www.ppiaf.org.

the countries' maturity to handle PPPs, upstream work strongly supports countries that need it the most, that is, those with a nascent enabling environment, as seen in Chapter 2.

The World Bank's upstream support to client countries' PPP agendas was delivered through a broad range of lending instruments. By type of instrument used across upstream and downstream, about two-thirds (67 percent) of the World Bank's work was delivered through specific investment loans (SILs), followed by adaptable program loans (APLs) with 11 percent and development policy loans (DPLs) with only 6 percent. Looking more specifically at projects that have an upstream component (but may also have a downstream component), the picture is similar. SILs again dominate, followed by DPLs, APLs, and technical assistance loans (TALs). Although TALs and DPLs almost exclusively address upstream work, APLs and SILs typically address both upstream and downstream issues. The less common instruments such as guarantees (PRGs), emergency recovery loans, and Financial Intermediary loans (FILs) were used mostly with downstream projects (Figure 3.2).

Except for SILs, country readiness drives the choice of instrument. SILs are used throughout all countries, regardless of their PPP readiness. For downstream work, SILs are more often used in developed than in nascent or emerging countries, however. In developed countries,

FIGURE 3.2 World Bank Instruments Use across Upstream and Downstream Work

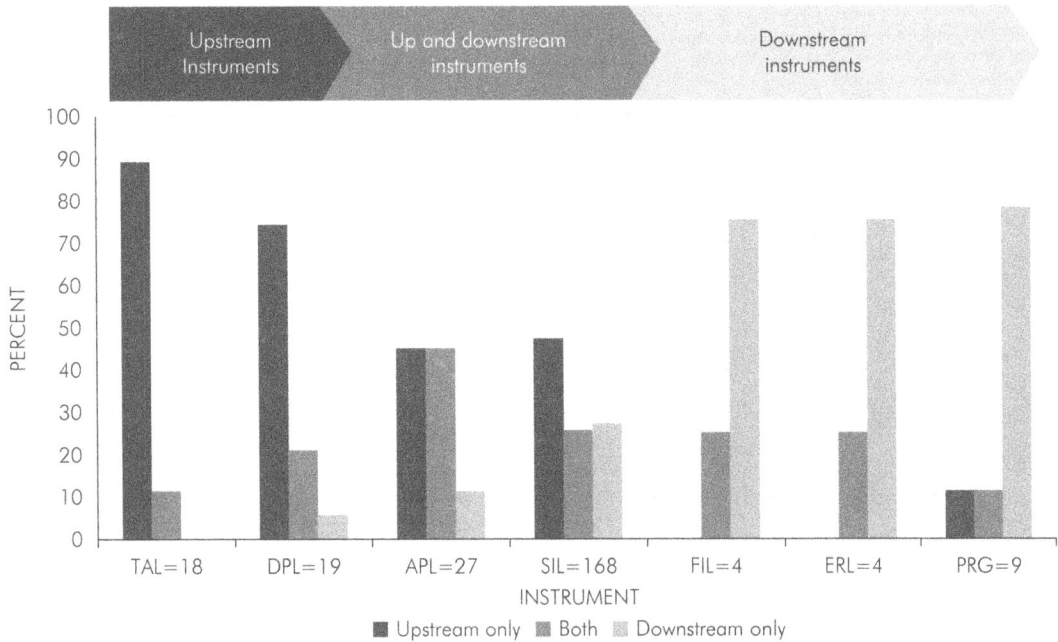

| | Upstream Instruments | Up and downstream instruments | Downstream instruments |

SOURCE: IEG.

NOTE: APL = adaptable program loan; DPL = development policy loan; ERL = emergency recovery loan; FIL = financial intermediary loan; PRG = partial risk guarantee; SIL = specific investment loan; TAL = technical assistance loan.

the basis for a PPP framework is better defined already and SILs seem to be used for specific interventions. APLs and DPLs are more often used in nascent and emerging countries to prepare the ground. The choice of instrument is therefore an essential factor in advancing the PPP agenda and needs to be made contingent of the country's readiness.

Focus and Results of World Bank Group Upstream Work

About half of the World Bank's (47 percent) and about one-third of PPIAF's (28 percent) upstream work focused on sector reform, often as a precursor to introducing PPPs. In addition to sector reform, capacity building and building consensus for PPPs were the next most frequently addressed enabling factors. The WBI's focus was on consensus building for PPPs (42 percent), followed by PPP capacity building (see Figure 3.3). There has also been significant support to the legal and regulatory framework in which PPPs operate. Nevertheless, in Senegal, even though the Bank helped the government develop a PPP law that excluded such an approach, its applicability has been effectively limited to a single PPP, with a new law being developed for other sectors that allows consideration of negotiated contracts.[3]

FIGURE 3.3 Objectives of World Bank Group Upstream Support

A. WORLD BANK UPSTREAM OBJECTIVES

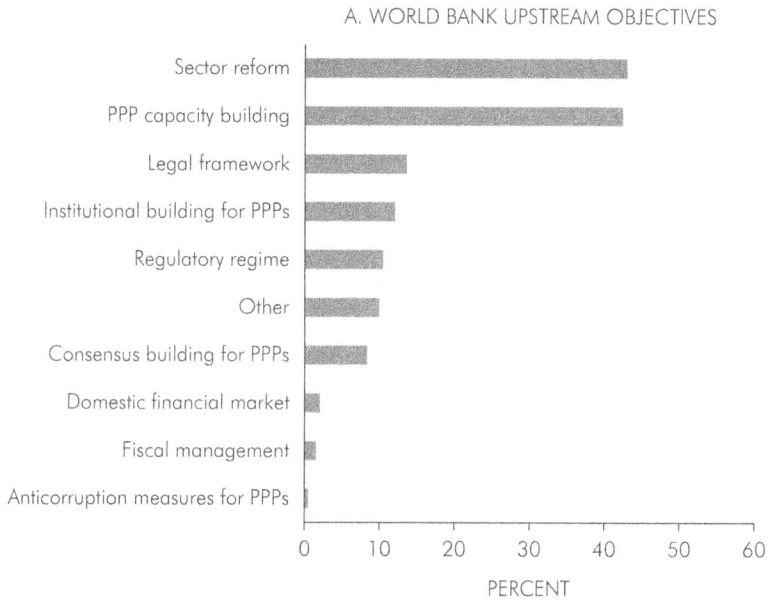

Sector reform
PPP capacity building
Legal framework
Institutional building for PPPs
Regulatory regime
Other
Consensus building for PPPs
Domestic financial market
Fiscal management
Anticorruption measures for PPPs

PERCENT

Total of 191 World Bank projects with upstream objectives.

B. WBI UPSTREAM OBJECTIVES

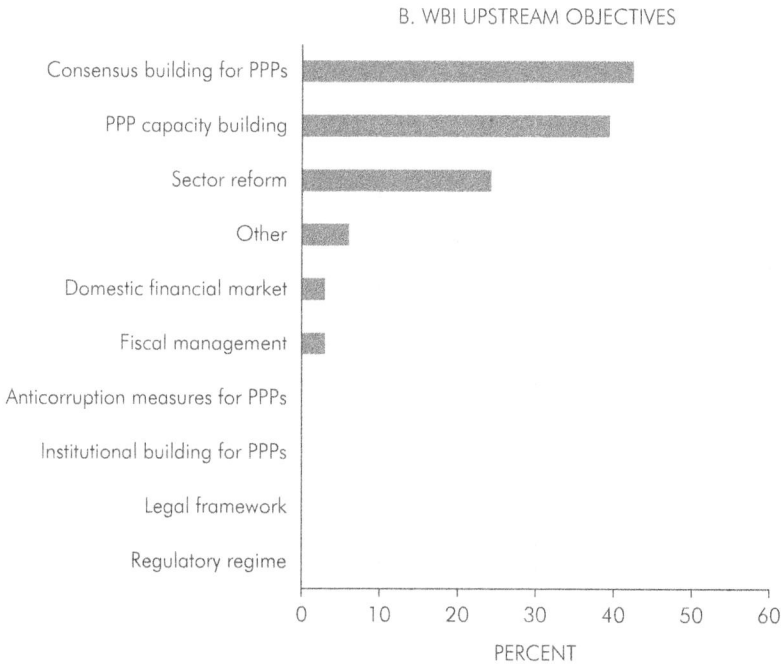

Consensus building for PPPs
PPP capacity building
Sector reform
Other
Domestic financial market
Fiscal management
Anticorruption measures for PPPs
Institutional building for PPPs
Legal framework
Regulatory regime

PERCENT

Total of 33 WBI projects.

Objectives of World Bank Group Upstream Support

C. PPIAF UPSTREAM OBJECTIVES

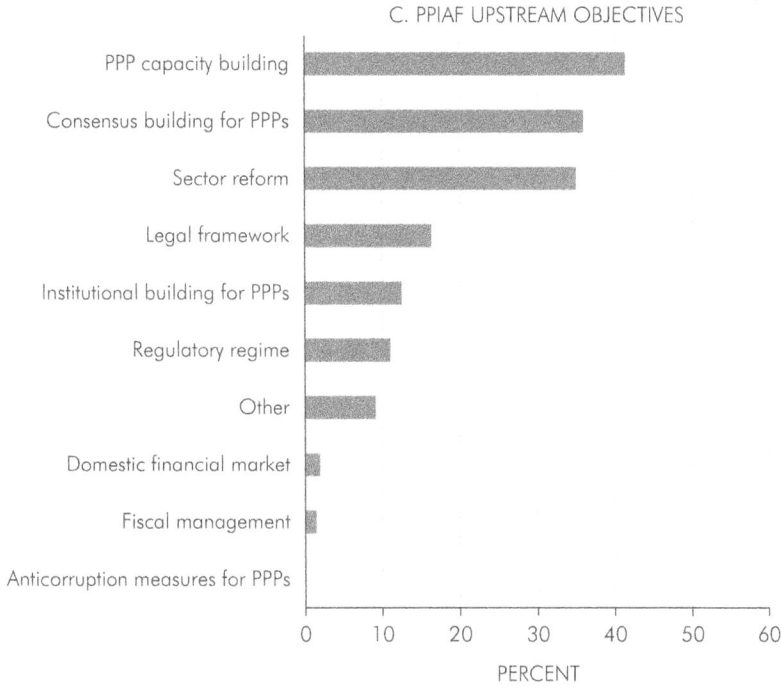

Total of 208 PPIAF activities.

SOURCE: IEG portfolio analysis of 173 World Bank loans, 204 PPIAF activities, and 33 WBI activities.
NOTE: PPIAF = Public-Private Infrastructure Advisory Facility; WBI = World Bank Institute.

Efforts aimed at improving fiscal management used to be rare. Across all World Bank Group institutions, systematic approaches to the client government's capacity to assess the fiscal implications of PPPs were rarely found during FY02–12. Contingent liabilities associated with PPPs need to be dealt with at two levels: ensuring an appropriate level of risk sharing upstream and ensuring adequate budgeting of liabilities during project implementation.

IEG's portfolio review indicates that although World Bank Group projects tend to give attention to ensuring adequate risk sharing, downstream contingent liabilities are rarely fully quantified at the project level. The nine country cases studies corroborate this and show that in selected cases the World Bank Group has actively been building the capacity of countries to assess PPP projects, and thus the ability to assess contingent liabilities. Recent efforts to systematize and introduce a framework for assessing fiscal implications of PPPs are a valuable contribution, with outcomes yet to be seen (Box 3.2).

Sector reform objectives were the most difficult to achieve because of their complexity and political nature. The World Bank is likely to have more leverage on client countries to advance sector reform than other institutions working on the upstream agenda—PPIAF or

BOX 3.2 World Bank Operational Note on Managing Fiscal Commitments from PPPs

There have been few cases of World Bank Group support for managing fiscal commitments. The importance of calibrating fiscal exposure in PPPs has been known for some time. Findings from IEG's nine country cases studies indicate that assistance has only been provided if requested by the government. In Colombia, for example, in the mid '90s, the Bank helped the government get a handle on contingent commitments (hidden exposure), which led to a rigorous, legally required procedure. In the Philippines the issue was flagged in a recent CAS, but no work was undertaken, partly because the government felt that it was not providing sufficient guarantees. Brazil has, on its own, established exposure limits for its state and local governments (both in aggregate and by project), and some states have already reached the limit, prompting calls for federal help.

A recent Finance and Private Sector Development Sector operational guidance note "Implementing a Framework for Managing Fiscal Commitments from Public-Private Partnerships" (World Bank and WBI 2013) could provide a basis for a more systematic approach by the Bank Group in advising clients and assessing risk. This framework was developed jointly with the WBI, based on the World Bank's experience in Ghana and Kenya, where it advised the government on roles and processes in assessing its commitments with regard to its—yet upcoming—PPP pipeline.

The note provided guidance to the formulation of specific components/subcomponents of the Ghana PPP APL and thus became an integral component of sector's lending program work in Africa. However, it remains unclear how this operational guidance note will be implemented across the World Bank Group, as it was not integrated in an overall PPP operational plan, nor were accountabilities for its execution spelled out.

SOURCES: IEG country case studies; World Bank and WBI 2013.

the WBI. Despite this, success on sector reform was only evident in about half of the cases (55 percent) for World Bank loans—an important finding, given that the country case studies indicate that proper sector reform was vital for successfully implementing a PPP agenda (see Figure 3.4). This statistical evidence from the portfolio review is corroborated by the country case studies, which found that sector reform efforts take longer than anticipated and tend to be exposed to political economy factor (see Drivers of Success).

Sector reform efforts were particularly prominent in the water and energy sector, indicating the heavy reliance on PPPs in reform in these areas. Of all projects where the PPP agenda was pursued through sector reform, about one-third (30 percent) were water and sanitation projects and one-fifth (20 percent) energy projects. Complex sector reform efforts—that is, those in energy, railways, and water—show overall relative low success, with 67, 63, and 50 percent of them achieving their objectives, respectively.

FIGURE 3.4 World Bank Achievement of Upstream Objectives and Evidence for Outcomes

A. WORLD BANK—SHARE OF OBJECTIVES MET AND OUTCOMES ACHIEVED

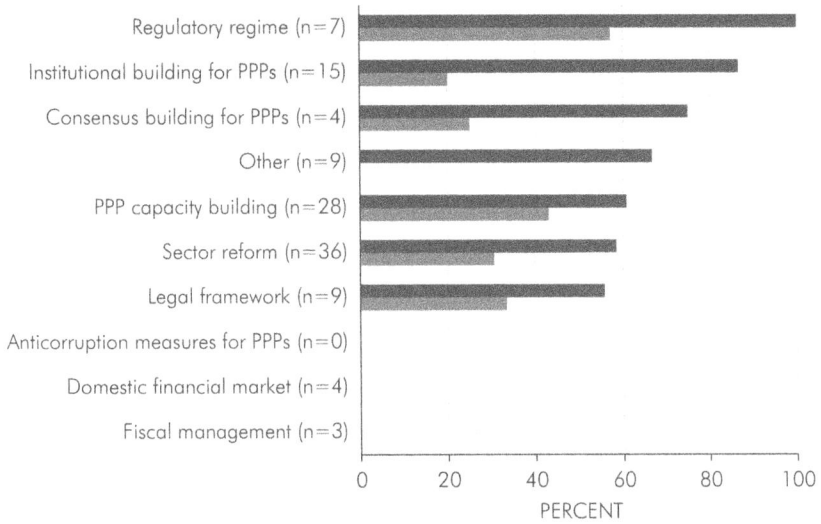

Regulatory regime (n=7)
Institutional building for PPPs (n=15)
Consensus building for PPPs (n=4)
Other (n=9)
PPP capacity building (n=28)
Sector reform (n=36)
Legal framework (n=9)
Anticorruption measures for PPPs (n=0)
Domestic financial market (n=4)
Fiscal management (n=3)

PERCENT

n=191 World Bank projects with upstream components. ■ % Objectives met ■ % Outcomes achieved

B. PPIAF—SHARE OF OBJECTIVES MET AND OUTCOMES ACHIEVED

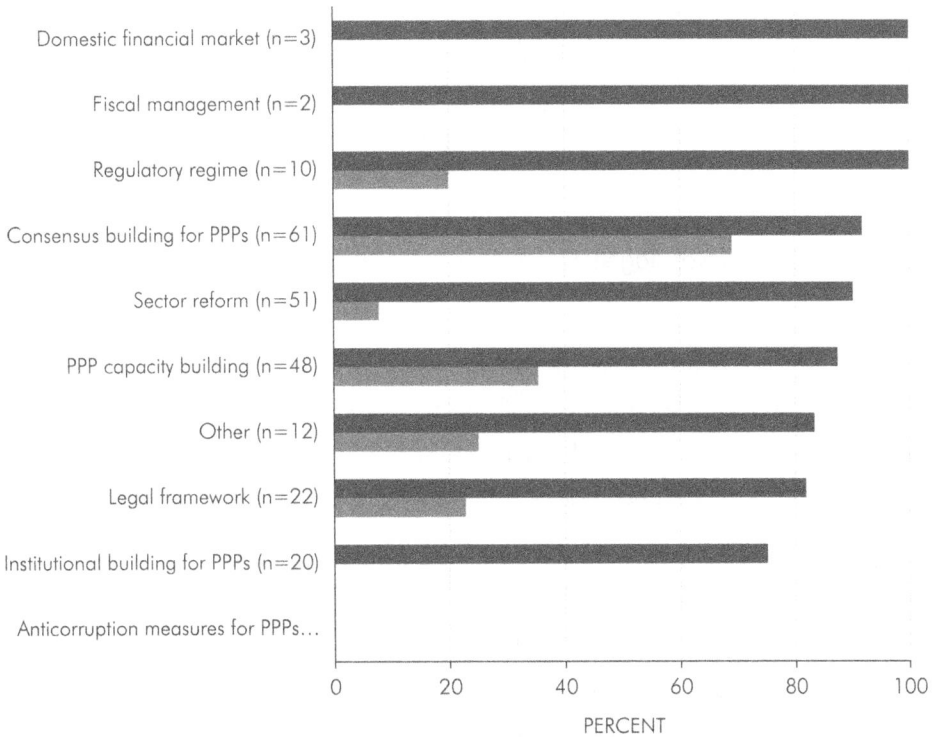

Domestic financial market (n=3)
Fiscal management (n=2)
Regulatory regime (n=10)
Consensus building for PPPs (n=61)
Sector reform (n=51)
PPP capacity building (n=48)
Other (n=12)
Legal framework (n=22)
Institutional building for PPPs (n=20)
Anticorruption measures for PPPs…

PERCENT

n=208 PPIAF activities ■ % Objectives met ■ % Outcomes achieved

SOURCE: IEG portfolio analysis.
NOTE: PPIAF = Public-Private Infrastructure Advisory Facility.

More narrowly focused efforts to build institutions for PPPs worked the best, with more than 81 percent of interventions achieving their objective.[4] Through such support the World Bank effectively contributed to establishing processes and institutions—for example, dedicated PPP units—advised successfully on interministerial coordination, and built capacity within these institutions. Similarly, building up consensus or installing regulatory commissions succeeded in about 75 percent of cases, respectively. Compared to relatively broad-based sector reform efforts, these types of upstream efforts are relatively targeted—which may be one of the reasons for their success.[5] Interestingly, apart from complexity, neither income levels nor regions are good predictors for success in upstream work.[6]

PPIAF and the WBI's self-reported results indicate a high level of achievement throughout all areas. For WBI and PPIAF, this evaluation has to rely on self-reported results measures.[7] The WBI regularly surveys participants of its capacity building seminars and workshops; PPIAF assess outputs, for example, preparation of PPP sector strategy, and their immediate outcomes, for example, adoption of such a strategy document by the client government.

For selected countries, IEG also assessed broader outcomes, albeit not validated independently (see Box 3.3). According to these data, PPIAF and the WBI have largely achieved their immediate objective, with 75–100 percent of their projects rated successful. These relatively good results do not vary greatly across sector or client country income levels. Their results were analyzed more in depth in the context of the nine country case studies. Case study evidence also indicates that PPIAF activities often complement the World Bank Group PPP agenda. For example, in the case of Brazil where PPIAF supported the development of a regulatory framework; or in the case of Ghana where PPIAF resources were used for a comprehensive country level diagnostic, which in turn allowed designing the PPP APL, currently under implementation.[8]

Looking at results across the various instruments used, DPLs and SILs tend to perform better. TALs and APLs were found to typically promote complex reforms in and were rated below average. By contrast DPLs often related to specific PPP upstream components, for example, introduction of a PPP unit or a PPP policy framework, and tended to score better (Figure 3.5).

Little is known regarding how far the upstream efforts also delivered the intended long-term outcomes. Although the reaching of objectives is usually well assessed at project closure (for World Bank) or completion of the activity (for PPIAF and WBI), less is known about reaching longer-term outcomes. For about one-quarter of cases there is evidence that PPP institutions and regulatory regimes are functioning and that consensus also led to action. Less is evident regarding to what extent PPP-related capacity was actually applied and sector reform led to

PPIAF supported the implementation of regulatory reforms in the power sector in Brazil. Brazil's power sector has changed from a model based on tariff-subsidized, government-owned utilities and a government-run grid to a hybrid competitive model with a mix of private and government-owned utilities, mandatory competitive auctions, and an independent regulator.

In 2002, PPIAF provided assistance to the Chamber of Power Sector Crisis Management (Câmara de Gestão da Crise de Energia Eletrica), which was organized by the Brazilian government to address urgent postcrisis issues regarding the sector's market and regulatory framework. PPIAF's team helped identify the critical issues and design a blueprint for the new energy auction model, through its technical assistance project. PPIAF's recommendation led to the adoption of a competitive market model based on bilateral contracts and mandatory energy auctions as a primary vehicle to introduce competition. This happened despite the strong political support for the adoption of the single-buyer model, where one company would purchase electricity from generators and sell it to the distributors.

PPIAF refined many of its initial recommendations with follow-up activities to help develop a new market and regulatory model for the Brazilian power sector. It also supported strengthening independent regulatory agencies. PPIAF conducted an independent assessment of regulatory roles and responsibilities of the Federal Electricity Agency and came up with 29 recommendations for strengthening the agency as the independent regulator.

Key success factors of PPIAF's support in the power sector include the high level of knowledge work and international expertise the World Bank has provided to Brazilian counterparts. PPIAF's knowledge work was also demand driven, where PPIAF has given the advice to the specific areas of regulatory reforms at the request of several ministries. Compared to other sectors, where PPIAF provided technical assistance such as irrigation projects, PPP projects in the power sector have a large pool of successful implementation.

SOURCES: IEG country case study; IEG 2013.

the wanted market structure and private sector participation (about one-third of cases).[9] As World Bank Implementation Completion and Results Reports (ICRs) are usually prepared at the time of project closure, many of these outcomes have not yet had time to materialize—or simply were not recorded.

Governments may also choose to benefit from Bank Group upstream assistance and subsequently go outside for their financing and developing. A government may take

FIGURE 3.5 Results by Type of Instrument

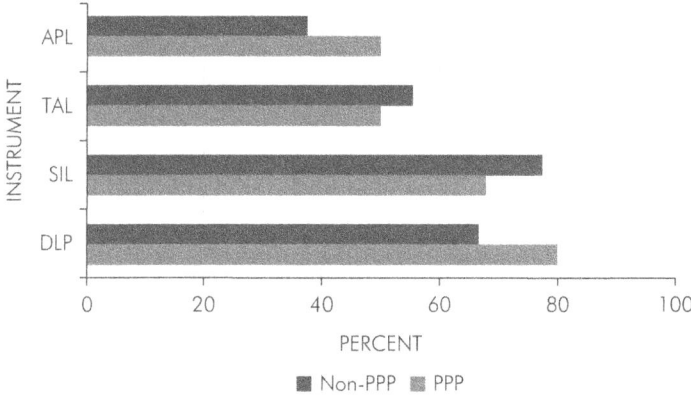

FIGURE 3.5 Results by Type of Instrument

SOURCES: IEG; ICR database.

NOTE: APL = adaptable program loan; DPL = development policy loan; SIL = specific investment loan; TAL = technical assistance loan.

advantage of Bank Group assistance in preparing the enabling environment and a specific project, but is then approached by a group that wishes to avoid competition entry. As observed in IEG's country case studies, lost opportunities for a PPP may also result from cases where PPP projects were given the go-ahead but subsequently were reversed when a foreign government came in with attractive terms and conditions that eventually turned the PPP back into a public investment.

Drivers of Success of Upstream Work

The most frequently found factors that influenced how far policy reform was successful were strong government commitment to sector reform and the availability of a capable and sustainable government champion to promote the PPP agenda. Frequent stakeholder consultation and active involvement of local staff likewise contributed to success of policy reform. By contrast, failure was generally associated with political uncertainty, power shifts during the project cycle, shift of government priorities caused by unforeseen exogenous events (for example, the Asian crisis), lack of stakeholder consultation, and project design factors. The country case studies corroborated these drivers of success and failure, which gave insights into the mechanics of these factors.

PPPs are basically about embracing market economy principles—ensuring political commitment, raising public awareness, securing stakeholder support, and identifying champions in a country are key to a PPP agenda. Upstream work was more successful when governments had clear objectives and demonstrated strong leadership and continuity. Lack of political commitment[10] and domination of government-close enterprises and state-owned enterprises was one of the leading causes for the low success of World Bank sector reform efforts, particularly in the energy and water sectors, according to the portfolio review and corroborated by the findings of the country cases studies. Invariably, understanding of the strengths and shortcomings of PPPs, political acceptance, and ability to foster sound transactions were the result of experience with private sector involvement that spanned decades (Brazil, Colombia, and the Philippines), and even then progress was hardly steady, with periods of reform often followed by regressive phases (Guatemala and the Philippines). Box 3.4 depicts several examples of successful and less successful working with governments that lack commitment and outlines lessons to be learned from this experience.

BOX 3.4 Drivers of Success and Failure in Creating and Maintaining Political Commitment and Awareness—Guatemala and the Philippines

Guatemala—Changing Priorities Stalling Transport Sector Reform Progress

The World Bank supported Guatemala as of 1998 through a TAL to structure, among other things, the transport sector, eventually introducing private sector participation. The component of this loan targeting the transport sector was not successful. After the successful implementation of the energy (and telecom) reforms, the government ran out of time. The following government changed priorities and did not have a majority in Congress. As a result, the transport sector reform was delayed until 2010 with the enactment of the new PPP Law. The transport sector is still dominated by public works, with emphasis on construction and entrenched sector interests. Furthermore, the country has very limited fiscal capacity because of low tax revenues. The regulatory and institutional framework is not ready to carry out PPPs. The following impediments prevented PPPs in the transport sector: (i) lack of political ownership and complex institutional setting; (ii) the small scale limits attractiveness to private sector participation; and (iii) cumbersome bureaucratic processes to obtain environmental licenses and land access permits.

The following lessons can be drawn from the World Bank's participation. The design of the World Bank TAL was too ambitious and complex and focused on too many sectors, given the country's political structure (four-year mandates without reelection) and long project life cycles (six to eight years). Second, although the World Bank's advice was still relevant to the country's objectives (developing transport infrastructure), the implementation cycle was not in line with the government's priorities.

continued on page 54

The Philippines—Working Around Changing Priorities Successfully

The Bank Group faced challenges in implementing its PPP agenda during 2003–09, as a result of poor governance. There were some notable successes in the early part of the period, such as completion of the Second Subic Bay Project, but IFC's support of Manila Airport was cancelled without disbursement. Overall, lending activity declined. Despite a long history of espousing a commitment to fight corruption, the country ranked poorly in international surveys on perceived corruption; coupled with the large public sector deficits, this undermined investor confidence.

The Bank turned to more intensive upstream work. Additional studies on public sector reform and the water sector were added, and the government passed the Procurement Reform Act, which was underpinned by a 2002 Bank study. The Bank also undertook a program of public information and education to give greater exposure to the challenges facing the country and influence the public's thinking, especially because many of the issues required political action.

These actions were effective in informing civil society and eventually building country ownership for reforms. The FY06–09 CAS adopted a "back to basics" approach, focusing on the ability of agencies to deliver services on the ground and make real implementation progress, rather than on sophisticated reform design. Regarding PPPs, both IFC and IBRD supported the Manila Water Company, and IFC undertook some power privatizations, but no other PPPs with World Bank Group involvement were launched, although both PPIAF and IFC Advisory Services provided advice on transactions. The Bank took a leadership role in the Philippine Development Forum that built on earlier Bank outreach efforts and sought to widen the consultative group process to include civil society, private sector, and other stakeholders. The Forum proved effective in building consensus among donors and country stakeholders on the issues confronting the country.

The outreach, coupled with strong upstream support on critical issues and a focus on service delivery, has enhanced the outlook for PPPs. A new PPP center, established in 2010, has established transparent preparation, evaluation, and oversight processes and is building a strong pipeline, although delivery has been slow. The challenge for the government now is to ensure this framework is speeded up and endures beyond a single presidential term.

The World Bank Group's close relationship with the government, despite differences on policy and transparency, allowed for candid dialogue, and meaningful actions. The Bank Group was able to deliver relevant upstream work, and focused service delivery downstream, and also allowed the Bank to make meaningful outreach efforts to the public, to highlight issues to build awareness of necessary reforms and political action.

SOURCES: World Bank 2004b; IEG country case studies.

Political commitment need not be taken as a given, but can be influenced. Evidence from country case studies indicates that the World Bank Group can address lack of or inconsistent political commitment. Factors that influenced political commitment were project life cycle synchronized with political realities on the ground and congruence of objectives; that is, project objectives should be in line with current government priorities, as in the case of Guatemala (Box 3.4).

Upstream work in the form of sector studies was helpful in the case of the Philippines as they focused the political attention on the right issues—and the public thinking, which may even be more important. Building institutions, albeit not directly focused on creating political commitment, can have as a side effect that the institutional roles and responsibilities become clearer and get codified, which can improve the authorities' readiness to make important decisions and deal with a complex PPP agenda, as it was the case in Colombia.

Privatization of state-owned enterprises has been a strong precursor to encouraging the PPP process, as it enhances competition and usually is accompanied by regulatory reform (Brazil, Colombia, and the Philippines). Indeed, in economies (or sectors) dominated by state-owned enterprises, PPPs are not embraced (Ghana, Guatemala, and Vietnam), as there is less competition, and regulation/oversight is unbalanced. Finally, even within the same country, PPPs could be successful in one sector and fail to gain a foothold in another because of uneven government commitment and consequent inattention to proper regulation and oversight—for example, water (Box 3.5) but not electricity in Senegal, or power but not transport in Guatemala. In China, PPPs have mainly worked in water, as other infrastructure sectors are dominated by state-owned enterprises.

Addressing regulatory failure has been key to the World Bank Group's upstream support so PPPs could gain a foothold, in particular in the energy and water sectors. As a general rule, a strong regulatory framework is a required for successful PPPs, as evidenced by IEG's portfolio analysis and the country cases. Particularly for electricity and water, a well-functioning authority appears to be needed to ensure tariffs that are fair and that recover costs and to ensure access; not surprisingly, most World Bank projects that aimed at advancing PPPs through sector reform were found in these two sectors.

In the Philippines water PPPs have been successful in metro Manila but have not taken a hold in other cities. There is a strong regulatory framework in place in Manila but not outside the city. In contrast, toll highways have been established both around Manila and elsewhere without awaiting the highway master plan (which has only recently been developed). In Ghana, initial progress on the regulatory front was reversed as the independent regulatory

Through lending and analytical work, including the Water Sector Project (closed FY04) and the Long-Term Water Sector Project (closed FY09), the World Bank supported comprehensive policy and institutional reform in Senegal in the water sector, commencing in the mid-1990s. The existing state-owned water utility was dismantled and replaced with a public asset-holding company that owns assets in the water sector, sets tariffs, and functions as the sector regulator. A framework engaging a commercial operator in water distribution was developed and a dedicated program was subsequently established to develop and implement an overall sector development strategy and coordinate interventions in the sector. These reforms were sustained and consolidated over the last 15 years.

Factors that drove the Bank's success in Senegal's water sector reflected several good practices: (i) guidance and support on the need to build consensus around reforms among stakeholders, including the government, unions, civil society, and donors; (ii) close support on the specific institutional, regulatory, and contractual framework of the PPP; (iii) effective adaptation of lessons of the experience from other parts of the regions; (iv) "permanent" Bank interaction with the client through field-based location of task team leaders and sector specialists and frequent headquarters missions; and (v) an effective Bank role as impartial "facilitator" as the new water company and partners adjusted to their roles and contractual obligations.

SOURCES: IEG country case study; World Bank 2004c.

commission turned into a stakeholder commission. In Senegal, a toll highway project has been supported as a stand-alone project. In contrast, its water sector performance has been based on meaningful regulatory reforms, and the electricity sector has suffered from the failure to establish an adequate framework.

The existence of at least some basic regulations is a necessary, but not a sufficient condition for PPP success; the framework must balance market requirements with technical principles and public policy objectives, such as pro-poor access, as well as optimal public sector risk exposure. Early reform efforts sometimes erred on the side of excessive public sector guarantees (Colombia, now corrected), high tariffs (electricity in the Philippines and Guatemala, subsequently reduced by subsidies), or unsustainable tariffs (Ghana (Box 3.6) and Senegal). These examples, however, showed also that launching a PPP agenda need not wait for perfect

BOX 3.6 Private Energy Generation Facing Regulatory Failure—Ghana

The World Bank entered into a sector reform dialogue as of 1998 through the Ghana Thermal Power Project and several analytical work elements, including one on energy tariffs and their poverty and social impacts. By project closure, a relatively robust regulatory framework was instituted, including the Public Utility Regulatory Commission and the Energy Commission. The Thermal Power Project also provided extensive capacity building to these regulatory commissions. During 1998–2004 tariffs actually increased by 350 and 250 percent. However, subsequent decisions by the government to absorb the tariff increases awarded by the Commission undermined the financial viability of the sector.

Although one private company had invested in the power sector since 1995, PPPs in the generation sector still face significant challenges because of, among other things, the ineffective regulatory regime. Despite World Bank capacity building efforts, the Regulatory Commission currently faces capacity constraints, as very little practical experience among staff exists, and consequently the regulatory process has lacked the requisite industry knowledge and confidence to meet the public and private sector needs and boost investor confidence; it operates a decision-making process that is not transparent (for example, not revealing the rate-setting guidelines in deriving tariffs) and suffers "stakeholder representation," rather than nomination based on qualification and experience. As a result, the sector suffers from electricity tariffs that are too low, as the automatic quarterly tariff adjustment mechanism was suspended.

The uneven application of tariff as a result of public outcry—as happened in 1998 and subsequent years and led to the government mandating the Regulatory Commission to withdraw increases or the government itself offering to subsidize end users—can be partly attributed to a low level of public awareness. When the government liberalized price setting in the petroleum sector, it undertook a professional campaign to explain the policy. This has not been the case on a sustained basis in the power sector.

The lesson to be learned for future regulatory reform efforts is that it is imperative that sustained public awareness campaigns become a key part of any World Bank program of sector reforms and that they engage competent professionals to institute and oversee these campaigns. In addition to the partly ineffective regulatory regime, the World Bank gave less and less attention to ensuring cost recovery tariffs as other issues such as privatization and radical sector reform came to the fore. Moreover, at the level of the Bank team there was a dilution of responsibilities as the number of the players was enlarged. This lack of consistent and strong dialogue may have contributed to an erosion of electricity tariffs between 2004 and 2007.

SOURCE: World Bank 2013.

regulation in place, but can also take the approach of incremental improvement, that is, where the implementation of PPP transactions helps identify changes needed.

In any case, a PPP agenda that emerges from a National Infrastructure Plan and or public investment management system will reduce uncertainty and should spur more competition in the process. The lack of such a framework has hampered transactions in Guatemala (Box 3.7), and Ghana is still coming to grips with integrating the various PPP opportunities and its national public investment priorities. And even in transport, PPPs can only be successful if there are enabling laws (such as BOT laws) and workable guidelines and policies on safeguards—where World Bank Group involvement has been beneficial (as in the Philippines).

BOX 3.7 The Institutional Framework for Managing PPPs—Colombia versus Guatemala

Colombia—Successful Institutional Set-Up

The World Bank Group helped Colombia twice (with 2003 and 2011 PPIAFs) with institutional reform, with full support from the government. The Bank Group and country learned mutually and improved the institutional design and the execution capability for PPPs. Colombia today has an institutional set-up that, although still evolving, is capable of undertaking PPPs.

The primary driver for success was the early and comprehensive support from the World Bank Group. World Bank support started in 2003 through the PPIAF with transport sector reform, the transition from public works to private concessions, and the establishment of the predecessor entity the National Concession Agency. Support included provisions of advice to the draft PPP law that was enacted in 2012 and subsequently used to process the fourth generation of road PPPs; it also included IFC Advisory Services support. The World Bank also advised on the organizational set-up of the PPP unit to ensure institutional and functional autonomy, conditions necessary for ensuring that pipeline development was carried out without interference and that actual transactions were handled in a transparent and neutral fashion.

The World Bank supported the government in the design of the agency and its coordination with other key agencies. In addition, the WBI strengthened the capacity of the National Infrastructure Agency and the National Planning Department staff. IFC also had a significant contribution in the regulatory and institutional reform process. The experience during the structuring of the IFC Ruta del Sol Project became the model for the new PPP law.

After the development of the PPP institutional framework, the government was committed to its PPP program. The National Infrastructure Agency had staff with strong technical capacity, using public-private comparator models for assessing PPPs, a stable budget allocation, and a sound approach to managing contingent liabilities. The unit has thus far handled a significant portfolio of infrastructure projects, including 25 road concessions covering 6,035 km, of which 875 km are already built; two railway concessions covering 625 km; two port dredging concessions (Cartagena, Buenaventura); and the airport concession in Barranquilla. It has an ambitious transportation investment plan estimated at $18 billion.

Guatemala—Insufficient Institutional Capacity with Focus on Immediate Quick Wins

The World Bank provided support in 1997–2002 through the TAL on transport sector reform, but the government did not follow up until 2010 with the enactment of the new PPP law. Although the World Bank provided regulatory advice on a concession law (2003 and 2006 PPIAFs), the concession law was never approved.

The PPP law lacks specifics. The institutional framework is also weak. There is a perceived lack of PPP operative capacity in the relevant agencies, that is, the Ministries of Finance and of Transport and the National Infrastructure Agency. The project selection process is not transparent, and there is no clear coordination with other government agencies. There is no agency with sufficient control and supervision. The transport sector is dominated by public stakeholders and there is no tariff control. The weak regulatory framework and institutional limitations severely constrain the country's capacity to carry out PPPs in the transport sector. The weak PPP unit was created without expertise from the World Bank. The objective of the government was not to achieve institutional reform, which it thought would come later, but to achieve quickly a "few success PPP projects" to demonstrate a "new way of doing business."

SOURCE: IEG country case studies.

In addition to sector reform, a PPP-specific enabling environment that included a minimum of an institutional framework, processes, and roles helped the PPP agenda take off. At the minimum, an institutional framework needs to be in place for approval of PPP projects, particularly when the public sector underwrites risk and (as in Brazil) to limit the amount of exposure underwritten by states and municipalities, as well as to ensure adherence to public policy objectives. Such a system includes transparent processes and institutional responsibilities for (i) implementing the PPP process from identifying PPP projects to the closure of the transaction and contract management; (ii) approving the most significant milestones, including fiduciary control functions; and (iii) instilling program oversight to ensure the right processes are followed. Such an institutional framework for PPPs needs to build on sound public financial management principles to ensure that fiscal exposure emerging from PPPs is adequately assessed, controlled, budgeted, and disclosed. Adequate knowledge and capacity is a prerequisite for all entities involved.

Whether a dedicated "PPP unit" at the country level is needed remains to be seen; identifying a sustainable "PPP champion," however, may facilitate interministerial coordination. Dedicated PPP units may serve well as the engine of PPP development; however, their existence and proactive engagement may easily imply implicit approval of PPPs as opposed to other procurement options.

Table 3.1 summarizes several more advantages and disadvantages of a dedicated PPP unit. In any case, it is likely to remain a balancing act of exploiting the advantages while containing the disadvantages. Vested interest can play a role in a country's PPP agenda as well—in both dedicated PPP units as well as other arrangements. These can delay the PPP process or be the root cause for lack of government commitment. Regardless of which set-up is chosen, the PPP champion seems to be an essential factor in advancing a PPP agenda and should be a neutral advocate for the public interest while creating a level playing field for the private investors.

World Bank Group–supported countries that have larger PPP programs generally have at least a PPP champion (or focal point). Both Colombia and the Philippines have stand-alone units but have had to restructure them to address corruption and make them more transparent and effective. In Guatemala, PPPs were hampered by a lack of an adequate institutional set up to manage PPPs until 2012. Line ministries also often have units to evaluate and process transactions, and sometimes the boundaries are unclear. In contrast, a lack of capacity (as in Guatemala and Ghana) leads to paralysis (Box 3.7).

For the location of PPP champions or units, there are generally three options: (i) within the regular departmental structure of the Ministry of Finance; (ii) in an individual line ministry that is predisposed in its functions to use PPPs, such as an infrastructure ministry; and (iii) as an independent government agency that collaborates with a secretariat in the finance ministry (or equivalent) (OECD 2010), including offices attached to a Ministry of Planning or the Prime Minister's office. Except for the last option, the solution need not necessarily include a dedicated PPP unit, as, for example, charging the Public Investment Unit with the role of a PPP champion, as is currently done in Ghana, may also work.

TABLE 3.1 Advantages and Disadvantages of a Dedicated PPP Unit

Advantages	Disadvantages
• A dedicated PPP unit can act as a knowledge center on PPP project preparation, negotiation and execution. • Centralization of knowledge can provide cost savings for government.	• Knowledge can be supplied by internal and external project advisors appointed directly by individual ministries/agencies with specific expertise in the relevant sectoral area and/or project issues.
• A dedicated PPP unit can help regulate the creation of PPPs by government organizations to ensure that they fulfill all requirements regarding affordability, value for money, and so forth.	• Line ministries/agencies together with the finance/planning ministry have expertise in assessing cost-benefits of projects and political prioritization of projects.
• A dedicated PPP unit can ensure that appropriate budgetary considerations are taken for PPP projects and that contingent liabilities are also evaluated.	• The closer a dedicated unit is to the relevant political leadership, the more susceptible it is to the political influence in deciding which PPP project should be initiated.
• A dedicated PPP unit can give a fillip to a country's PPP program, soliciting projects, attracting potential partners/ investors, building trust and good will with private partners.	• Establishing a dedicated unit may imply an implicit approval of PPP and weaken the case for other viable procurement methods.
• A dedicated PPP unit can separate PPP policy formulation and implementation.	• PPP policy can be formulated by the same authority that does so for traditional procurement. • A dedicated unit may not separate policy formulation and implementation if it can directly fund PPP projects.

SOURCE: Adapted from OECD 2008.

World Bank Group–supported PPP programs have been influenced by subregional market trends, making countries scramble to prepare for them. In Latin America, as public investment became more constrained in the aftermath of the debt crisis, private sector involvement in infrastructure grew rapidly, with the rising tide lifting individual countries whether they were ready or not. Colombia's early PPPs were done in response to this trend, and mechanisms were not in place to properly regulate government support; this led to excessive guarantees—which in turn led to well-conceived policies to measure and limit public exposure. In a similar vein, more recently the large infrastructure gap and limited public resources in Africa have prompted an interest in PPPs as a means to raise finance for what were traditionally public sector investments.

The design of PPP component(s) and how related knowledge products are delivered matters—suggesting that the PPIAF resources should be used more strategically. At times, the PPP agenda did not advance because of complexity, as in Guatemala, where PPP upstream work was cobbled together in several sectors under one loan. However, a public sector development loan worked in Colombia, and in Ghana a PPP APL has been recently put in place to advance such operations. In both these cases, however, the project design was not only adopted to local conditions through in-depth diagnostic work but also built carefully on existing structures, including on a strong series of sector reform efforts and the lessons that had been learned. At other times, PPP activities were embedded in somewhat disconnected operations—in the sense of having different counterparts and objectives than the partnership itself—such as a PPP program in a public management reform program (see Box 3.8).

BOX 3.8 Lessons on How to Embed PPP Components—Ghana

Early attempts by the World Bank to advise on a PPP program in Ghana failed. The Public Sector Management Reform Project, approved 2004, was the first comprehensive attempt to build a PPP program in Ghana. The development of a strategy for enhanced public-private cooperation was seen as a first step to operationalize this objective. Eventually, a PPP strategy was developed. The outcomes were rated unsatisfactory for the following reasons: (i) too complex a project design embedded in an inappropriate framework, that is, sector-specific reform efforts in a public sector management framework, (ii) insufficient evidence of sustained government commitment, and (iii) unrealistic time frame and elections.

Currently the World Bank and the government of Ghana are working on a comprehensive PPP program. As of the financial crisis in 2008 the government showed increased interest in expanding the role of the private sector in the economy, including in financing infrastructure. To promote this approach, the government recognized that it would first have to create an appropriate policy, legal, regulatory, and institutional environment. The World Bank and PPIAF responded by launching a series of comprehensive studies, including a systematic readiness diagnostic and benchmarking with Ghana's peer countries, which eventually led to the approval of a World Bank APL PPP project. This latest PPP APL builds on a systematic effort on sector reform in energy, water, and transport and takes a comprehensive approach with specific milestones, integrating institutional and legal issues as well as emphasizing capacity. As it was only approved in 2012, outcomes have yet to materialize.

SOURCES: World Bank 2004a; IEG country case study.

Careful thought needs to be given to how best to design PPP interventions to ensure dialogue with the right government counterparts, and where knowledge and capacity exists or can be developed quickly. In Vietnam, for example, knowledge products aimed at the government were fragmented and have not made much of a dent in the catalyzing transaction level activities. In this regard, although PPIAF's work was useful, timely, and of good quality (especially with very relevant just-in-time studies and project preparation activities), it is unclear if deployment of resources is adequately strategic. Being flexible and responsive to requests for studies certainly is a good thing, but it may miss the opportunity to fully exploit carefully designed approaches fitting strategically into the PPP agenda. A more strategically oriented approach to utilize PPIAF resources, with filters to evaluate the strategic thrust of PPIAF interventions and a more systematic linkage to CAS undertakings, may be able to achieve a broader and richer set of results than the current approach, which is driven mainly by project-level preferences.

Capacity, regulations, and incentives tend to make PPPs at the subnational level successful. World Bank Group–supported PPP programs exhibited differences between PPPs managed at the national government level and those managed by local units. PPPs at the national level depend on the success of national laws and regulations, national ownership and capacity, and credibility of undertakings. Similar factors play a role in success at the local government level, but local politics also plays a role.

Where decentralization is accepted and states and municipalities have strong capacity, clear regulations, implicit or explicit incentives tied into an accountability structure, and sizable markets, PPPs at the subnational level tend to work well (Brazil and China). However, in countries where markets may be fragmented (such as the water market in Colombia, Guatemala, and the Philippines), local government units do not have adequate capacity (Guatemala) or the regulatory frameworks do not cover local government units, so performance of PPPs is generally weaker. In the Philippines the Bank is currently working on consolidating water districts and establishing a water regulator for a more conducive climate for meaningful private sector participation. Conversely, the broad approach of the World Bank Group has allowed IFC to support PPPs at the local government level, even when upstream reform efforts at the national level have had mixed results (China).

A lack of skills and resources for the preparation of a PPP pipeline and bankable PPP projects is a serious limitation across all World Bank-supported countries. PPPs are more complex than public sector operations and to the extent that they employ project financing, they can also be more challenging than simple corporate finance. Countries with adequate capacity have gradually undertaken them and in some cases have developed institutions that evaluate projects and develop a pipeline (Colombia and the Philippines). In other countries, even where assistance with upstream issues such as regulations and laws has been supported by the Bank, PPPs have been slow to take off, because of a lack of capacity (China, Ghana, Guatemala, and Vietnam). More engagement in capacity building appears needed, and the World Bank Group (the World Bank or IFC Advisory Services) could play a role in develop oversight and competition processes and institutions to develop and execute a PPP pipeline.

Conclusion

Upstream support to client countries' PPP agenda was mostly delivered through sector reform efforts. Capacity building for PPPs, creating consensus, and building the legal and institutional framework for PPPs were the next most frequently addressed enabling factors across World Bank, PPIAF, and the WBI. Although World Bank Group projects tend to give attention to ensuring adequate risk sharing, downstream contingent liabilities are rarely fully quantified at the project level. Recent efforts to systematize and introduce a framework are valuable contributions, with outcomes yet to be seen.

Sector reform, although the most important type of upstream support, was the most difficult to achieve. Despite the World Bank's leverage and country presence, success on sector reform was only evident in 55 percent of World Bank loans—an important finding, given that proper sector reform is necessary to implement a PPP agenda successfully. Sector reform efforts were particularly prominent in the water and energy sectors, indicating the heavy reliance of PPPs in reform in these areas. Sector reform failed often because of the complexity and political implications of projects; project design and unrealistic timing on the side of the World Bank were factors contributing to failure as well. The choice of lending instrument is another essential factor in advancing the PPP agenda and needs to be made contingent of the country's readiness.

Relatively narrow interventions, for example, the efforts to build institutions for PPPs, worked the best. Similarly, building up consensus or regulatory commissions succeeded more often. Compared to relatively broad-based sector reform efforts, these types of upstream efforts are relatively targeted—which may be one of the reasons for their success. Also PPIAF and the WBI's self-reported results indicate a high level of achievement throughout all areas, and PPIAF was found complementing the work of its Bank Group partner institutions.

The most frequent factors influencing how far policy reforms were successful were strong government commitment to sector reform and the availability of a capable government champion to promote the PPP agenda. Active involvement of local staff contributed likewise to success of policy reform. Privatization of state-owned enterprises has been a strong precursor to encouraging the PPP process, as it enhances competition and usually is accompanied by regulatory reform. Technical assistance upstream had a positive role in creating government commitment, as did institution building efforts, because they clarified roles and processes for making important PPP-related decisions.

Addressing regulatory failure has been key to the World Bank Group's upstream support so PPPs could gain a foothold, in particular in the energy and water sectors. In addition to sector reform, a PPP-specific enabling environment including a minimum of an institutional framework, processes, and roles helped the PPP agenda take off. Whether a dedicated "PPP unit" at the country level is needed remains to be seen; identifying a "PPP champion," however, may facilitate interministerial coordination. The design of PPP component(s), if and how they are embedded in a World Bank lending operation with complementary knowledge products, matters and suggests that PPIAF resources should be used more strategically.

On the side of the countries' governments, a lack of skills and resources for the preparation of a PPP pipeline and bankable PPP projects is a serious limitation across all World Bank-supported countries. For subnational PPPs to be successful, capacity, regulations, and incentives need to be in place and embedded in a clear accountability system.

Notes

[1] The concept of sector reform can often entail elements that do not necessarily enable PPPs. For example, in the transport sector, the introduction of a road fund would form part of a reform package to ensure adequate maintenance. Although this is important to the transport sector as such, the existence of a road fund will not determine if and how to process with a single toll road. What is needed in most sectors, however, is the financial viability of the sector surrounding the PPP. For example, in the energy sector, the financial viability of the off-taker of an IPP is a precondition for any private sector engagement in power generation. This analysis hence focuses on the factors relevant to PPPs.

[2] With the exception of four IFC investments that had some upstream elements.

[3] The relative weight of these upstream components remained more or less unchanged over the evaluation period (FY02–12). The only exceptions were that a few efforts to improve fiscal management and local capital markets did occur more recently, that is, in FY07–12.

[4] Note that for several of these cases the number of observations is low, hence the statistical representativeness limited.

[5] In general, evidence for meeting objectives of project components specific to PPPs was available in about 50 percent of cases. In the remaining half, ICRs did not report on progress in these areas at all as either (i) the component was too small given the overall project envelope or (ii) progress took longer than anticipated and could only be assessed beyond project closure. Project closure also marks the end of systematic project-level monitoring, which also explains why little is known on outcomes of policy reform efforts.

[6] Results of the World Bank's upstream work seem not to be aligned with the income gradient of the recipient country, as LICs and UMICs exhibit higher success (70 and 60 percent, respectively, meeting their respective objectives) than LMICs, at 38 percent. Hence the concept of country income seems not a good predictor of success of upstream work—neither does region. In Sub-Saharan Africa, where PPPs are the least prominent, World Bank upstream work was the most successful, with 73 percent meeting their objectives, as opposed to Latin America and the Caribbean, with 57 percent, and the Middle East and North Africa, with 50 percent.

[7] These are not embedded in a structured results monitoring and evaluation framework as lending or investment operations.

[8] Assessing complementarity of WBI activities is challenging, as these are typically very small and documentation on outcomes is scarce.

[9] The EIU rating scheme that scores countries according to their PPP maturity dates only back for about three years so that the effectiveness of World Bank's upstream support could not be tested if it affected the country's overall maturity.

[10] Although there is no metric to measure the extent of political commitment, the term subsumes decisiveness, leadership, continuity, and will of the political elite in a country. For the analysis, political commitment was judged based on the assessment of ex post project-level evaluation reports (XPSRs, PCRs, ICRs, PERs, and so forth.)

References

CEE Bankwatch Network. 2008. *Never Mind the Balance Sheet: The Dangers Posed by Public-Private Partnerships in Central and Eastern Europe.* Prague: Central and Eastern Europe Bankwatch Network.

Hammami, Mona, Jean-Francois Ruhashyankiko, and Etienne B. Yehoue. 2006. "Determinants of Public-Private Partnerships in Infrastructure." IMF Working Paper, WP/06/99, Washington, DC.

High Level Panel on Infrastructure. 2011. *Recommendations to G20—Final Report.*

IEG (Independent Evaluation Group). 2013. *Brazil CPE, FY 2004-11: Evaluation of the World Bank Group Program.* Washington, DC: World Bank.

Irwin, Timothy C. 2007. *Government Guarantees: Allocating and Valuing Risk in Privately Financed Infrastructure Projects.* Washington, DC: World Bank.

OECD (Organisation for Economic Co-operation and Development). 2008. *Public-Private Partnerships: In Pursuit of Risk Sharing and Value for Money.* Paris: OECD.

———. 2010. *Dedicated Public-Private Partnership Units—A Survey of Institutional and Governance Structures.* Paris: OECD.

Sadka, Efriam. 2006. "Public-Private Partnerships: A Public Economics Perspective." IMF Working Paper WP/06/77. Washington, DC: IMF.

Ter-Minassian, Teresa. 2004. *Public-Private Partnerships.* Washington, DC: International Monetary Fund.

World Bank. 1998. "Contingent Liabilities—A Threat to Fiscal Stability." PREM Notes, Economic Policy, No 9, Washington, DC.

———. 2004a. "Ghana—Public Sector Management Reform Project." Implementation Completion and Results Report No. 27651, World Bank, Washington, DC.

———. 2004b. "Second Subic Bay Freeport Project." Implementation Completion and Results Report No. 27282, World Bank, Washington, DC.

———. 2004c. "Senegal—Water Sector Project." Implementation Completion and Results Report No. 30800, World Bank, Washington, DC.

———. 2013. *Energizing Economic Growth in Ghana—Making the Power and Petroleum Sectors Rise to the Challenges.* Energy Environment Review No. 79656, Washington, DC.

World Bank and WBI (World Bank Institute). 2013. "Implementing a Framework for Managing Fiscal Commitments from Public-Private Partnerships." Operational Note, Washington, DC.

4

Did Public-Private Partnerships Deliver?

HIGHLIGHTS

• Available data indicate positive effects of PPPs, in particular when measured in terms of development outcomes. But evidence is weak and limited when it comes to the users' side of PPPs. The least amount of information is available regarding how PPPs affect the poor—a particular concern, given the new dual strategic objective of "shared prosperity" in the World Bank Group's 2013 strategy.

• In addition to providing finance and catalyzing other financiers, IFC investments added value during due diligence or as an honest broker of the government's interest.

• IFC-supported PPPs generally do very well. Its thorough due diligence contains effectively sponsor and market risk. Its PPPs are located in countries with well-developed enabling environments. As a consequence, IFC-supported PPPs exhibit not only consistently higher development outcomes ratings, but also stronger than average business performance and higher investment income. IFC investment can hence afford to increase its risk appetite by extending investments into countries with a less-tested enabling environment, so-called "emerging" countries and—to the extent the market opportunities exist—also in "nascent" countries.

• IFC Advisory Services has demonstrated high value added. About half of the projects result in contract award, with the shortfall mostly because of government volatility and the pioneering nature of the transactions. IFC Advisory Services can play a more proactive role in securing government commitment upfront.

- IFC established *IFC InfraVentures* to fund the early stages of project development in IDA countries. But it is questionable whether it will solve the problem of project preparation for high-volume mainstream PPPs.

- MIGA guarantees helped increase investors' confidence, improve their capacity to raise capital, lower financing costs, and mediate disputes with government. MIGA's political risk insurance brought PPPs into nascent and emerging PPP countries.

- The World Bank Group does not stay sufficiently engaged throughout the lifespan of a PPP.

- Bank Group–supported transactions often created a market for PPPs through their demonstration effects and at times helped shape the regulatory environment.

This chapter examines if and to what extent PPPs have contributed to improved access to infrastructure and social services. The analysis focuses on PPPs that benefited from World Bank Group support during project preparation, structuring, and bidding, and that received financial support by means of equity, debt, or guarantees.

To assess the success rate of PPPs, IEG developed sector-specific indicators to capture what constitutes success for the various types of PPPs, keeping in mind product differences across the Bank Group. These indicators were developed in broad consultations from World Bank sector experts and were applied both during the portfolio review and in country case studies (see Appendix B). The indices measure performance of PPPs along the dimensions of creating or improving access, quality, efficiency, financial soundness, fiscal aspects, and access for the poor.

World Bank Group Support to Structuring and Financing PPPs

World Bank Group support to structuring and financing PPPs is provided by IFC investments, IFC's Advisory Services, MIGA, and the share of World Bank support that focus on PPP transactions, for example, through project preparation and PRGs. Table 1.1 provides an overview of projects with focus on PPP downstream support.

Which type of PPP is used varies from sector to sector. Overall, concession models and design, build, operate (DBO) schemes dominated in terms of types of PPPs. A concession grants a private firm the right to operate a defined infrastructure service and to receive revenues from it, usually against a concession fee. Such structures are particularly frequent in the transport sector. DBO schemes are second most frequent, mostly encountered in energy generation, but also in transport (ports, airports, and roads) (Figure 4.1). In the water sector, the PPP uptake faces still many challenges; lease and management contracts prevail, as they typically do not involve ownership of assets—often a concern in this sector. When comparing the use of the various types of PPPs across World Bank Group, performance-based contracts appear more frequently in the World Bank's portfolio, with most other types evenly distributed.

The World Bank Group emphasized PPPs in water, ports, and railways stronger than the market. According to the private participation in infrastructure[1] database—which is used as a proxy for "market"—almost half of PPPs occur in energy (47 percent), followed by toll roads (17 percent). The World Bank Group's priorities with regard to which sector to support differ from the market, as reflected in the PPI database. Although the Bank Group has also supported the energy and road sectors, it has placed more emphasis than the market on water (both the World Bank and MIGA), ports (IFC investments and MIGA),

FIGURE 4.1 Type of PPPs in World Bank Group Operations

A. TYPES OF PPPs ACROSS WORLD BANK GROUP INSTITUTIONS

B. TYPES OF PPPs IN THE ENERGY SECTOR[a]

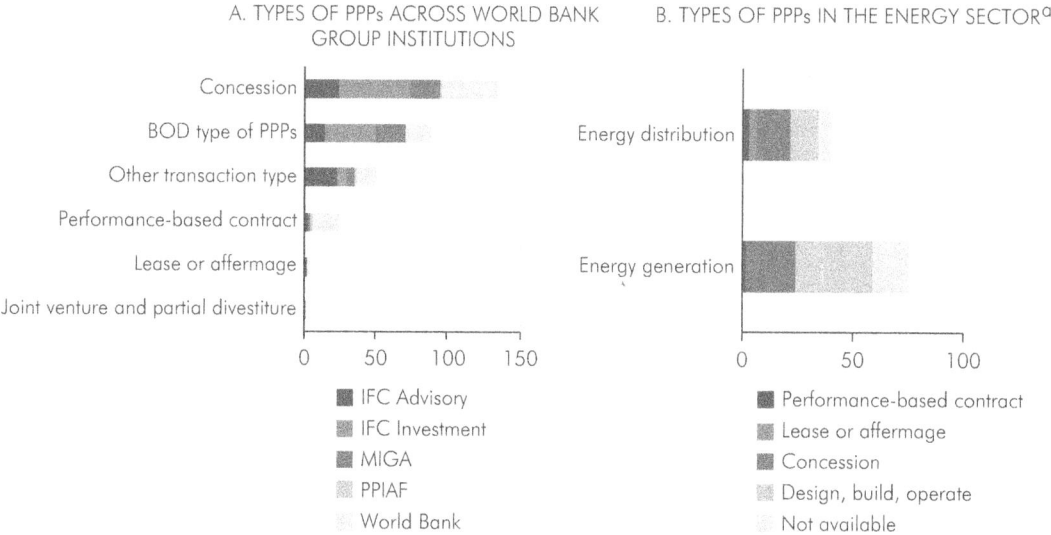

Concession
BOD type of PPPs
Other transaction type
Performance-based contract
Lease or affermage
Joint venture and partial divestiture

0   50   100   150

- IFC Advisory
- IFC Investment
- MIGA
- PPIAF
- World Bank

Energy distribution

Energy generation

0   50   100

- Performance-based contract
- Lease or affermage
- Concession
- Design, build, operate
- Not available

SOURCE: IEG.
NOTE: MIGA: Multilateral Investment Guarantee Agency; PPIAF = Public-Private Infrastructure Advisory Facility.
a. n = 14.

railways (IFC investments and World Bank), and airports (mainly IFC investments) (see Figure 4.2).

IFC investments in PPPs grew, with a total of 176 investments between FY02 and FY12, a significant share of its infrastructure portfolio. Collectively, they amount to $6.2 billion in original commitments. IFC's investments in PPPs represent 41 percent of total infrastructure and 9 percent of total IFC investments. Although volatile between years, total IFC investments in PPPs have more than doubled, from $186 million in FY02 to $470 million in FY12. PPP-targeted investments grew until 2008, when the financial crisis hit. However, support significantly increased in the following years and rose to a new high in FY11 (see Figure 4.3). In summary, the volume of investments in PPPs during the five-year period FY07–12 was about three times higher than the preceding period (FY02–06), with $3.8 billion FY07–12 compared to only $1.2 billion during FY02–06. IFC's investments in PPPs are concentrated in UMICs and more than a third occurred in Latin American and the Caribbean.[2]

In addition to its investments, IFC also provides advice on designing and implementing PPP transactions to national and local governments, regardless of sector. The mandate of IFC's business line focusing on structuring PPPs ("C3P") extends not only to PPPs, but also to management and lease contracts, restructuring, and privatization of state-owned

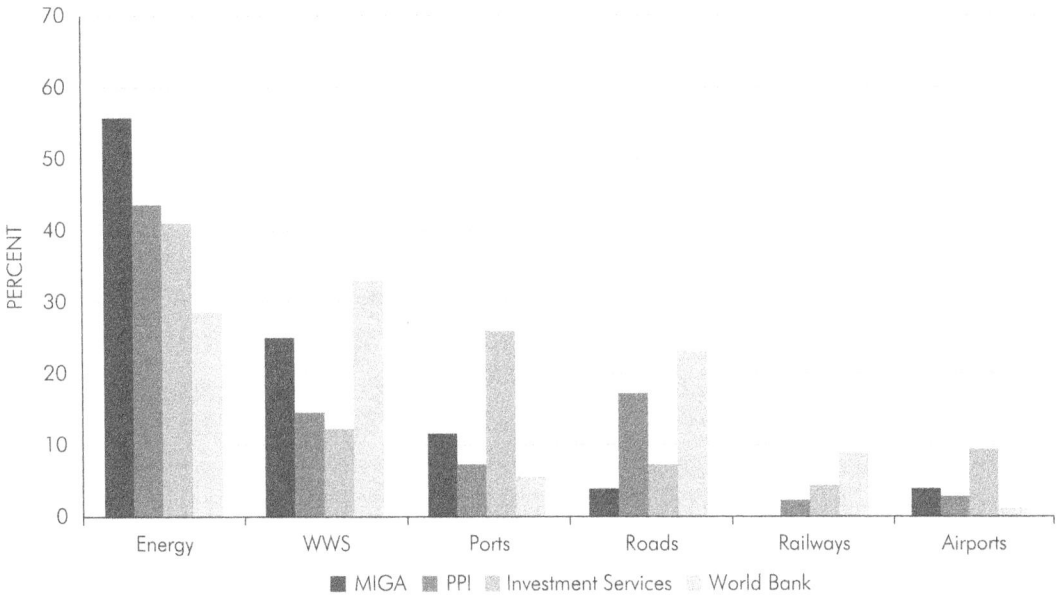

FIGURE 4.2 Sector Priorities in PPPs: World Bank Group Response versus the Market (per PPI database)

SOURCE: IEG.

NOTE: The PPI database was adjusted to fit the definition used in this evaluation. PPI = private participation in infrastructure

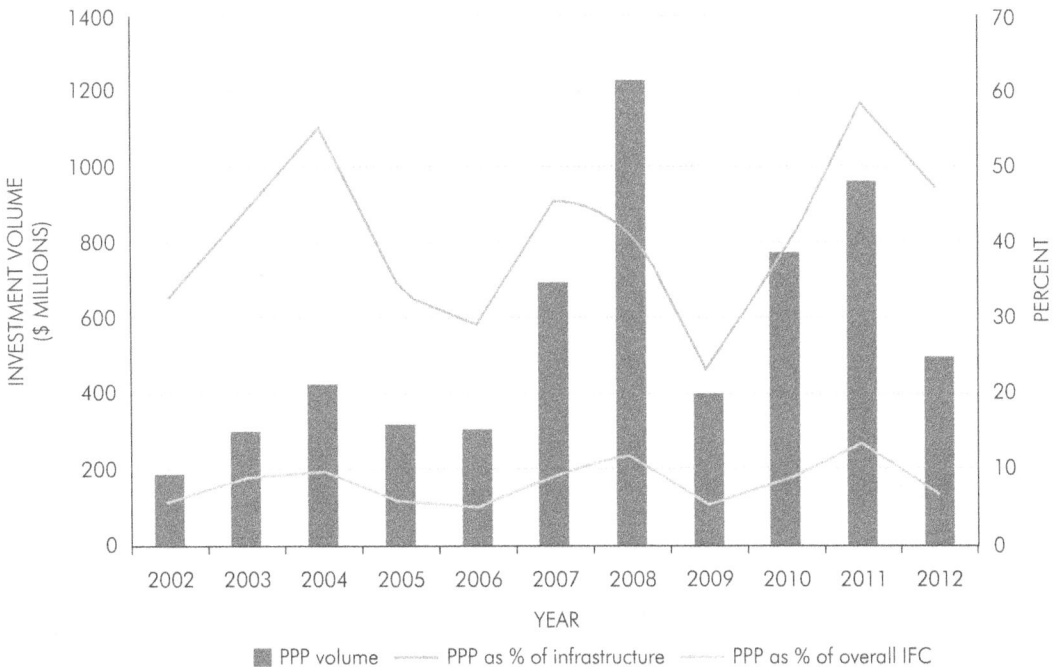

FIGURE 4.3 IFC's Investments in PPPs, FY02–12

SOURCE: IFC.

NOTE: Volume = original commitments.

enterprises and upstream advisory work (regulatory, legal). Using this evaluation's definition of PPPs, the business lines of IFC advisory services PPP has supported 140 services related to PPPs between FY05[3] and FY12, increasing in absolutes and relative values since FY05.

These 140 advisory services were largely in support of transactions. About 14 percent of these 140 advisory projects focused on transactions but had some minor upstream component, such as conducting feasibility studies or advising on specific legal issues related to the transaction. Seven percent (ten projects) of IFC's PPP advisory services projects addressed upstream issues exclusively (without an immediately related transaction). Of this seven percent, most work was geared toward capacity building, workshops and seminars, sector studies, and consensus building. Collectively, IFC advisory on PPPs comprise about 11 percent of IFC's total expenditure of advisory services and about 10 percent by number. Total IFC expenditure for advisory services in PPPs has increased over time from $6 million in FY05 to $28 million in FY12 (Figure 4.4). In contrast to IFC investments, IFC Advisory Services in PPPs are found mainly in LMICs and are concentrated in Sub-Saharan Africa.[4]

FIGURE 4.4 IFC's Advisory Services in PPPs—Volume of Funding of Services, FY02–12

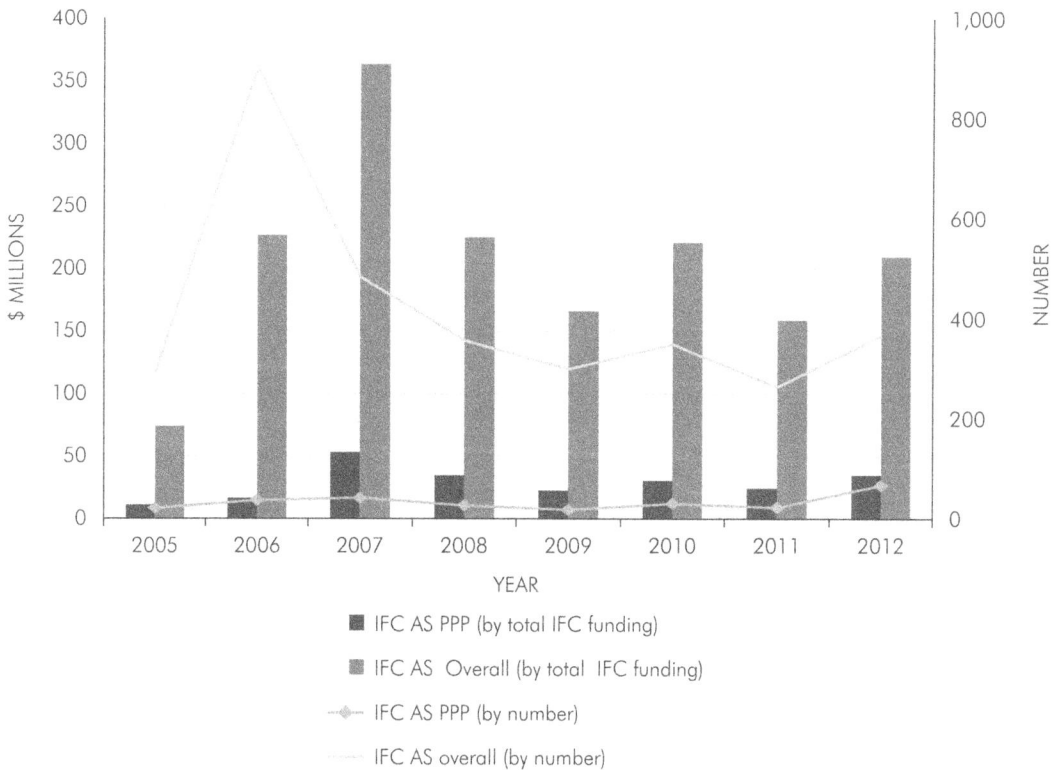

IFC AS PPP (by total IFC funding)
IFC AS Overall (by total IFC funding)
IFC AS PPP (by number)
IFC AS overall (by number)

SOURCE: IFC Advisory Services database by project as of October 31, 2012.
NOTE: Volume = IFC funding. AS = Advisory Services.

MIGA provided PRI through guarantees for 81 PPP projects, amounting to $5.1 billion gross issuance between FY02 and FY12—nearly half of its total guarantee volume issued during this period. The volume of MIGA guarantees issued for PPP projects represents 95 percent of total infrastructure volume and 50 percent of total guarantee volume (gross). Looking at projects approved, MIGA's guarantee volume issued (gross) in support of PPPs increased almost twofold during the last 10 years, from $1.7 billion during FY02–06 to $2.7 billion during FY07–12 (Figure 4.5). Similar to IFC investments, most of MIGA's guarantees in PPPs were in MICs and more than a quarter in Latin America and the Caribbean and Sub-Saharan Africa.[5]

MIGA's ability to insure stand-alone debt made it easier to provide non-honoring of sovereign financial obligations coverage and was also a factor behind the increase in PPP volume in FY11 and FY12. MIGA's ability to offer this coverage resulted in its backing of several large PPP projects in FY11 and FY12. This coverage is the newest type of guarantee and the least common, totaling 1 percent of the total number of guarantees. Transfer restriction and expropriation are the most common guarantees, comprising 55 percent of all and followed by war and civil disturbance and breach of contract with 22 percent and 21 percent, respectively.

The World Bank supported PPPs in increasing numbers through advising on transactions and finance. In total, 353 World Bank projects were found to target PPPs during

FIGURE 4.5 MIGA Guarantees to PPPs—Volume of Guarantees Issued (gross), FY02–12

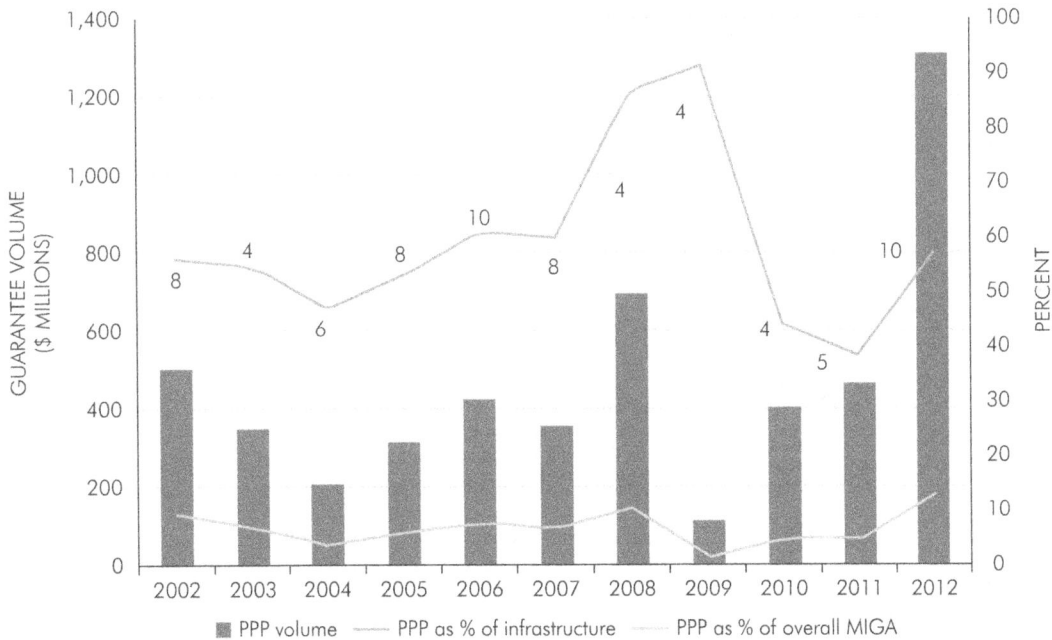

SOURCE: MIGA database.

NOTE: Volume = gross guarantee volume.

FY02–12. Of these, 231 were reviewed in detail, identifying 128 projects with downstream components,[6] approved or exited between FY02 and FY12. Collectively, downstream lending components had a total PPP volume of $7.6 billion.[7] World Bank downstream lending represented 11 percent of total infrastructure and 3 percent of total World Bank investments.

Looking at projects approved during FY02–12, the volume of investments in PPPs during the five-year period (FY07–12) was about three times higher than the preceding period (FY02–06), with $ 4.4 billion in FY07–12, compared to only $ 1.8 billion during FY02–06 (Figure 4.6). This rise can largely be attributed to an increase in lending in water and energy, where investments increased from $ 0.5 billion and $0.4 billion in FY02–06 to $1.5 and $0.7 during FY07–12, respectively. Half of the World Bank's downstream lending in PPPs is concentrated in LMICs and occurred more often in Sub-Saharan Africa and Latin America.[8]

The World Bank Group has also applied innovative approaches, such as output-based aid, in an effort to expand the concept of PPPs into delivery of basic service to the poor. This type

FIGURE 4.6 World Bank Transaction Support to PPPs, FY02–12

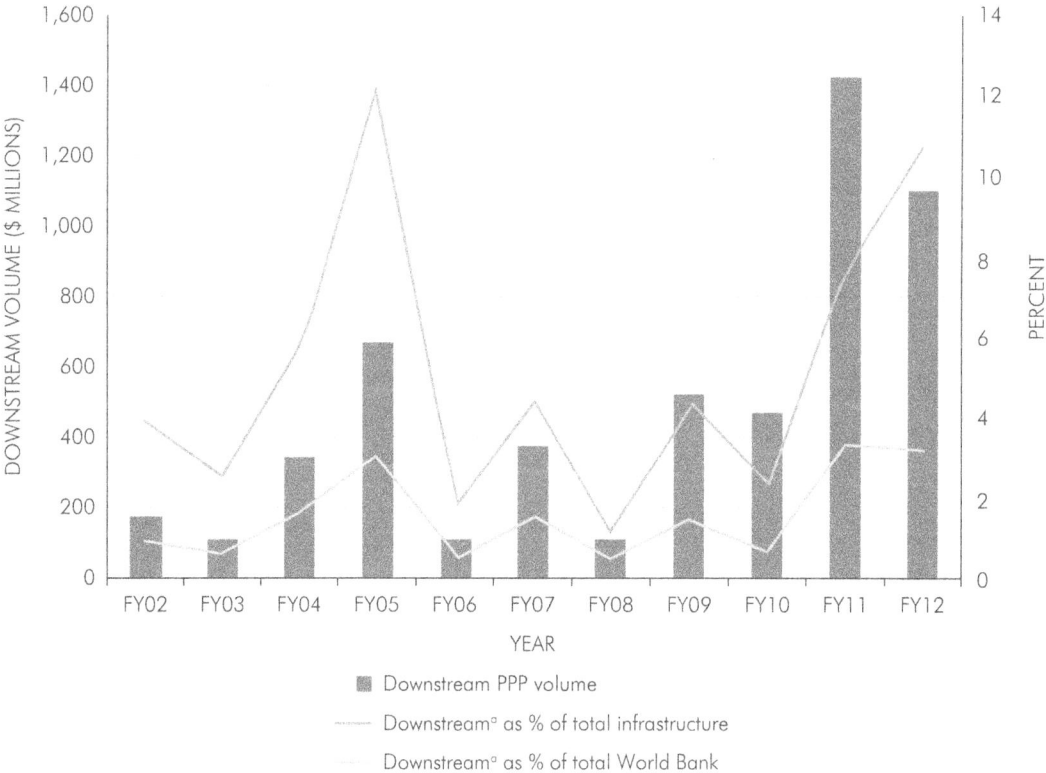

Downstream PPP volume
------- Downstream[a] as % of total infrastructure
------- Downstream[a] as % of total World Bank

SOURCE: World Bank database.
a. Downstream figures have been extrapolated to mimic entire population.

of aid, introduced in the World Bank Group in 2002 through the Private Sector Development Strategy, is a results-based mechanism that ties the disbursement of public funding in the form of subsidies to the achievement of clearly specified results that directly support improved access to basic services, such as water supply and sanitation, access to energy, health care, education, communications services, and transportation.

In 2003, the Global Partnership on Output-Based Aid was launched as a World Bank–administered, donor-funded pilot program to mainstream output-based aid. In support of this approach, IFC's Board approved the Performance Based Grant Initiative and with it the allocation of retained earnings ($97.8 million) for output-based aid, supported infrastructure projects, executed by the Partnership. By December 2013, only 7 (out of a total of 34) output-based aid projects had PPP components, of which only two were closed.

Results of World Bank Group Support to PPPs

According to project development outcome ratings, PPPs are successful. IFC's investments, MIGA guarantee projects, World Bank loans are subject to a regular results monitoring and evaluation.[9] Development outcomes are assessed of these private sector operations at the time of operational maturity, project completion, or, for World Bank loans, at project closure, that is, once the loan is fully disbursed. Using predetermined criteria the development outcome is scored. This score builds on the business performance of the respective PPP—a good business performance is a requirement for positive development outcomes. According to these criteria, PPPs are largely successful, with more than two-thirds of projects rated satisfactory or better. A full 83 percent of IFC's investments are rated satisfactory or better, 62 percent for MIGA and 66 percent for World Bank. IFC's investments in PPPs significantly outperform their other infrastructure investments and the portfolio overall of which 69 and 61 percent are rated satisfactory or better, respectively.

Looking at project development outcome ratings per sector, IFC investments has been successful in most cases, with an average of 83 percent rated satisfactory or better. The worst performing sectors in IFC investment portfolio were railway and road PPPs, with only 50 percent and 60 percent successful, respectively.

By contrast, World Bank has placed greater emphasis on projects in sectors such as waste water management with 32 percent compared to 15 percent of the market (per the PPI database) and railways with 9 percent compared to two percent in the market sectors that require significant reforms and public investment to make them viable. Success of these projects is below average in water and waste management, with 59 percent success and energy distribution with only 33 percent success. This lowered the average development outcome rating to about 66 percent satisfactory or better. For MIGA, the evaluated sample of projects is yet too small to report on sector-specific performance. For IFC advisory, project success ratings relate to the extent to which supported transactions reach contract closure (see below).

The high rate of success of IFC's investments in PPPs should not lead to the conclusion that all other national or local PPPs necessarily perform well. IFC is an *active* investor and as such assesses projects very thoroughly and is skilled at structuring them and selecting reliable sponsors. IFC also stays engaged during the lifetime of a PPP. These PPPs take place in countries where the enabling environment is already well established, as discussed in Chapter 2. PPPs that do not benefit from IFC's support therefore cannot be expected to be equally successful; this also applies to PPPs where World Bank may be engaged prior to bidding, for example, by financing needed up-front investments. As the World Bank itself is not the investor, the active—and in IFC's case, very positive—role of an investor should not be taken for granted.

PPPs should better be measured in a multifaceted manner. The development outcomes ratings contained in project-level evaluation reports, for example, Expanded Project Supervision Reports (XPSRs) or ICRs, are important evidence when assessing PPPs; however, judging PPPs solely on these ratings does not shed sufficient light on important aspects of public service delivery. For instance, it remains unknown if access was increased or was also improved for the poor. Development outcome ratings do not necessarily address quality of service data or efficiency data on the company. Fiscal implications would go unrecorded as well as affordability issues. Hence, to judge PPPs more holistically, more dimensions need to be assessed. And as PPPs are long-term arrangement, often subject to contract renegotiations, these aspects should also be monitored beyond the early years of operations—ideally throughout the entire lifetime of a PPP.

Existing World Bank Group monitoring systems need to be strengthened to better assess the breadth of PPP effects. Neither project-level evaluations nor other corporate monitoring systems, for example, IFC's Development Goals (IDGs) or its Development Outcome Tracking System (DOTS), closes the data gap. Both focus heavily on access related figures: Typically these systems collect data on the number of customers reached or passengers transported. For the World Bank, no systems exits at all that would track performance of PPPs post project closure. To do justice to the broad effects of PPPs, a wider set of outcome indicators should be kept track of throughout the life of a PPP. IFC advisory is currently in the process of institutionalizing a post-implementation monitoring, which is likely to help building up a database on actual PPP performance. Going forward, it will be important that projects subject to any post-implementation monitoring should be chosen on the basis of a stratified random sample to avoid selection bias; and fiscal effects should be captured in manner consistent with the recently adopted Operational Note (World Bank and WBI 2013).

In addition, World Bank Group as well a country authorities could learn from in-depth studies of selected PPP engagements to see if and how they contributed to economic growth and shared prosperity (Figure 4.7). Monitoring and evaluation systems are resource intensive and need to be embedded in corporate reporting systems—that should anyway collect the referred outcome data on a regular basis—and national statistics services. In light of the existence of IFC's systems (IDGs and DOTS), strengthening them—and transferring IFC's experience also to the World Bank—may be more economical than instilling new ones.

The discussion below first summarizes PPP performance along these additional key dimensions of access, quality, efficiency, financial soundness, fiscal aspects, and access for the poor. Data are assessed before and after, but without a counterfactual, as usually a comparable service provision without PPP does not exist. Subsequently, the development outcome ratings are discussed for each institution in their context to complement the picture.

Most data were available for access. Data were extracted from 173 PPPs that the World Bank Group supported (Table 4.1). For about half (53 percent) of projects, data are available for at least one dimension; there were no projects for which data were available along all dimensions. More data were available on access and less on pro-poor and fiscal effects.[10]

FIGURE 4.7 Elements of a PPP Monitoring and Evaluation System

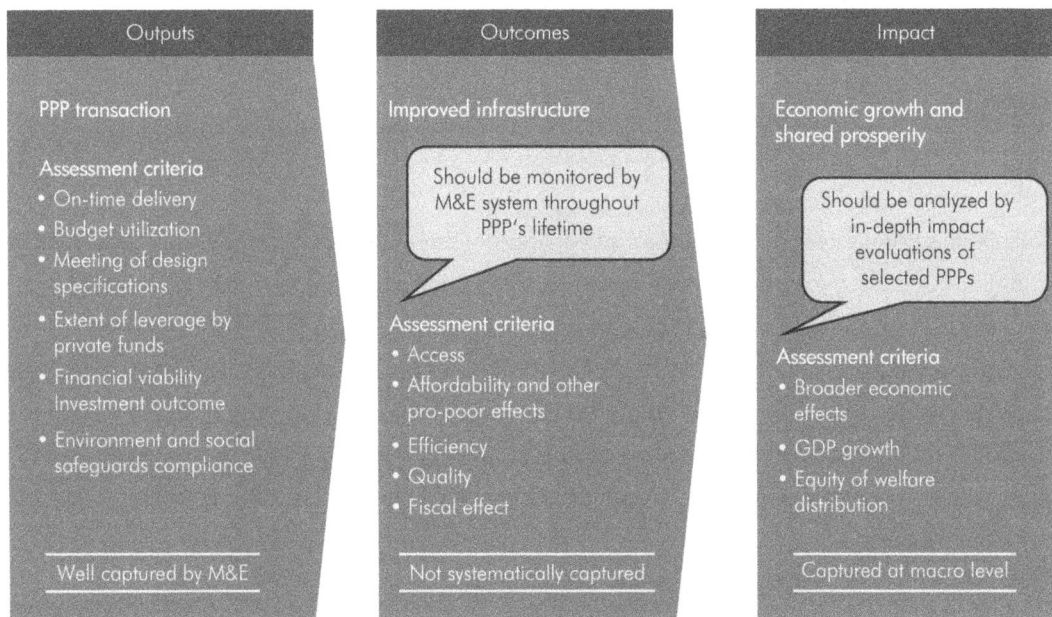

Outputs	Outcomes	Impact
PPP transaction	Improved infrastructure	Economic growth and shared prosperity
Assessment criteria	_Should be monitored by M&E system throughout PPP's lifetime_	_Should be analyzed by in-depth impact evaluations of selected PPPs_
• On-time delivery		
• Budget utilization		
• Meeting of design specifications		
• Extent of leverage by private funds	**Assessment criteria**	**Assessment criteria**
• Financial viability Investment outcome	• Access	• Broader economic effects
	• Affordability and other pro-poor effects	
• Environment and social safeguards compliance	• Efficiency	• GDP growth
	• Quality	• Equity of welfare distribution
	• Fiscal effect	
Well captured by M&E	_Not systematically captured_	_Captured at macro level_

SOURCE: IEG.
NOTE: E&S = environmental and social; GDP = gross domestic product; M&E = monitoring and evaluation.

TABLE 4.1 Availability of Results Data for World Bank Group–Supported PPPs

	IFC Investments	IFC Advisory Services	MIGA Guarantees	World Bank Loans/PRGs
Total number of PPP projects	147	105	62	128
Of these, number of operationally matured/closed PPPs (and for World Bank loans classified as "major")	99	n.a.	47	27
PPPs with results data—at least one dimension	60	6	12	20
PPPs with results data—all dimensions	0	0	0	0
Access	50	5	6	14
Pro-poor	5	0	1	3
Quality	14	2	3	10
Efficiency	17	3	3	8
Financial	43	1	4	6
Fiscal	6	3	2	1

SOURCE: IEG.
NOTE: For IFC advisory services, data are based on the six available post completion reports on PPPs. Objectives Pursued with PPPs. n.a. = not applicable; PRG = partial risk guarantee.

Despite the Bank Group's central goal of fighting poverty—reaffirmed by the new strategy's dual goal of ending extreme poverty and promoting shared prosperity—little is recorded on the effects of PPPs on the poor. Studies that assessed, for example, the effects of tariff reforms on the poor were found as part of World Bank's upstream policy work during the nine country case studies. But actual data on the effects of PPPs on the poor—for example, better access through expansion into poor areas or subsidy schemes targeting the poor to improve affordability—are not systematically recorded. In general, the scarcity of data makes it difficult to conclude at the portfolio level.

Primary objectives pursued with PPPs are increased efficiency and improved access; rarely was access for the poor a specific goal. A multiple set of objectives can be pursued with PPPs, as pointed out in Chapter 1. Among the six most commonly identified objectives, World Bank

FIGURE 4.8 Objectives Pursued through PPPs

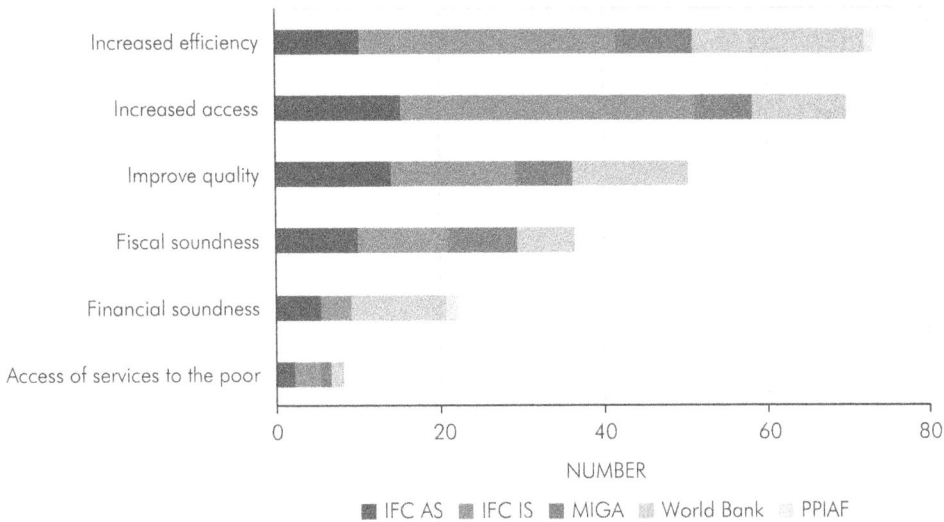

SOURCE: IEG.
NOTE: IFC AS = Advisory Services; IFC IS = Investment Services; PPIAF = Public-Private Infrastructure Advisory Facility.

Group projects envisage to primarily improve efficiency of operations and access of services. Access of services to the poor are rarely indicated as an explicit objective, which may also explain why data were not collected in this important area. The relative importance of these six objectives remains about equal across all World Bank Group entities active downstream (Figure 4.8).

ACTUAL RESULTS OF PPPS

Improved access was generally achieved. More often than not, the objective of improving access to infrastructure was achieved, in case data were available: 93 percent of World Bank projects, 66 percent of IFC investments, and 61 percent of MIGA projects. In most cases access figures drove overall performance, including cash flow; it is hence not surprising that this indicator is reported most frequently. Also in the case of PPPs supported by IFC advisory services, access was in most cases where there were data collected, but with the overall low availability of actual performance data, this is not representative of its overall portfolio.[11]

The extent to which PPPs benefited the poor cannot be assessed in a systematic manner, as large data gaps exist. Confirmation that access did improve for the poor was only recorded in about 10 percent of cases, where improved access was documented (Figure 4.9), according to the portfolio analysis.

FIGURE 4.9 Performance Indicators for IFC, World Bank, and MIGA-Supported PPPs

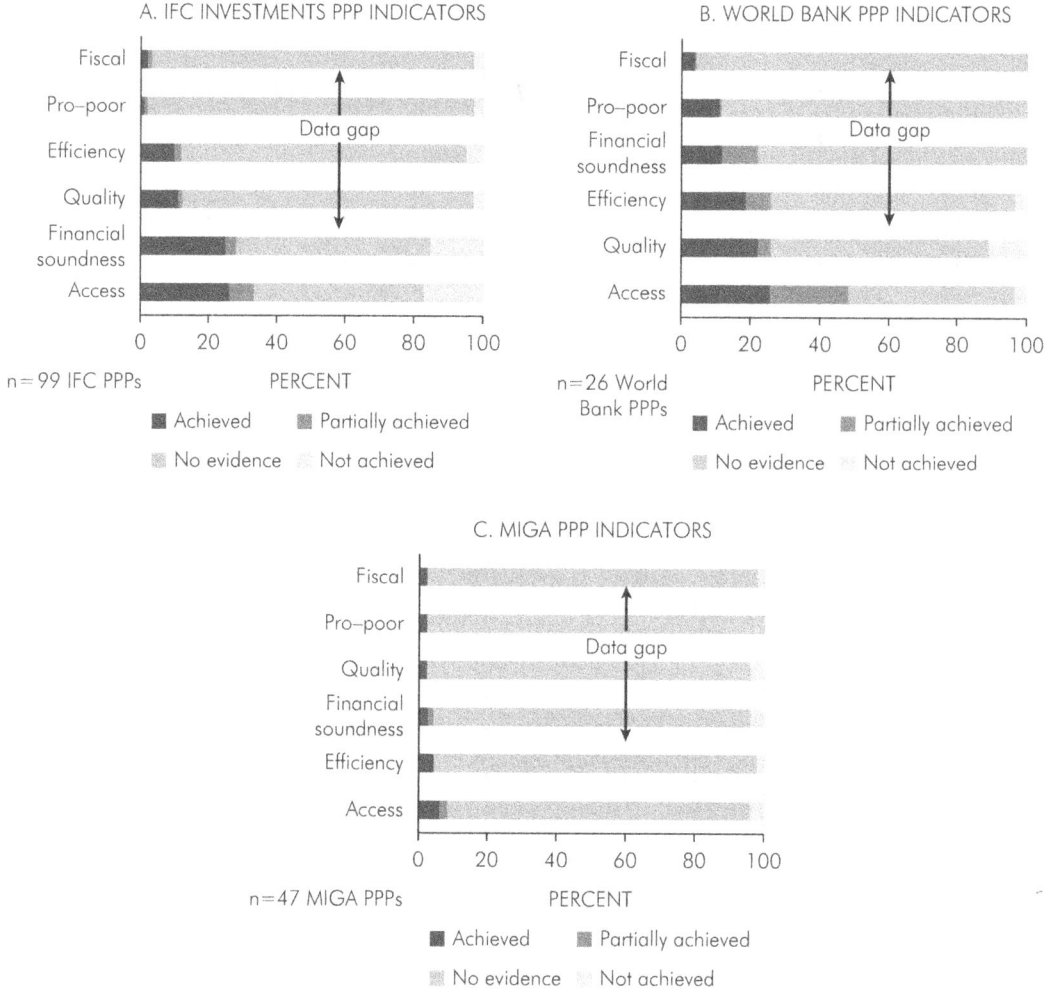

A. IFC INVESTMENTS PPP INDICATORS

n = 99 IFC PPPs   PERCENT

■ Achieved   ■ Partially achieved
 No evidence   Not achieved

B. WORLD BANK PPP INDICATORS

n = 26 World
Bank PPPs   ■ Achieved   ■ Partially achieved
                  No evidence   Not achieved

C. MIGA PPP INDICATORS

n = 47 MIGA PPPs   PERCENT

■ Achieved   ■ Partially achieved
 No evidence   Not achieved

SOURCE: IEG.
NOTE: MIGA = Multilateral Investment Guarantee Agency.

In addition, IEG's country case studies provided selected evidence on how pro-poor issues were integrated in the design and implementation of Bank Group–supported PPPs. These range from IFC's advisory support to a PPP hospital in a poor urban community in Bahia, Brazil, which is expected to improve health care for the poor (Hospital do Suburbia); to introducing smart cross-subsidy schemes for water distribution to allow 500,000 poor users to gain access, as it was the case in the Triple AAA Barranquilla investment by IFC in Colombia; to the World Bank's energy reform work in, for example, Guatemala which increased electrification in poor rural areas from 56 to 70 percent through a TAL or in Ghana where the Bank's energy sector reform work reflected the results of a Poverty and Social Impact Analysis of Electricity Tariffs (ESMAP 2005). For more examples, see Box 4.1.

In the water sector, the economic cost of alternatives to piped water, especially in urban areas is quite stark. As a result Manila Water Company tariffs are not subsidized even in poorer areas (unlike some other countries, such as Colombia). This has the advantage of a transparent system, which reduces the likelihood of rent-seeking behavior. In contrast, some households are too poor to even afford the connection fee to have pipes laid to their homes. To address this issue, the World Bank Group's Global Partnership for Output Based Aid undertook a pilot with the water company to provide water connections for 28,000 households. The grant of $2.8 million, provided connections at a cost of about php2476 each, of which the householder was responsible for about php600, which could be paid in installments. The pilot has proven very successful, and the government is planning to scale up the effort nationally, and also include sanitation.

In transport, on the one hand, the World Bank Group–supported North Luzon Expressway started operations by tripling tolls, met by stiff public resistance in the initial years, but eventually accepted (and tolls were reduced a few years later, when the deal was restructured to convert foreign exchange obligations to local currency). On the other hand, to stimulate access by the poor to the highway, the expressway company designed the toll for mini passenger buses, so called, jeepneys as a flat daily rate, instead of the per entry toll used for other vehicles. As a result, jeepneys are able to get on and off the highway to pick up and drop off passengers, and bus traffic has grown to be a significant portion of total traffic: Bus share of traffic grew from 0.9 percent in 2004 to 7 percent in 2010, as total traffic continued to grow.

In the electricity sector, keeping rates affordable is a challenge. Philippines' cost of electricity is relatively high compared to neighboring Indonesia and Vietnam, and China (but not in comparison to other regions). The government has nonetheless refrained from providing large-scale subsidies to the sector (as has Indonesia) which has been good for the financial stability of the sector. However in the off-grid areas, the government subsidizes electricity rates, as a result of IFC advisory advice in the context of the privatization, by keeping them at a fixed level and paying the difference to the generator. Although there is pressure to reduce rates generally, this would mean a greater reliance on coal, in a system that is currently more or less balanced between geothermal, hydro, and thermal generation. Instead the government is looking to photovoltaic and other renewable sources for small generators as a way of reducing costs to poor communities, but with limited success thus far.

SOURCE: IEG county case study.

Specific data on access for the poor are scarce, but there is some evidence that PPPs delivered "broader" benefits to the poor. A review of broader benefits to the poor revealed evidence beyond the mere question of access to improved infrastructure. But large data gaps still remain. For World Bank PPP projects, there was evidence of broader benefits to the poor in 42 percent of cases; for IFC investments in 39 percent and MIGA in 20 percent of its projects. Examples of such evidence included PPPs that provided job opportunities or benefit to migrant workers from the poorest areas through job creation. Note, however, that the fact that evidence was found in only 20–42 percent of PPPs does not necessarily mean such broader effects were absent in all other cases; it rather reflects the weaknesses of the monitoring records.

Where data were available, financial, efficiency, and quality improvements can also be confirmed. About 70–100 percent of World Bank PPPs achieved or at least partially achieved improvements in the financial situation, efficiency, and quality, but these relatively good results are based on available data for only 20 transactions. For IFC investments, financials (that is, business success), efficiency, and quality were satisfactory in about 65–70 percent of cases. Although business success has been recorded systematically for all IFC investments that were evaluated (about 50 percent have an XPSR), quality and efficiency data were only recorded in about 15 percent of cases. Fiscal effects appear insufficiently monitored, and in the few cases where fiscal implications were recorded, they were typically in the form of government revenues or concession royalties and were more often positive than negative (Figure 4.9). As there is no requirement to report on efficiency and quality data, they may be biased toward reporting positive outcomes; that is, data are only reported in case they show positive results.

A statistically nonrepresentative but in-depth assessment of 22 PPPs conducted as part of the 9 country cases studies provides more insights into the performance of World Bank Group–supported PPPs. Country case study missions were conducted in nine countries; as part of these missions, policy reform aspects were assessed as well as the performance of all supported PPPs. A particular effort was undertaken to collect a comprehensive set of primary data for 22 PPPs. Projects were reviewed in Brazil, China, Colombia, Ghana, Guatemala, the Philippines, Senegal, Uganda, and Vietnam. IFC Investment Services participated in twelve projects, IBRD/IDA in seven, MIGA in seven, and IFC Advisory Services in four; several projects involved more than one entity. Table 4.2 provides details on sectors and types of these 22 PPPs. Albeit not representative, the findings indicate good results:

• **Virtually all the projects were successful in increasing access**, either directly (water, transport, electricity distribution) or indirectly through additional power generation to alleviate severe shortages. Generally, the indicator exceeded or came very close to targets, corroborating IEG's assessment of the portfolio analysis, which showed that about 60–70 percent of projects achieved their objective with regard to access (Figure 4.9).

TABLE 4.2 PPPs Assessed In Depth, by Sector and Type of PPP

	DBO	Concession	Lease/ Affermage	Mixed Ownership	Performance Based Contracts	Total
Energy distribution	1	3				4
Energy generation	5	1				6
Ports		1				1
Railways		1				1
Toll roads		1				1
Urban transport					1	1
Water, waste management	3	1	1	1	2	8
Total	9	8	1	1	3	22

SOURCE: IEG.
NOTE: DBO = design, build, operate.

- **Quality indicators were also good for most projects.** Water projects returned good outcomes with regard to water quality and availability for the most part. Some projects provided better results than comparable public sector projects, a port gained international certification, and a sewage treatment plant won an international award. The exceptions were a power generation project, which was shut down for 21 months because of technical issues and an inability to access fuel supply and a railway project, which had trains run intermittently and more expensively so traders used trucks instead of the freight train for transporting goods between the two countries. In contrast, two power generator projects increased reliability and reduced brownouts substantially. At least with regard to World Bank projects, this appears in line with data from the portfolio review, which showed that about half of World Bank projects showed positive evidence on quality (and none negative). For IFC and MIGA, data on quality were scarce, partly because quality is not necessarily a cash flow driver and hence is used less frequently in Expanded Project Supervision Reports or Project Evaluation Reports to create a compelling case.

- **Indicators for efficiency were mixed.** Some projects exceeded benchmarks and targets, others performed less well. Indicators were also diverse, which makes direct comparisons harder. But for example, in water, some projects were very efficient (in terms of collection rates and responsiveness) and costs, while others had disappointing output to worker ratios, or did not reduce non-revenue water adequately. Similarly, in electricity generation, while two projects had excellent efficiency rates (in terms of collection rates and reduction of commercial losses), three others suffered from high output costs and long construction delays. For this small (and unscientific) sample, one could conclude that efficiency was about average—a result that is counter-intuitive, given that efficiency is often touted as a prominent advantage of private sector participation. Again, data on efficiency were mainly available for World Bank projects at the portfolio level, with about 40 percent positive indications and about 5 percent negative.

- **The pro-poor indicators for water supply were mostly positive**, with targeted access to poverty areas, and in some cases cross-subsidies in rates. A Global Partnership on Output-Based Aid pilot to subsidize connections to poor households was successful in one project and is being scaled up nationally. However, in one case tariffs were increase drastically, and there were no targets for connections to poor households. Pro-poor indicators were also high in transport (increase in bus access, mobility for the poor, and economic development in a port area) and in electricity distribution—where a large number of poor (half of all new connections) gained access to electricity for the first time. Pro-poor access was not measured for most power generators but in one case was rated high, because the tariff was subsidized, and the generator was providing free electricity and water to a nearby school. No corroboration with data from the portfolio review is possible on this dimension.

- **With few exceptions, most projects were financially sound**, showing profitability and strong margins. In one electricity-generation project, however, the profitability of the sponsor was marred by a costly transfer from the government, because of defects in the power purchasing agreement. Another such project ended in default, because of both technical problems as well as a fuel price increase. The first sponsor in a railway project did not have the financial capacity and experience to manage a railway rehab project. Although the project has been restructured, it is still operating significantly below capacity.

- In contrast, other generation projects are doing well. In the transport sector, the port and toll road are in strong financial condition (both types of concessions are rarely unprofitable) but the bus rapid transit systems in smaller cities are financially weak, as projected passenger levels have not materialized. Water supply projects were generally profitable, despite the absence of government subsidies. The exception was the experience of several small municipalities that were supported under one project. In that case, profitability was weak and unsustainable without municipal and government subsidies. As the latter two cases demonstrate, adequate market size is important for project sustainability.

Drivers of Success and Failure of PPP Performance

GENERAL DRIVERS OF SUCCESS AND FAILURE

Country maturity drives PPP success. The analysis of development outcome ratings[12] and the maturity[13] of the host country revealed that these indicators correlate positively. Several country-level attributes are needed for a successful PPP: protection against regulatory failure, an institutional framework to manage the PPP process, operational maturity in terms of building a track record of successful PPPs, a good investment climate, and financial facilities.[14] The better these are in place, the higher the chances of PPP success. This correlation applies to both IFC investments and World Bank projects, even though the effect is much less pronounced for the latter (Figure 4.10).[15,16]

In addition to country maturity, PPPs need a sound business case, a competent sponsor, and government commitment to be successful. These essential attributes, along with the above referenced regulatory risk, became evident from the 22 PPPs studied in depth for the nine country cases studies. For example, in the Philippines water PPPs are successful in metro Manila but failed elsewhere, because of fragmented markets outside Manila and lack of uniform regulation. A similar situation of fragmented markets was observed in Colombia. In addition, initial water PPPs were not successful because they were generally sponsored by construction companies with little knowledge of water operations.

In Senegal, PPPs in the electricity sector failed (Box 4.2), but the toll road was successful. In contrast, in Guatemala the road PPPs were unsuccessful, whereas the energy sector registered satisfactory progress. There was strong political support in Senegal for the road work,

FIGURE 4.10 PPP Development Outcomes and Country-Level Maturity

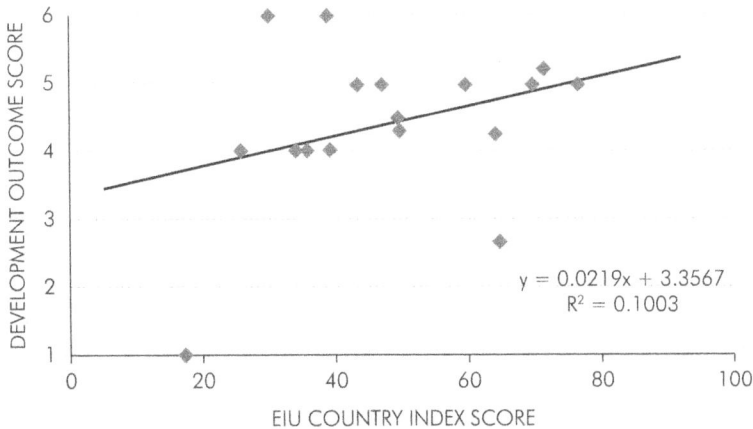

$$y = 0.0219x + 3.3567$$
$$R^2 = 0.1003$$

SOURCES: IEG ratings of XPSR Evaluation Notes and ICR Reviews.
NOTE: EIU = Economist Intelligence Unit.

IFC-supported PPPs in Senegal's power generation helped add generation capacity but have been substantially undermined by underlying sector weaknesses. The two independent power producers in which IFC invested helped increase generation capacity in Senegal by 125 megawatts, or 20 percent of Senegal's installed capacity. However, both producers saw substantial technical, operational, and financial difficulties. Both project companies defaulted on their loans, largely because of payment delays by SENELEC.

IFC eventually recovered its loan to GTI Dakar in 2013 but its equity stake was written off. Both plants produce high-cost energy and both were affected by technical problems caused by factors such as machinery not adapted to local conditions, poor fuel quality, and instability in the grid. For example, the GTI Dakar plant required naphtha fuel, which was not available in Senegal. The plant consistently operated at levels well below expected capacity. At one point it failed to produce any power for two years but continued to receive payments because of contractual arrangements, where "capacity payments" were made to service the project's debt directly from SENELEC's largest customers. The concession agreement for the second power producer, Kounoune, corrected some of the flaws in the contract and was better balanced. However, the plant's productive capacity and financial viability were undermined by technical problems, issues in fuel supply, and payment delays on the part of SENELEC.

Although successive governments in Senegal have shown commitment to engaging the private sector, the experience with PPPs in the energy sector has been marred by difficulties. Factors undermining the PPP experiences include the following:

- The lack of financial viability of SENELEC, the public distribution utility and off-taker, caused largely by the high cost of diesel power generation in Senegal. An inefficient monopoly on the supply of refined oil has added to costs of generation.

- Some weaknesses in the management of SENELEC, including ambivalent and uneven views on the role of the private sector in generation; lack of experience and know-how in negotiating the initial IPP contract in 1996.

- Lack of familiarity with the country on the part of both IPP sponsors. Although the sponsors were both well-established and experienced international operators, this was their first investment in the country or the Africa Region. Both projects suffered long operational delays and technical difficulties caused by the unsuitability of machinery and equipment to local conditions.

- Lack of a strong, independent regulator. The first IPP was implemented without an independent regulatory.

SOURCE: IEG country case study.

as well as an enabling PPP law, both absent in Guatemala, and a fairly robust regulatory framework for electricity in Guatemala, absent in Senegal. Tariffs need to allow (at least) recovery of costs to attract the private sector, and in energy, the power purchaser must be reliable; several of the small power utilities in the Philippines that were not privatized (advised by IFC Advisory Services) faced unreliable power purchasers.

As a general rule, the presence of a strong regulatory framework was necessary for projects to succeed in the water and power sectors; in the transport sector (ports, airports, and roads) project-level parameters on pricing and oversight, along with the legal framework governing PPPs, seemed to be sufficient. Despite this, an overall master plan for roads made the pipeline more transparent and allowed potential bidders to survey their options. Although much less frequent (and more work needs to be done in the Bank Group on PPPs in these fields), it also appears that one-off transactions in sectors such as health and education seem to work without the need for overall frameworks.

Factors that inhibited PPPs included overly time-consuming government reviews (often the result of suspicious authorities and inadequate public sector capacity to vet transactions), quality of sponsors and managers, politicization of the process (sometimes accompanied by no-transparency and corruption), and poor or unbalanced incentives for the private sector in project agreements. PPPs were also inhibited in sectors dominated by state-owned operations, or where markets were fragmented.

Factors that increased the chance of success included government (local or national) commitment, competent operators, and transparent procedures for project preparation, bidding and award. The need for a robust legal and regulatory framework emerged also as one of the key findings of a recently conducted IEG Cluster Study of PPPs in Africa (IEG 2013a). The focus of the World Bank Group's upstream policy support to countries with a less developed enabling environment is hence an important contribution to making PPP globally more successful. The strategic resources allocation emphasizes these "nascent" PPP countries, as seen in Chapter 2.

Cross-sector approaches as envisaged by the World Bank Group 2013 strategy need to be rooted in sector reform. To the extent that the World Bank Group plans to apply multi- or cross-sectoral approaches, as indicated in its latest strategy (World Bank 2013b), these need to be rooted firmly in reform progress in individual sectors.

A cross-sectoral approach, as applied in Colombia and Guatemala in the late 1990s and more recently in Ghana, appears promising, as managing the PPP agenda is a cross-cutting issue, spanning line ministries in charge of policy making in the various sectors, public procurement, and fiscal management. In particular, the 2012 APL for Ghana's PPP program emerges from 15-plus year history of dealing with sector reform issues across energy, water, and transport—with limited success (World Bank 2013a); it builds on several cross-sectorial diagnostic studies assessing Ghana PPP "readiness" and benchmarking the country with its peer countries (AICD 2010). The APL provides the needed cross-sectorial assistance to allow Ghana to build up its "infrastructure for PPPs" while pressing for the much needed progress at the level of the individual sectors. But it is too early to assess any outcomes at this stage.

Long-term alignment of private and public objectives contributed to PPP sustainability, with fair regulation providing incentives. Especially in the water sector, PPPs have been successful when sponsors have had substantial technical and operational expertise as well as knowledge of local conditions and have gradually grown their concessions. Colombia (Barranquila) and Senegal ensured service was affordable with cross subsidies as necessary; they continued to increase access and increased profitability gradually by expanding connections, enabled by appropriately structured regulation (for example, cross-subsidy formulae in Colombia and Senegal) (Box 4.3).

IFC INVESTMENT-SPECIFIC DRIVERS OF SUCCESS AND FAILURE

In addition to providing finance and catalyzing other financiers, IFC investments added value during due diligence or as an honest broker. In PPPs, when engaged early, IFC Investment Service has been helpful in several ways. Its Environment and Safety guidelines provide comfort to the sponsor and reduce delays, as was the case the North Luzon Expressway highway in the Philippines, and it introduced safeguards standards in the wastewater sector in China. It helped to develop a smart collection system for a water distribution system in Colombia reflecting poor people's availability of cash (Box 4.3). It also introduced the first waste-to-energy project in China. Several such projects followed. IFC participation can boost investor confidence and play the role of an honest broker with a weak regulator.

BOX 4.3 IFC Investment in Water—Successfully Improving Access and Quality

The IFC investment in a Colombian water company improved access and quality of service and increased efficiency and sustainability in water sector. In 1996, the Baranquilla municipality entered into a concession contract with an *Empresa mixta*—or *mixed ownership model*—whereby a minority portion of the water company was sold to a private partner who then operates the company under a management contract.

IFC invested in the company in 2002. Since then, the number of equivalent customers increased 50 percent, the volume of water doubled, the water coverage increased from 94 to 99 percent, sewage coverage increased from 80 to 96 percent, and the efficiency ratios improved mainly with regard to uncollected bills, a rate that was reduced from about 20 percent to 4 percent, and number of employees per 1,000 clients was also reduced. With regard to access to the poor, almost 80 percent of its customer base is from low-income strata. Cross-subsidization helps the company keep prices within reach. By Colombian law, water tariffs are designed so that higher-income households pay more for services than lower-income ones. Specific rates are negotiated with federal regulators, on a cost plus basis. Also, the federal government provides subsidies based on the number of people being billed and the rates being charged. In the case of Triple A, about 20 percent of revenues come from the municipal government through transfers from national government.

Success factors in the water distribution PPP in Triple A Barranquilla are varied. First, the sponsor has substantial technical and operational knowledge as well as knowledge of local conditions—the company is owned by a Spanish operator that brought innovation and technology, and the company is run entirely by Colombian nationals with an effective management strategy to improve efficiency and reduce costs. Second, depoliticized government revenue transfers were a factor. Triple A was not receiving the subsidy amount that was required but the operator was able to ring fence the transfers that came from the central government directly to a fiduciary. This allowed secure, stable flow of the transfers to the company and eliminated political interference.

Third was local/municipality commitment to improve water and sanitation system problems of the city. Fourth, a cross-subsidy program across groups within the water distribution network enables low-cost access to water for the poorest, without undermining the financial viability of the system. And last, to improve collections, the company developed a comprehensive system to facilitate and encourage payment among low-income customers, acknowledging the reality that many low-income families in Barranquilla live day-to-day on small amounts of cash earned from informal occupations.

SOURCES: IEG and Expanded Project Supervision Report.

IFC-supported PPPs tend to be less risky than other infrastructure investments, owing to a thorough due diligence. The risk profiling of IFC's investments in PPPs revealed that PPP investments tend to be less risky than other IFC investments in the infrastructure sector when it comes to project risk factors, such as sponsor and market risks (see Appendix D for methodology). In general, IFC's PPP projects are associated with better-quality sponsor[17] and less market risk[18] exposure than non-PPP projects. This is because the due diligence process screens out weaker sponsors, and normally structures the deal to make the project sustainable, that is, with contractual arrangements (for example, off-take agreements) to minimize revenue fluctuations. There is no difference between PPP and non-PPP projects, with 58 percent of PPPs being greenfield investments, compared to 55 percent of all infrastructure investments.

Looking at the country risk,[19] IFC's investments in PPPs take place in comparable countries as do IFC's infrastructure investments overall, that is, in lower-risk countries with Institutional Investor Country Credit ratings of around 35–55 (Figure 4.11). Not only are these countries lower risk, according to these ratings, but the countries in which IFC's investments mostly occur are also the ones with a well-established enabling environment (55 percent in countries that the EIU rated "developed" on PPP maturity).[20]

The thoroughness of IFC's due diligence is also reflected in the high work quality ratings for IFC investments in PPPs. IFC's PPP investments are better managed with regard to overall work quality, screening, and appraisal as well as supervision and monitoring than other IFC

FIGURE 4.11 Risk Profile of IFC's Investments in PPPs, Compared to Other Infrastructure Investments

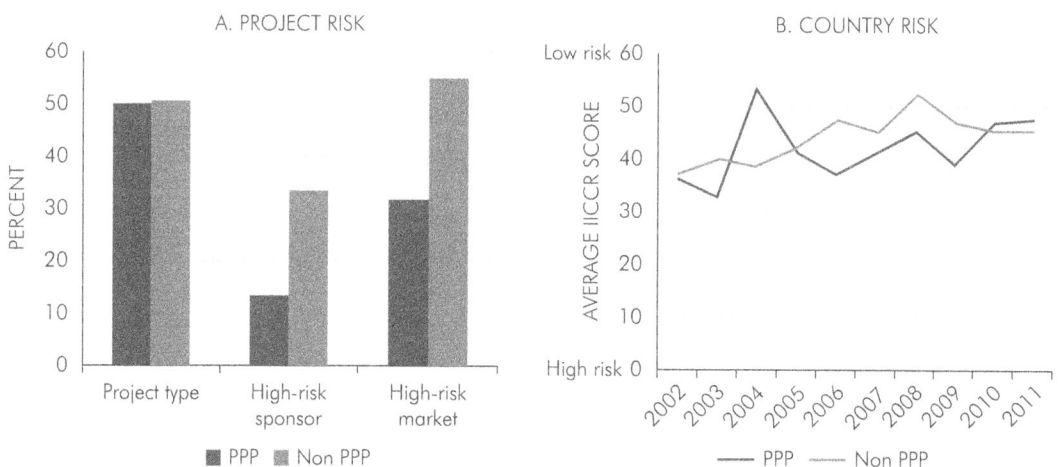

SOURCE: IEG.

NOTE: Project-related risk factors have been analyzed systematically only for IFC investment thus far. Hence, subsequent sections will only discuss country risk factors. IICCR scores are weighted average (by numbers of projects) per year. IICCR = Institutional Investor Country Credit Rating.

infrastructure investments (Figure 4.12).[21] With regard to IFC's role and contributions, PPPs are rated lower than other infrastructure investments, albeit on an overall high level. Those PPP projects that were scored less than satisfactory were rated so because of low non-financial additionality, for example, deficiencies in standard-setting and work-related issues, and low financial additionality.

As a consequence, IFC-supported PPPs exhibit consistently higher development outcomes rating than other infrastructure investments—and significantly higher ratings than the rest of the portfolio. A full 83 percent of IFC investments in PPPs are rated satisfactory or better, compared to 69 percent for IFC investments in infrastructure (non-PPP) and 61 percent for the remaining sectors. PPPs show better performance not only according to the overall rating, but also when it comes to the various factors that constitute development outcomes, that is, business success, economic success, environment and safety, private sector development effects, and even investment outcomes for IFC's account (Figure 4.12).

IFC's PPPs also exhibit higher-than-average business success and investment outcomes. Risk is adequately priced in PPP deals. IFC prices risk into the loan package for debt or the equity valuation for an equity deal, based on the understanding of the market situation, management quality of the sponsor, and expected profit margin, along with country- and sector-specific factors. IFC's due diligence screens out weaker sponsors and mitigates market risk by sound structuring of the deal. *Financial* results confirm that IFC is doing a good job at due diligence and pricing, as most PPPs outperform the other infrastructure deals both in terms of business success and investment outcomes for IFC (Figure 4.12).

FIGURE 4.12 Development Outcomes and Work Quality—IFC-Supported PPPs and Infrastructure Projects

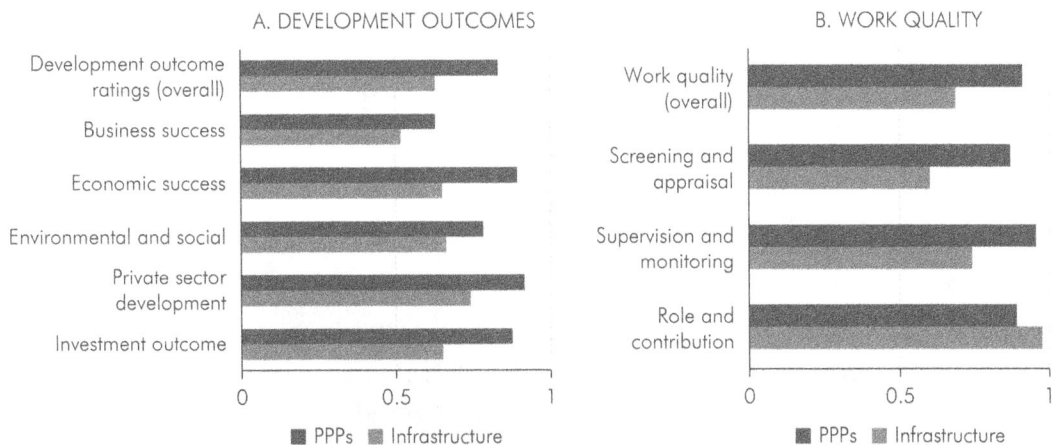

SOURCE: Expanded Project Supervision Reports.
NOTE: All data from IFC Investment Services. n = 46.

A similar constellation of thorough due diligence and consistently (very) high success ratings were also found in the recently issued IEG evaluation on the World Bank Group's support to transport (IEG 2012). That study found that more than 85 percent of IFC's transport investments[22] —of which a majority were PPPs—were found sustainable with regard to business performance and management quality. The study concluded that IFC's due diligence was very thorough; it also concluded that investments tend to occur later than for other private investors that engage in a country's reforming sector, that is, after regulatory regimes had been tested by other pioneering investments.

Analysis of the timing of IFC's transport investments in an overall sector reform pathway revealed that only about 29 percent took place in the early stages of private sector participation, which is less than or equal to seven years after countries opened the transport sector for private investors. Earlier IFC engagements, such as first-of-a-kind concession arrangements, demonstrate that private sector participation is possible in untested regulatory regimes or in distorted markets that are the result of the competition of a large state-owned enterprise.

But the majority of IFC's investments took place *after* that crucial transition phase. That transport study also found that it is possible for IFC to invest earlier in a sector reform process without compromising on project success. Even when IFC invested earlier in sector reform processes—and thus took on more complex and riskier investments—success ratings remained unchanged.[23]

The findings of this evaluation, corroborated by a recent IEG transport study, seem to indicate that IFC investment could afford to expand into countries with a less tested environment or partner more with non-blue chip sponsor. Taking all facts together (strong investment activities in countries with already proven PPP track records and well-established frameworks, that is, developed PPP countries, and above-average development outcomes, business performance, and investment outcome ratings) suggests that IFC could afford to increase its risk appetite in investments. Taking on risk in a smart manner could be accomplished by, for example, partnering with more non-blue chip partners, that is, by taking on more sponsor risk or going into countries where the enabling environment is less well tested, that is, emerging PPP countries.

It is important to note at this point that investing in countries with less development enabling environments, that is, in countries that are rated emerging with regard to their PPP maturity, does not compromise success. A full 88 percent of IFC's investments into emerging countries are rated satisfactory or better, comparable with those PPPs in already developed countries where 86 percent are satisfactory or better. PPPs in both emerging and developed countries are doing substantially better than IFC average portfolio of which 65 percent is rated satisfactory or better.

To the extent that market opportunities exist, IFC can also explore increasing its investments in "nascent" countries where still 50 percent of their investments had satisfactory or better development outcome ratings. Originating a higher share of IFC's PPP portfolio in emerging—and possibly nascent—countries will demonstrate to other potential investors that private sector participation in infrastructure is possible (and lucrative).[24]

"Smart risk taking" as envisaged by the 2013 strategy (World Bank 2013b) will therefore help IFC increasing its development footprint. Instilling and nurturing a culture of informed risk-taking along with the needed institutional structures (including a policy) will enable taking on higher-risk—and potentially transformational—PPP projects. As part of this, IFC should consider moving parts of its PPP business into emerging countries; pioneering PPP transactions in these countries will not only set important demonstration effects, but also stimulate reform upstream. It hence appears that IFC would benefit from a review of the framework it uses to strategically decide where to do business, including incentives, to identify avenues that would allow IFC to take on more—and smart—risks when engaging in PPPs.

A country diagnostic may be helpful in determining the role IFC investments should have given a country's stage of maturity with regard to managing PPP. At the level of the World Bank Group, determining which institution should play which role is essential to ensure leveraging the comparative advantages of them. World Bank's public sector focus and close country ties often help moving forward the country's policy reform agenda, while IFC and MIGA support specific transactions through finance and guarantees, once reforms have progressed. To better direct the array of World Bank Group products and services toward those countries that are at the right stage of their maturity of handling PPPs, a Bank Group-wide country diagnostic is called for. Such a diagnostic would also indicate where PPP markets are already sufficiently mature so its financing needs can be served by commercial banks—the time for IFC to move out.

A related issue is shrinking business opportunities for IFC Investment Services as commercial banks increasingly become more prominent financiers, especially in UMICs in established sectors. In the Philippines IFC Investment Services has not been involved in any of the national toll highways or in the water projects outside metro Manila. In Brazil it has been crowded out by the state development bank but has succeeded in small distribution utilities. Looking to the future, IFC Investment Services may need to look for business opportunities that have a demonstration effect in areas that have had little PPP involvement to date, such as off-grid power, electricity distribution, secondary ports, and smaller water systems, and more involvement in LMICs and LICs.

IFC has been strengthening its efforts in project development of PPPs in IDA countries through *InfraVentures*. One of the major constraints identified by all nine country case studies was project preparation. Once PPP projects have been developed, there is generally no lack of finance, nor is there a lack of potential project opportunities to start with—an experience shared by other multilateral project development facilities (Palmer 2013). At the preparation stage, capacity with the public sector and initial funding are found lacking. And preparation costs can be substantial—often ranging from 5 to 16 percent.[25] In particular, in IDA countries, where infrastructure investment needs amount to $300 billion annually through 2015, about 12 percent of gross domestic product on average, the need for private finance appears particularly significant. With *InfraVentures* and its IDA focus, IFC established a mechanism to address this constraint by funding the early stages of project development to increase the pipeline of bankable projects in IDA countries (Box 4.4).

Both the niche market occupied by its projects and the slow pipeline raises the question of whether *InfraVentures* will solve the problem of project preparation for high-volume mainstream PPPs in IDA with overall investment needs of $300 billion annually. Despite the vast market for potential PPPs, *InfraVentures'* pipeline built up very slowly. Since its inception in 2007, *InfraVentures* handled 25 projects[26] with an average commitment of $2.2 million

---

BOX 4.4 IFC's *InfraVentures*—A Mechanism to Support PPP Project Preparation

IFC's Global Infrastructure Project Development Fund (*InfraVentures*) provides (i) risk capital to fund the early stages of the development of infrastructure projects in IDA countries through a variety of financial instruments and (ii) expertise in critical areas of the project development, to successfully bring private and PPP infrastructure projects to the financing stage. Its volume amounts to $100 million for the five-year fund life.

InfraVentures' mandate consists of investing in infrastructure projects in IDA countries. For each project, *InfraVentures* can currently fund up to $4 million of project development expenses at an early stage, typically 20–30 percent of the amount required. In return, it takes an equity stake in the project after financial closure. Additional debt and equity funding for construction can also be mobilized from other partners.

InfraVentures funding can be allocated, among other things, to feasibility studies, economic, social, technical, or environmental studies, for managing stakeholder relationships, financial modeling, or legal expenses. Through this early support, *InfraVenture* has the potential to structure PPP projects to reduce risk and make them bankable.

SOURCES: Global Infrastructure Project Development Fund Board Paper (Annex 4), Project No. 25792, September 2007; IFC *InfraVentures* presentation, January 2013; IFC *InfraVentures*—Proposals for Renewed Mandate, Presentation, May 2013.

per project. Of these, none has reached financial closure for construction finance to date. Project development took longer than anticipated, that is, three to five years, as opposed to initially assumed two to three years—a trend that reflects the experience in IEG's country case studies, where project preparation was often stalled by government commitment, sector reform issues (Ghana, Senegal) or safeguards issues (Uganda).[27]

The Special Initiative for Infrastructure, approved by IFC's Board in 2011, is another effort that emphasizes infrastructure in Africa. The private sector has historically played a smaller role in infrastructure in Africa than in other regions. The Special Initiative was envisaged to complement and expand IFC's efforts in this area at a time when more governments were ready to contemplate private delivery of infrastructure and PPP than before. The initiative focuses primarily on expanding the flow of bankable transactions in infrastructure, working closely with IDA in particular, especially in those countries that are making major efforts to expand private infrastructure. Preliminary results indicate a build-up of a medium-term pipeline in several countries, including Cote d'Ivoire, Ghana, Mozambique, Nigeria, Senegal, and Uganda, where at times all three World Bank Group institutions collaborate.

IFC ADVISORY SERVICES: SPECIFIC DRIVERS OF SUCCESS AND FAILURE

The focus of IFC Advisory Services is to bring PPP transactions to commercial and financial closure. In practice, this means to bring a successful completion to what is usually a two-phase process, wherein option reports and recommendations on transactions structure carried out in the first phase ("phase 1") lead to a second implementation phase ("phase 2"), in which IFC would help organize a transparent, competitive bidding process, to result in a successful bid and award of concession ("contract closure"). It is desirable, though not always easy to guarantee, that the winning bidder be able to secure financing ("financial closure").

In carrying out these transactions, IFC makes use—to the extent possible—of retainer and success fees. For the most part, these are employed to ensure the commitment of the client, as well as to ensure that IFC does not knowingly distort the market through provision of subsidized services. Fees do not cover a significant proportion of IFC's costs: the largest share (about 50 percent) comes from donor contributions. In addition to specific transactions, IFC also seeks to expand the PPP market through studies, workshops, and policy reform assistance.

Assessment of success for IFC Advisory Services focuses on bringing PPP transactions to contract closure. A systematic record to assess the extent to which IFC advisory services lead to successful PPPs is being built. With the exception of few PPPs (six), for which IFC has commissioned a third party to conduct postcompletion evaluations, IFC's completion reports have documented only activities up to the transaction closure—with very little evidence beyond and into the actual life time of a PPP. Hence, most of this assessment focuses on bringing a transaction to a successful contract closure.

Although almost all transaction cases (97 percent) reviewed delivered the specific advice for phase 1, about half resulted in an award of a contract, a prerequisite for creating a successful PPP. Assessment of the delivery chain for PPPs more carefully (Figure 4.13) reveals that the process often gets stalled after phase 1 and before or at the stage of bidding—a point that only 70 and 60 percent of all transactions reach, respectively. Once the bidding is completed, contract closure is likely to happen but is not guaranteed; 51 percent of projects reach this stage.[28]

Among projects that led to contract closure, the largest success factor is government commitment and IFC's role. Government commitment was cited as a success factor in 76 percent of the projects that were successful, followed by IFC's role and contribution, found in 52 percent of the projects as a success factor. Collectively, these two factors led to success in 86 percent of projects. An important aspect of IFC's role and contribution rests with its strength in financial structuring and market analysis and testing, where client governments and other international financial institutions have fewer comparative advantages.

FIGURE 4.13 IFC Advisory Services Success along the PPP Delivery Chain

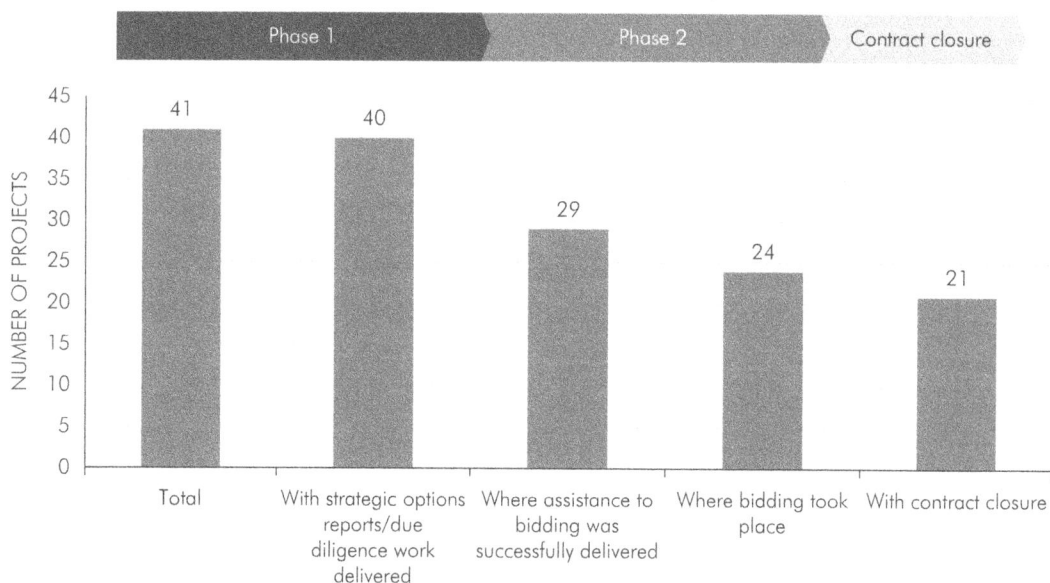

SOURCE: PCRs and IEG validated Project Completion Reports.
NOTE: n = 41. IEG identified 156 PPP-targeted transactions by IFC Advisory Services C3P, approved during FY05–12, of which 79 are closed. Of these, 41 are transaction advice with the objective of commercial/contract closure (or commercial closure in another term) and have PCR documents. The remaining are studies, workshops, and knowledge management products that do not aim at contract closure of a specific PPP transaction.

For example, IFC advisory teams conduct market soundings early on and continue the dialogue with investors throughout the PPP preparation process to get a sense of how the terms/conditions/requirements can be structured to facilitate a successful transaction. In a few cases, IFC teams also engaged a further upstream than the actual transaction and helped conduct project viability gap analysis and value for money analysis, and present different structuring options with various viability gap funding (capital subsidy) and fiscal impact scenarios. These upstream efforts were clearly the minority of IFC advisory work, which largely focuses on getting transaction closed.

IFC's value added is also demonstrated by its ability to adjust and balance government objectives with the needs of a bankable transaction that would interest the private sector. The IFC team emphasized ensuring that a project's risks were correctly allocated to the party that could best handle them, and to structure a project so that mechanisms are in place to adequately respond to all possible contingencies over the life of a project.

Other consultants can do the same job; however, IFC's name and reputation for transparency and competitive bidding help to kick start pioneering PPP projects and attract sufficient numbers of bidders. In the Syria Independent Power Producer Project, for example, once IFC got involved, 16 international and reputable firms successfully qualified for the project, citing IFC involvement as the reason for their willingness to bid on the project. The government had launched a first round of prequalification for the project; however, that had resulted in only one party successfully prequalifying/submitting a request for quote.

The nine country case studies corroborate IFC Advisory Services high added value, for the individual transaction as well as for the wider PPP and private sector development agenda. IFC Advisory Services supported many "first of a kind" concessions and contributed to model contracts, as in Colombia, and innovations, such as economic equilibrium concessions. In a few cases, broader effects can be observed, for example, on increasing competition and lowering transport costs.

In the Philippines, IFC Advisory Services succeeded in bringing to closure a utility privatization that had earlier been unsuccessfully attempted, by engaging with the regulator from the start and innovating financing that minimized risks to the potential sponsor. It has also acted as adviser on high-profile transport projects, and in the non-grid areas, it took on challenging privatizations of small generators and successfully completed one.

In Brazil advisory work it set new standards that removed barriers, increased international participation, and lowered tariffs. During the evaluation period, it was practice of IFC Advisory Services to exit transactions at financial close, but some clients has have observed that extending its role beyond that point, as an honest broker, could facilitated faster

BOX 4.5 The Role of IFC Advisory Services in Brazil

IFC Advisory Services played an important catalytic role by successfully introducing new standards to PPP transactions in the transport sector and breaking new grounds by advising the first health and education PPPs. In contrast, Brazilian transaction advisory firm Empresa Brasileira de Projetos concentrates on more standard PPP projects like ones in the power sector. Empresa Brasileira de Projetos was established in March 2009 jointly by the National Bank of Economic and Social Development and Brazilian banks. PPPs and concession transactions were following the PPP models established by Brazil's Private Sector Partnership Program, for example, in the transport sector. Its work has been recognized by KPMG. KPMG selected two projects as among the 100 most innovative infrastructure projects in 2011. These two projects served as models of how PPPs can improve health and education for underserved population in Brazil.

Coordination with other development banks has been successful in Brazil, led by the effort of IFC Advisory Services. A number of IFC's PPP Advisory Service projects are financed under the Brazilian Private Sector Partnership Program, a partnership of IFC, the National Bank of Economic and Social Development, and the Inter-American Development Bank. The goal of the Partnership Program was to realize PPP and concession projects so to increase the private sector participation in infrastructure financing in Brazil. Another of its objectives was to develop the capacity of Brazilian government for PPP work.

Since the National Bank has been the dominant player for financing infrastructure projects including PPPs, it is important for IFC to engage the National Bank to transfer knowledge of structuring PPPs and project finance transactions. IFC has been leading the program in terms of providing a technical expertise and the Inter-American Development Bank was only involved in providing funding to the program.

SOURCES: IEG country case study; IEG 2013b.

implementation (Box 4.5). In response, IFC advisory introduced a new post-transaction support product in 2012 helping client countries building capacity for contract monitoring or in case of renegotiations.

Conversely, among projects that failed to reach contract closure, the top driver of failure was political and economic risk factors, such as replacement of top government officials, civil wars, and economic crises, which contributed to the failure of 50 percent of the projects. The second driver of failure is lack of government commitment, which affected 45 percent of these projects.

Collectively the two factors contributed to the failure in 75 percent of these projects. It seems that lack of government capacity and the pioneering character of a PPP project do not affect project success significantly. However, it should be noted that overall 40 percent of IFC advisory projects have a pioneering character, that is, are either the country's first PPPs or a first-of-a-kind PPP.

Of projects where government capacity was weak, over half of them reached contract closure, which indicates that IFC advisory capacity can handle the process. In Albania and Liberia power projects, for example, government capacity was weak but the projects succeeded because of government commitment and IFC's strong role.

Inherent country risks only marginally explain the contract closure rate of 50 percent. Profiling PPP transactions reveals that IFC Advisory Services tends to operate in medium-risk countries, that is, in countries with an Institutional Investor Country Credit Rating (IICCR) of between 30 and 45. Compared to IFC investments, country risks are only slightly elevated for IFC Advisory Services.[29] Compared to other IFC Advisory Services business lines, the country risks are comparable (Figure 4.14).[30] However, PPPs supported by IFC advisory services are found mainly in LMICs (59 percent of projects) and are concentrated in Sub-Saharan Africa (21 percent)—to a higher extent than IFC investments. Although no official rating with regard to these countries' maturity to manage PPPs exists (they, for example, have not been rated by the EIU), one could safely assume that many of them are more in the nascent or emerging state of developing PPP frameworks. This may in part explain why about 50 percent of PPPs do not reach contract closure.

FIGURE 4.14 Risk Profile of IFC Advisory Services PPP Compared to Other IFC Advisory Services Business Lines and Investments

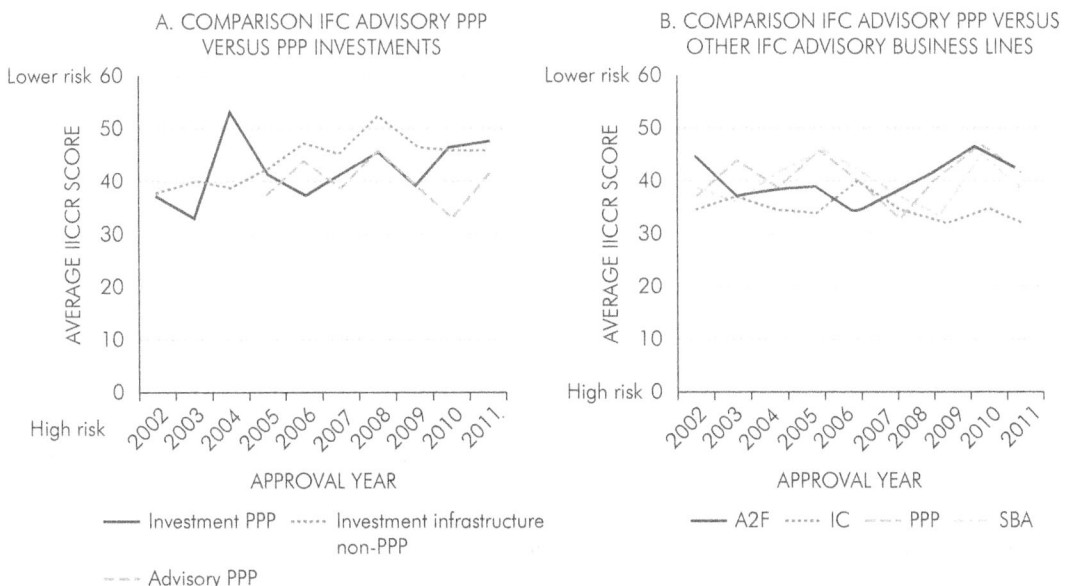

A. COMPARISON IFC ADVISORY PPP VERSUS PPP INVESTMENTS

B. COMPARISON IFC ADVISORY PPP VERSUS OTHER IFC ADVISORY BUSINESS LINES

SOURCE: IEG.

NOTE: A2F = Access to Finance; IC = Investment Climate; IICCR = Institutional Investor Country Credit Rating; SBA = Sustainability Business. IICR scores are weighted averages (by numbers of projects) per year.

IFC Advisory Services' business model can help explain why half of its mandates result in contract closure for a PPP. The reason half of projects reach financial closure has to do with the circumstances advisory services are implemented in. Unlike IFC's mainstream investments, in which the client is a private sector company, advisory services deal directly with governments as clients. Lacking the close relations—and (financial) leverage—that the World Bank would normally have with governments through its lending tools and the country dialogue, IFC is in principle able to secure commitment from its clients only by virtue of the commercial fee-paying nature of its assignment; this may not be significant in terms of the quantum of fees it can reasonably charge.

An important lesson is that more upfront work should be undertaken to better assess client commitment and to determine the areas of support and opposition to a project within the client government. Such work could occur before signing the Financial Advisory Services Agreement. For projects that involve commitments from multiple stakeholders, IFC should engage in a premandate assignment to identify and map stakeholders and engage in discussions with them to determine their support for the projects. It is also important to ensure that the client has real decision-making authority and is not a source of technical expertise/ oversight that still needs to go elsewhere for decisions on points of project implementation.

A dedicated project champion from the clients end and the formation of steering committee with all decision makers are good ways to help strengthen commitment from various stakeholders. This is likely to require more field presence of staff who can technically engage in such business development activities with key policy makers—that is, senior staff. Efforts to increase awareness about the circumstances under which PPPs can present a solution for infrastructure constraints and how PPPs work, would be important components of such upfront work. Similar awareness efforts have recently been undertaken by IFC when hosting a competition, jointly with the Infrastructure Journal and funded by PPIAF, to identify the "Top 40 PPPs in Emerging Countries" (IFC 2013).

Systematic country diagnostics on PPPs could help identifying the right entry point for such upfront work. Upfront stakeholder consultations and business development efforts are likely to be resources intense, not only in terms of cost, but also time. A careful assessment would be required to understand the trade-offs between increased resources allocation to this sort of business development and the subsequently (hoped for) positive effects on the political economy. A Bank Group-wide systematic country diagnostics for PPPs will be helpful in assessing as of which stage intensified stakeholder consultations and business development would be justified, given a country's level of maturity (see also Chapter 5).

More proactive dialogue with civil society stakeholders should be part of this increased upfront work. When the project team reached out to stakeholders beyond the client, such as civil society organizations, local communities to build support and overcome political obstacles, the probability of success was higher; this finding was corroborated further by the IEG Cluster Note on PPPs in Africa (IEG 2013a). Regular meetings with key stakeholders during project implementation as part of client relations strategy is an important ingredient to success. In the case of TKL Advisory in Kenya, client trust, confidence, and commitment were enhanced by the fact that IFC had previously worked with the client. Another example is IFC Advisory Services for the Comoros, where a phased-level approach allowed the project to move ahead with phase 1 at least, despite initial resistance of the companies.

Recently, IFC advisory introduced a new product, PPP Upstream Work. This is intended to cover (i) assessing and prioritizing potential PPP projects; (ii) within the context of a specific PPP transaction, reviewing and recommending changes to legal/regulatory frameworks; and (iii) disseminating global knowledge and lessons learned on PPP transactions, primarily among government officials. This new offering will likely contribute to closing the deal gap for PPPs (see later in this chapter), but IFC advisory may still have to strengthen it upfront stakeholder work, as delineated above.

IFC Advisory Services has been intensifying its collaboration efforts with the World Bank. Of 45 self-assessed IFC PPP advisory projects, 73 percent present at least one form of collaboration. The most common type of collaboration is informal collaboration, which happens in 49 percent of the projects. This type of collaboration varies significantly from providing information technology—related equipment for government steering committee, exchanging technical information, and reviewing technical studies to informal talks with World Bank staff, especially on sector and country strategies.

More formal types of communication also occur, for example, in 31 percent of IFC advisory projects there was a World Bank staff member participating in the execution team of the advisory project (for example, toll roads in Brazil and Colombia and ports in Mauritius and India). A similar proportion of projects (29 percent) have World Bank Group staff participating in quality at entry meetings. In about 18 percent of projects, the mandate was brought by the World Bank or there is a PPIAF study associated. Only 9 percent of the projects have an IDA loan/technical assistance associated with the mandate.

Such World Bank Group-wide collaboration made IFC Advisory Services transaction support more successful. In about a quarter of IFC Advisory Services projects that led to PPP contract closure, such collaboration was a key success driver. In the IFC Advisory Albania KESH Electric Power Project, the close cooperation of IFC and the World Bank in coordinating among stakeholders and in achieving political commitment and donor community consensus facilitated the acceleration of policy and regulatory reform, which helped structure a transaction conducive to the private sector. Organizing and coordinating among all the government institutions and their respective advisors was crucial, especially during the PPP transaction preparation phase.

In the Cape Sierra Hotel Project in Sierra Leone (a concession project), IFC greatly benefited from collaborating with other parts of the World Bank Group. For instance, IFC leveraged the World Bank's sector-specific experience and contacts within the government to bring the transaction to commercial closure. Government decisions in a conflict-affected state often rest with key individuals, and the IFC advisory team used this established network to get and keep the ball rolling. This need was particularly evident after the failed initial tender, when it became critical to rebuild stakeholder support at high levels to continue with the transaction. Also, early collaboration with IFC investment services and MIGA was instrumental in increasing the attractiveness of the project to potential investors. During the marketing phase of the transaction, concern over the recent civil war and the related question of political stability was a common refrain from potential investors. By engaging with IFC investment services and MIGA early on, the team offered potential investors a robust portfolio of World Bank Group services, which encouraged many investors to participate in the tender process.

MIGA SPECIFIC DRIVERS OF SUCCESS AND FAILURE

MIGA guarantees helped effectively increase investors' confidence, improve their capacity to raise capital, lower their financing costs, and mediate disputes with government. The review of the available 13 Project Evaluation Reports identified evidence that in at least half of the cases MIGA had a crucial role, albeit not statistically robust evidence for its entire portfolio—see Box 4.6.

MIGA's PRI did not necessarily allow PPPs to get structured in higher-risk environments, but covered for specific risks. Looking at the country risks associated with PPPs in terms of IICCR ratings indicated that MIGA-supported PPPs are located in countries comparable to IFC's investments in PPPs, that is, in countries with an IICCR score of 35–50. This appears to

---

BOX 4.6 MIGA's Role in Getting PPPs Off the Ground

MIGA's political risk insurance has contributed to PPP projects getting off the ground (or even to their success), as evidenced in multiple country cases.

In Guatemala and the Philippines, early involvement by MIGA at a time of uncertainty help to mobilize finance for a large PPP, but there has been no involvement since then. In Brazil, several guarantees were secured for transmission, but more than half were with the same investor. Attribution is also difficult given MIGA's relatively small contribution, even when its involvement is in a single subsector, as in power transmission in Brazil, given the large presence of others, including state-owned utilities.

Shenzhen Water (Group) Company Ltd., China, was the first large-scale PPP to focus on integrated network water and wastewater services—an untested area for private investment and management in China at the time the guarantee was issued. The MIGA guarantee increased investors' confidence in its investment decision-making process for this project. Particularly considering the project's size and time horizon, international sponsor Veolia had high expectation for MIGA's deterrence effect and, to a lesser extent, mediation services if needed.

Similarly in the Costa Rica project Compañía Hidroeléctrica Doña Julia S.A, a BOT run-of-river hydroelectric power plant, MIGA's support was critical to its success, as one of the project's principal equity contributors required MIGA coverage for its investment; the principal lender also required MIGA coverage for its shareholder loan to the project because of its small country limits in Costa Rica.

Likewise, the investor would not have proceeded with the Ormat Momotombo Power Project in Nicaragua without the MIGA guarantee. MIGA coverage allowed the company to raise commercial debt for their investment in Nicaragua and having multilateral participation in the project helped to lower the cost of funds. At the time of underwriting, Nicaragua's sovereign credit risk rating made the cost of borrowing prohibitively expensive without some form of insurance.

In the case of Asia Power (Private) Limited, Sri Lanka, even with the involvement of four bilateral and multilateral institutions that offered concessional financing and the readiness of the IBRD to fund the project, MIGA support was important to the guarantee holder because of the high political risk associated with the country. MIGA's participation in the project also supported and complemented IFC's involvement and ensured that IBRD's 1996 blueprint for the country's infrastructure sector program was implemented. The project had been identified as priority in the IBRD's pipeline for its Private Sector Infrastructure Development Loan in 1996.

SOURCES: IEG country case studies; MIGA.

indicate that investors either take out MIGA's coverage for political risk for specific project risks (as comparable IFC PPP investments seem not to need it), or that investors feel comfortable with IFC's risk coverage that comes with any investment implicitly (Figure 4.15).

MIGA's PPPs, however, are located in less risky countries than other MIGA projects, which are hosted in countries with an IICCR score of 18–40. Still, evidence suggests cases where MIGA's guarantees did effectively allow the investor to enter countries where specific risks were high, for example, the Hydelec BPA in Madagascar and Cotecna Destination Inspection Limited in Nigeria. Madagascar has had a long history of expropriation. In the 1970s the socialist

FIGURE 4.15 Risk Profile of MIGA PPPs and IFC Investments in PPPs, Three-Year Rolling Average, FY02–12

A. MIGA PPPs VERSUS MIGA INFRASTRUCTURE PROJECTS

B. MIGA PPPs VERSUS IFC IS PPPs

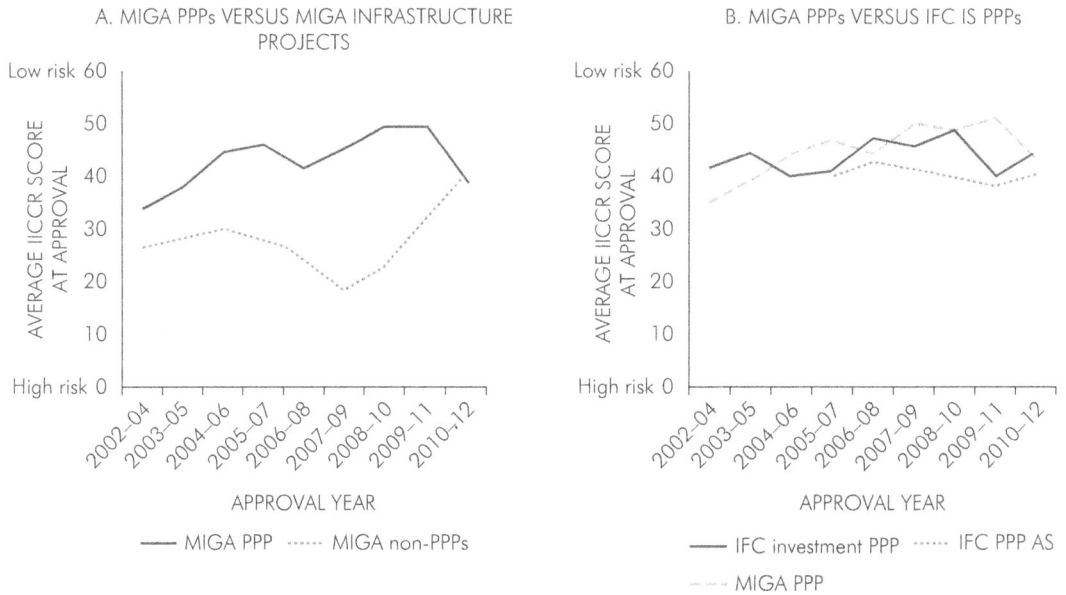

APPROVAL YEAR

—— MIGA PPP ······ MIGA non-PPPs

—— IFC investment PPP ······ IFC PPP AS
– – – MIGA PPP

SOURCES: IICCR, IEG.
NOTE: IICR scores are weighted averages (by numbers of projects) per year. AS = Advisory Services; IICCR=Institutional Investor Country Credit Rating.

government expropriated all foreign assets; more than 25 years later some claims are still not settled. Within this context and given the dearth of foreign investment in the country, MIGA played an important role in promoting future investment flows. MIGA's PRI was also essential for undertaking PPP projects in Nigeria, which has a history of reviewing and changing contract terms whenever a new government, particularly the opposition party, takes over.

MIGA's support to PPPs was strong in countries that are about to build up their enabling environment. As Chapter 2 showed, MIGA-supported PPP are frequently located in countries that have little experience with PPPs, that is, those that are rated by EIU as nascent and emerging. In both categories, MIGA was able to support disproportionally more PPP than indicated by FDI flow and general PPP prevalence. This indicated that MIGA was effective in bringing PPPs into frontier areas.

MIGA-supported PPPs have also been more strategically relevant than their other infrastructure projects. Development outcomes and work quality ratings were about the same for PPPs and other MIGA projects. The ratings of MIGA projects at the point of reaching operational maturity indicate that MIGA PPPs perform on a par with the rest of the MIGA infrastructure portfolio. However, MIGA-supported PPPs show significantly higher strategic

FIGURE 4.16 Development Outcomes and Underwriting Quality—MIGA-Supported PPPs and Infrastructure Projects

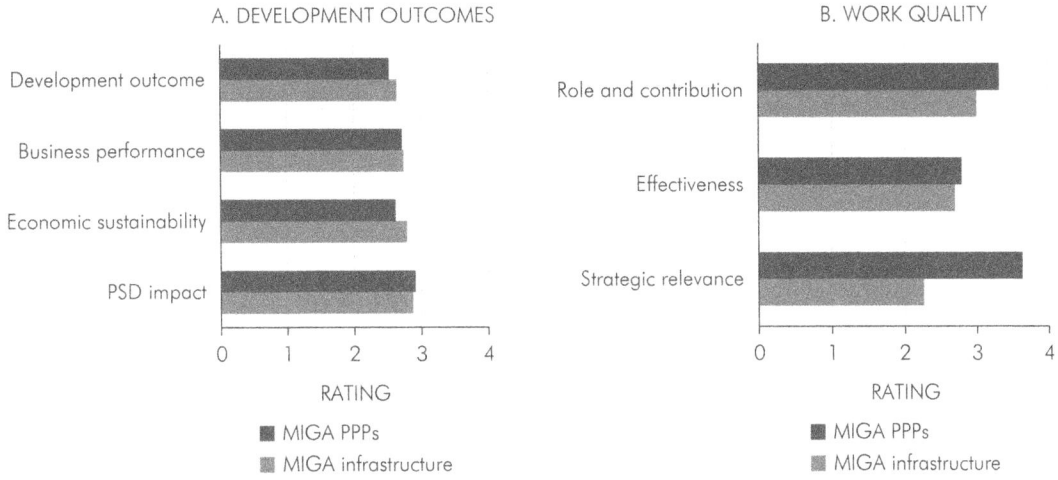

SOURCE: MIGA.
NOTE: n = 13. PSD = private sector development.

relevance than other infrastructure projects (Figure 4.16). This corroborates MIGA's useful role in bringing PPPs to nascent and emerging PPP countries.

MIGA's mediating capacity played a role as well. MIGA's Role and Contribution in the OrPower 4 project in Kenya was "excellent" because of its active role in mediating the disputes between Ormat (the sponsor) and the government. For MIGA the efforts paid off when it did not have to pay a claim and when it convinced Ormat to proceed with phase 2, covered by a MIGA guarantee. Ormat considered MIGA's guarantee as critical for the implementation of the project. They particularly appreciated MIGA's willingness to assist them in discussions with the government.

Similar to all World Bank Group PPP transactions, regulatory failure and political economy factors were at times the root causes of failure. For example, in the Hydelec power plant in Madagascar, which was envisaged to be a peaking power station, continued constraints on the country's generation capacity resulted in the plant being used almost for base load generation. This resulted in increased overall prices of electricity generation. Because of political pressures to restrain full cost pass-through of generation to end users, the off-taker was required to subsidize electricity prices—resulting in near bankruptcy. Although the project has modestly increased electricity supply, its sustainability remains unclear.

WORLD BANK-SPECIFIC DRIVERS OF SUCCESS AND FAILURE

World Bank engages in inherently more risky countries, which may explain why its projects show lower development outcome ratings. With 62 percent of its downstream supported

FIGURE 4.17 Country Risk of World Bank Downstream PPP Transactions

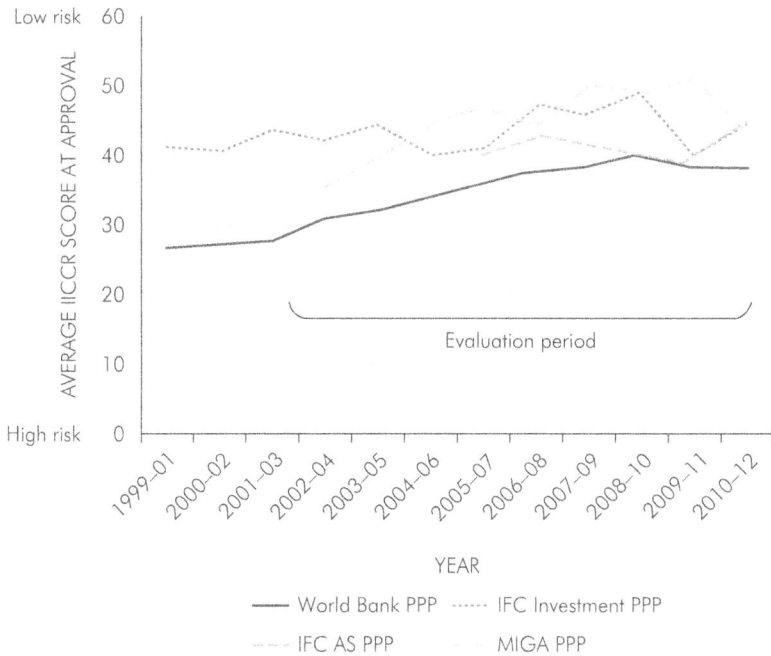

SOURCES: IEG; IICCR.
NOTE: AS = Advisory Services. IICCR = Institutional Investor Country Credit Rating.

PPP transactions rated satisfactory or better, the World Bank clearly lags behind the success rate of IFC's transactions, of which 83 percent were successful. This could be first explained by the country risk of a World Bank PPP project. Countries where the World Bank implements its downstream PPP transactions have a significantly worse IICCR rating than countries in which IFC or MIGA engage (Figure 4.17). Although World Bank countries became less and less risky over time (since 1999), they still have IICCR ratings between 28 and 40.

Second, the World Bank engages more in countries that have less developed PPP frameworks: a full 19 percent of World Bank downstream projects are in nascent countries, compared to only 6 percent of IFC PPP investments. Third, the World Bank's engagements tend to be determined by long-term lending programs, which usually leave the Bank with little freedom in what and with how to engage—whereas IFC can select projects based on sponsor quality and project risk.

Although World Bank PPP transactions appear sufficiently well designed, their implementation is cumbersome. Looking at the World Bank's performance in ensuring quality at entry and supervision (per ICRs), PPP projects rank equal to other infrastructure projects. This seems to indicate that the manner in which the World Bank manages its PPP projects is fine, or at least on a par with its general portfolio of infrastructure projects. However, looking more closely at

FIGURE 4.18 World Bank PPP Outcome Ratings and "Project Flags"

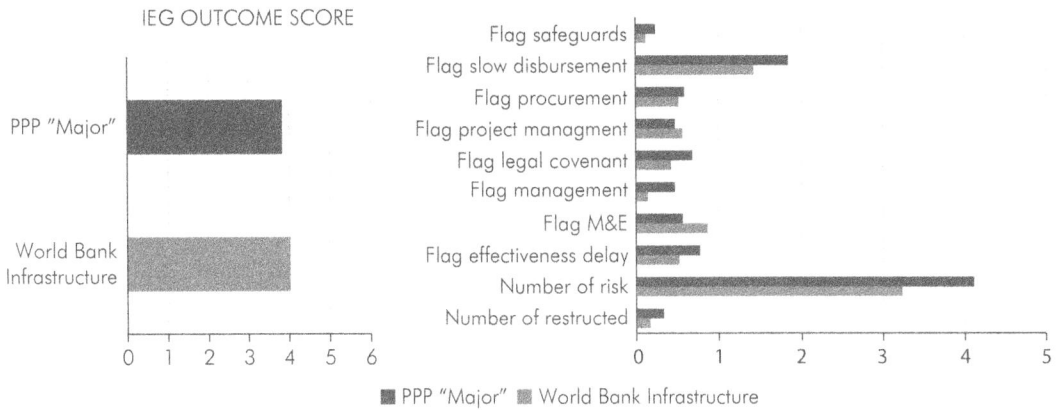

IEG OUTCOME SCORE

SOURCE: World Bank.
NOTE: M&E = monitoring and evaluation.

the implementation process reveals that World Bank PPP projects are more cumbersome: they are flagged more frequently for slow disbursement[31] and delays,[32] being at risk,[33] subject to project restructuring, procurement,[34] and safeguards issues (Figure 4.18). This corroborates the qualitative findings made during the country case studies on World Bank downstream support.

Leading factors for delays and failure include overly complex project design, unrealistic timeframes, and, at times, the implementation of safeguards. World Bank PPP projects often set unrealistically narrow timeframes to start with, that is, a timeframe that forces reform measures into a World Bank project cycle, instead of acknowledging the complexity and political nature of such processes. Government commitment plays as important a role for World Bank transactions as it does for IFC and MIGA projects. Adhering to environmental and social (E&S) safeguards also delays project implementation. Once flagged—and World Bank PPP projects get flagged more often than other infrastructure projects (Figure 4.18)—E&S assessments and needed midcourse corrections can take a long time. Eventually, the Bank Group does a good job in implementing them, as evidenced by the E&S ratings of World Bank, IFC, and MIGA PPP projects. However, the delays caused may, at times, cloud the appreciation of benefits received from the project (Box 4.7).

However, compliance with E&S safeguards also delivered valuable public benefits. The relatively high rate of World Bank projects flagged for E&S issues and implementation delays seems to indicate that adhering to E&S safeguards can come at the detriment of pace. This is corroborated by qualitative findings from case studies (Box 4.7). Despite these implementation delays, E&S safeguards clearly delivered public benefits. A closer look at World Bank downstream projects revealed evidence[35] that most of those projects that had E&S information (82 percent) also achieved their E&S safeguards objective. Social benefits

The Bujagali Hydropower Project is the first independent power producer in Uganda, a country that had 2 percent of its population with access to grid-supplied electricity and one of the lowest electricity consumption per capita in the world when the concession was awarded in 1995. With funding support from the World Bank, IFC, MIGA, numerous bilateral agencies, and the private sponsors, the project serves as a prime example of the complexity in financing PPP projects in developing countries.

The World Bank Group contributed mainly by providing finance and guarantees and managing the environmental and social aspects of the project:

1. Convening power of the World Bank Group and leveraging of resources secured full financing for the project. IDA partial risk guarantee, IFC loans and MIGA PRI exposure accounted for 44percent ($395 million) of the $902 million actual project cost. Leveraging of World Bank Group resources secured $437 million from other international financial institutions, providing sufficient comfort to the new private sponsor and private lenders to invest $70 million in Bujagali Electricity Limited, the project company.

2. Adoption of strict technical and E&S standards and procurement rules. Best industry standards and practice were applied in the technical design, procurement, construction, operation and maintenance of the power plant. The World Bank required compliance with its Safeguard Policy and Environmental Guidelines; IFC and MIGA also required compliance with their E&S Performance Standards. Feedback from Uganda's environment authority appreciated that the World Bank Group raised the bar of the country's E&S standards. A carefully designed resettlement plan for 34 affected families, extensive local community consultations, and a multi-stakeholder observer group with nongovernmental organization representation were critical elements of the project's accountability structure.

3. Off-setting mechanism to address the irreversible environmental damage caused by the project. The Indemnity Agreement between the Ugandan Government and World Bank established a Sustainable Management Plan to ensure that the natural habitat of Kalagala Falls (8 kilometers downstream from Bujagali Falls) and the spiritual values of the community are protected and conforms to sound social and environmental standards. This conditionality is tied to the continuation of the World Bank's engagement in Uganda.

Bujagali began commercial operations in August 2012. The power plant is operating at full capacity but daily dispatch to Uganda Electricity Transmission Company Limited (UETCL) ranged from 125 megawatts to 200 megawatts because of transmission bottlenecks. Residents, businesses and industries connected to the grid have reliable electricity since commissioning, according to electricity distributor Umeme Limited. Bujagali Energy Limited (BEL) has received timely payments from the electricity transmission company and end-user tariffs had been cost-reflective since 2012. The project is in compliance with Uganda's environmental legislation and IFC's and MIGA's E&S Performance Standards. E&S issues identified at appraisal are regularly monitored; implementation progress is routinely supervised by the lenders consortium.

However, Bujagali's demonstration effect may not be as positive as hoped for. Public perception about the long delay in project completion (1995–2012) has clouded the appreciation of benefits from improved electricity flow and in having a "gold-plated" hydropower plant in the country. Although the project encountered problems and changed private sponsors, government officials and the public associate the delays with World Bank Group's stringent requirements and accountability processes and procedures. Stakeholders perceive that the World Bank Group was more concerned about compliance with its institutional requirements than about delivering results. Disappointment over the PPP model as a means of alleviating power supply shortage was also palpable because of the muted interest from the private sector in financing other power generation projects in the country.

In September 2013, the Ugandan government announced the award of three hydropower projects, two of which are twice the capacity of Bujagali Hydropower Project, to Chinese companies financed by Chinese state-owned banks. The 600 megawatts Karuma, 600 megawatts Ayago, and 180 megawatts Isimba Hydropower Projects were awarded as public sector projects instead of using the PPP model. Karuma is expected to come on-stream in 2016.

SOURCE: IEG country case study.

can be seen for example through the application successful resettlement process framework, or through addressing key social impacts of rail operations on neighboring population. Environmental benefits were seen in most of the cases through adequate implementation of the environmental management plan of the project. Note, however, that for all 37 World Bank downstream projects, 20 had no E&S-related infromation contained in the ICR.

The World Bank has recently reformed the application of its E&S safeguards standards. On June 26, 2012, the Board of Executive Directors approved adoption and application of World Bank Performance Standards to be used for Bank financing or support (for example, partial risk guarantees), which is destined to projects, or components thereof, that are owned, constructed, and/or operated by the private sector, in place of the World Bank E&S safeguard policies. Technical assistance for preparatory work for private sector engagement in PPPs would be eligible, as well as investment operations that include medium- or long-term management contracts, affermage/leases, privatizations, concessions, and projects within the BOT family. At this stage, however, it is too early to assess the effects of this reform on the PPP agenda.

Data on the actual long-term performance of PPPs are rare. Compared to the large amount of World Bank support to policy reform (Chapter 3), actual transaction support was limited to 22 cases; of these, data existed for an even more limited sample on access, efficiency, quality, and financial performance. This is linked to the business model of the World Bank's downstream support: more than half of World Bank projects with a downstream component also have an upstream component. In such cases, the World Bank typically advises on policy reform aspects leading up to a government efforts to engage in PPPs—and in a few cases the Bank advises the government on transactions. PPP transactions, in the overall scheme of events, occur toward the end of a series of reform measures. Projects are typically closed at that stage. Subsequent ICRs are carried out at project closure, which—for most PPPs—is too early to know about the exact PPP structure, not to mention about data on access, efficiency, and quality. Hence, ICRs contain little information about actual PPP success.

EMERGING CROSS-CUTTING ISSUES

Staying engaged beyond financial closure of a PPP is a strategic necessity. The recently adopted World Bank Group strategy identifies as one main element "performance and learning reviews to identify and capture lessons from implementation to determine midcourse corrections and end-of-cycle learning and accountability and help build the World Bank Group's knowledge base" (World Bank 2013b). Although it may be debatable where the "end-of-cycle" is for PPP projects, assessing project success at an early stage, for example, at contract or financial closure does not capture actual performance of PPP operations. Currently, World Bank–supported PPPs are monitored until the closure of the World Bank loan; at that point most PPPs have reached only contract closure stage or are under construction. IFC- and MIGA-supported PPPs are monitored until operational maturity, which is typically 18 months after financial closure.

If the World Bank Group plans to intensify its PPP support as envisaged in its latest strategy, it needs to put arrangements in place that allow to monitor the performance of its PPPs throughout major parts of their lifespan.[36] This may also help identify if World Bank Group support is called for during the implementation of a PPP contract. Post-implementation support by the Bank Group may be warranted for a variety of reasons, including providing capacity building for monitoring PPP contracts or providing support for renegotiation or during rebidding processes. IFC Advisory Services has recently (2012) expanded its service offerings to include such support under *postadvisory mandate support*.

In a similar vein, World Bank Group knowledge products and services—though they deliver high value added for PPP— are currently undermonitored. Upstream policy reform is of utmost importance for the success of PPP; however, its effects are difficult to assess, as they are not embedded in a results and monitoring framework. The IEG evaluation *Knowledge-Based Country Programs: An Evaluation of the World Bank Group Experience* (IEG 2013c) recommended that the Bank Group "monitor closely implementation and results to track progress toward mutually agreed outcomes and mitigate the risk of fragmentation and loss of strategic focus …. " It also found that World Bank knowledge services were not monitored and evaluated consistently. Where monitoring and evaluation was better, knowledge services results were more likely to be achieved, probably reflecting a link between monitoring and evaluation and knowledge service quality. The evidence of this evaluation provides extra weight to that recommendation.

Demonstration and replication effects may be at times as important as the actual transaction. Ample evidence from the country case studies indicates that a single PPP transaction may have broader effects by setting an example of a pioneering project in a relatively untested environment and hereby attracting the interest of other potential investors. For example, in Colombia, the Transmilenio Bus Rapid Transit Project, supported by World Bank lending, led to six such projects in other cities in Colombia. In Guatemala, the first downstream geothermal PPP project in the country, supported by IFC and MIGA, was replicated in two subsequent geothermal PPPs. In China, IFC's 2004 investment in China Green Energy (Cayman) Ltd. offered a good example of demonstration effects achieved through an investment in a waste-to-energy power project on a build-down-operate basis. Not only did this project introduce environmental and social standards, six to eight private investors entered the market within five years of IFC's investment.

PPP transactions can also positively influence the regulatory framework. In Brazil, for example, IFC advisory service was successful in introducing "performance-standard" contracts to a transport PPP transaction and the Hospital do Surburbio, a health PPP. It also introduced the Equator Principles and IFC's Social Standards for expropriation and resettlement rules, subsequently applied to other road concessions.

With the Ruta del Sol transaction, IFC Advisory Services paved the way for the PPP law and its contracts are used as models for current concessions in Colombia. The involvement of IFC and MIGA in Guatemala's Orzunil I Geothermal Project encouraged additional strong private sector investment, that is, leveraging private sector funds, with Orzunil's capital structure serving as a model for subsequent geothermal projects. In Albania, IFC advisory services assisted the government in setting up a regulatory framework conducive to private sector participation while acting as lead advisor on an electricity sector projects.

Key to most successful cases was the close cooperation of IFC and the World Bank in coordinating among stakeholders and in achieving political commitment and donor community consensus when it facilitated the acceleration of policy and regulatory reform. For more lessons, see also Box 4.8.

BOX 4.8 Demonstration and Replication Effects in the Philippines

In toll roads, IFC and MIGA were deeply involved in North Luzon Expressway, along with the Asian Development Bank. The project came at the end of the Asian financial crisis, and except for a small equity portion, most of the commercial lending was covered by MIGA, IFC b-Loans, and export credits. With investor confidence returning, both IFC and MIGA exited the project within a few years, but their involvement was crucial in the early stages, not only for the financial support but also to lay down markers for adequate social and environmental safeguards that were implemented as part of the project.

A similar situation prevails in the electricity sector. Several PPPs have been undertaken in the past decade, but only one has been supported by the Bank Group. Nonetheless, the success of these ventures can be attributable to the upstream efforts to define an electricity law and provide incentives for private participation. IFC has also indirectly contributed to the success of PPPs by participating in several privatizations of generators—which reduce the market power of the public sector and hence make private generation more feasible.

In the water sector, despite the successes of the Manila water companies, its demonstration effect, to influence similar operations in other water districts, has been weak. The Manila case is rather unique in the Filipino context, as other water districts are much smaller, and moreover the special regulatory arrangement for Manila's water companies is not easily replicable. Thus despite the success of water PPPs in Manila, there is scarce replication of this approach outside the capital.

Comparing the water and energy sectors, the lesson is clear: A robust regulatory framework that encourages private participation, even without demonstration projects, is more conducive to encouraging similar project starts than a pristine project developed in a regulatory system that is specific to a certain set of circumstances and that is not easily expanded.

SOURCE: IEG county case study.

Conclusion

According to the development outcome rating of project evaluations, PPPs are largely successful. More than two-thirds are rated satisfactory or better; IFC-supported PPPs lead, with 83 percent rated satisfactory or better. The high rate of success of IFC's investments in PPPs should not, however, lead to the conclusion that all local or national PPPs necessarily perform equally well. IFC's active role in structuring and supervision was a major success factor—likely absent in cases without IFC's engagement.

But PPPs need to be measured in a more multifaceted manner to shed more light on important aspects of public service delivery, for instance, access, pro-poor aspects, and quality of service delivery. But such data are rare. The existing monitoring and evaluation systems primarily build on a PPPs business performance. Project-level evaluations and IFC's Development Goals and DOTS measure mainly the operational aspects of a PPP that are relevant to cash flow. Fewest data are available on pro-poor and fiscal effects; access has the most data available.

In view of the Bank Group's central goal of fighting poverty—reaffirmed by the new 2013 strategy's dual goal of ending extreme poverty and promoting shared prosperity, and in light of the intent to increasingly pursue PPPs—there is an urgent need to introduce a more systematic way of monitoring PPPs; such a system should not only capture better the end-user aspects of PPPs, but should also monitor PPP performance beyond the early years of operational maturity. Existing systems, such as IFC's IDGs or DOTS would have to be strengthened—and possibly expanded to the World Bank—to better assess the breadth of PPP effects.

For example, the development goals or DOTS only partially close the data gap. Both focus heavily on access related figures: Typically these systems collect data on the number of customers reached or passengers transported. For the World Bank, no systems exist at all that would track performance of PPPs after project closure. To do justice to the broad effects of PPPs, a wider set of outcome indicators should be kept track of throughout the life of a PPP, as envisaged by IFC advisory's post-implementation system, which is currently being implemented. In addition, the World Bank Group and country authorities could learn from in-depth studies of selected PPP engagements to see if and how they contributed to economic growth and shared prosperity. Monitoring and evaluation systems are resource intensive and need to be embedded in corporate reporting systems—that should collect the referred outcome data on a regular basis anyway—and national statistics services.

Improving access was generally achieved. When data were available, financial, efficiency, and quality improvements could be confirmed for the majority of cases, but data on efficiency and quality were scarce. A statistically non-representative but in-depth assessment of 22 PPPs conducted as part of the nine country cases studies albeit not representative indicates good results along all dimensions, except for efficiency where results were mixed. It cannot, however, be assessed how far PPPs benefited the poor, as large data gaps exist. Confirmation that access did improve for the poor was only recorded in about 10 percent of cases. Beyond reaching the poor through improved access to infrastructure, a review of broader benefits showed that evidence for such effects, for example, employment effects, was found in 42 percent of World Bank PPPs, 39 percent of IFC investments and 20 percent of MIGA's guarantees.

Country maturity drives PPP success. The analysis of development outcome ratings[37] and the maturity of the host country revealed that these factors correlate positively, both for IFC's investments and World Bank projects, though much less for the latter. As a general rule, the presence of a strong regulatory framework was necessary for projects to succeed in the water and power sectors, but in the transport sector (ports, airports, roads) project-level parameters on pricing and oversight, along with the legal framework governing PPPs, seemed to be adequate. Hence cross-sector approaches as envisaged by the World Bank Group 2013 strategy would have to be rooted in sector reform. In addition to country maturity, PPPs need a sound business case and a competent sponsor to be successful.

IFC investments, in addition to providing finance and catalyzing other financiers, added value during due diligence or by acting as an honest broker. IFC-supported PPPs tend to be less risky than other infrastructure investments, because of the thorough due diligence. This thoroughness is also reflected in the high work quality ratings for IFC investments in PPPs. As a consequence, IFC-supported PPPs exhibit consistently higher development outcome ratings than other infrastructure investments—and significantly higher ratings than the rest of the portfolio.

Risk is adequately priced into IFC's deals for PPPs—resulting in an even higher-than-average business success of the PPP project and investment outcome for IFC. Chapter 2 also showed that IFC-supported PPPs are located often in countries with already well-established enabling environments, and less in emerging or nascent countries. Supporting more PPPs in emerging countries will not decrease their success rate; even increasing its—currently very small— investment portfolio in nascent countries is likely to maintain the overall very high success rate of greater than 80 percent at a still very reasonable level.

The findings of this evaluation, corroborated by the recent IEG transport study, seem to indicate that IFC investment could afford some more "smart risk taking," as envisaged by the 2013 strategy *A Stronger, Connected, Solutions World Bank Group* (World Bank 2013b). This could help supporting more PPPs in countries that need IFC's support the most, that is, those that are only now building up their PPP frameworks and have a limited track record of implementing PPPs.

The focus of IFC Advisory Services is to bring PPP transactions to commercial and financial closure. Although almost all transaction cases (97 percent) reviewed delivered the specific advice for phase 1, about half resulted in the award of a concession, a prerequisite for creating a successful PPP. Among projects that led to commercial closure, the largest success factors are government commitment and IFC's role. IFC's value added is also demonstrated by its ability to adjust and balance government objectives with the needs of a bankable transaction, which would interest the private sector. Lacking somewhat the long-term and close relations, in-depth policy dialogue, and financial leverage that the World Bank would normally have with governments may also explain this pattern; so can the fact that IFC advisory operates a lot in LMICs and Sub-Saharan Africa, where one could expect relatively untested PPP frameworks. IFC advisory's experience in these countries could therefore inform IFC investments regarding the country and market's readiness and help leading their investment more into emerging—and even nascent—countries.[38]

Another important lesson is that more upfront work should be undertaken. More proactive dialogue with civil society stakeholders should be part of this increased upfront work. A Bank Group-wide systematic country diagnostic for PPPs may help determine the right entry point for IFC's upfront work.

MIGA guarantees helped effectively increase investors' confidence and improve their capacity to raise capital, lower their financing costs, and mediate disputes with government. Looking at MIGA's effectiveness, underwriting quality for PPP projects is on a par with the quality of underwriting of other MIGA projects. Similar to all World Bank Group PPP transactions, regulatory failure and political economy factors were drivers of success and failure. MIGA's PRI allowed coverage for specific risks to be obtained and was effective in helping establishing a track record of PPPs in countries that need support the most, that is, those that are in the process of building up their PPP frameworks.

MIGA-supported PPPs have been more strategically relevant than their other infrastructure projects, corroborating their important role in nascent and emerging PPP countries. Strengthening MIGA's role in Bank Group-wide efforts and benefiting from its role appears to be the way forward when bringing PPPs to more nascent and emerging countries.

Sixty-two percent of World Bank support to downstream PPP transactions was successful. This means that, measured by their overall development outcomes, PPPs are quite successful, but significantly less successful than IFC's investments in PPPs of which 83 percent are rated satisfactory. But the World Bank takes on significantly more country risk. Countries in which the World Bank engages tend to have worse IICCRs, and a higher share of them are nascent countries (19 percent, compared to 6 percent for IFC investments). Furthermore, PPP projects are markedly more difficult to implement than normal infrastructure projects. They are often restructured, delayed or flagged for procurement issues. This stems for the rather complex nature of PPPs projects which in half of the cases combine upstream policy work and downstream transaction support.

Leading factors of failure are overly complex project design and an unrealistic timeframe to start with, that is a timeframe that forces reform measures into a World Bank project cycle, instead of acknowledging the complexity and political nature of such processes. As with IFC and MIGA, government commitment plays an important role. Adhering to E&S safeguards also contributed to slow implementation to the extent that it sometime clouded the appreciations of project benefits. But implementing these safeguards was important and delivered public benefits.

Staying engaged beyond financial closure of a PPP is a strategic necessity. The current practice stopping monitoring of PPPs once the contract is awarded or a few months into their life span is insufficient. If the World Bank Group plans to intensify its PPP support as envisaged in its latest strategy, arrangements are needed to monitor the performance of PPPs throughout major parts of their lifespan. This may also help to identify if World Bank Group support is called for during the implementation of a PPP contract, for example should a need for renegotiations arise.

Demonstration and replication effects of individual PPPs may be at times just as important as the actual transaction. Bank Group engagements led to subsequent follow-up investments in PPPs by other investors thus demonstrating that they created a market for PPPs. Frequently Bank Group–supported PPP transactions also helped shape the regulatory environment, often facilitated by close Bank Group-wide collaboration and stakeholder involvement.

Notes

[1] The Private Participation in Infrastructure database is used as a proxy for all PPP projects in developing countries, that is, as a proxy for "the market." This database has been adjusted and only PPP projects that fall under PPP definition have been included.

[2] More than half of PPP investments can be found in UMICs and in non-IDA countries (with 53 percent each). Conversely, LICs accounted for only 7 percent of IFC's PPP investments. Investments are also concentrated regionally in Latin America and the Caribbean, which has 38 percent by volume (and 44 percent by number). The remaining volume has been flowing more or less evenly into the other regions, with 18 percent (13 percent by number) in Europe and Central Asia, 16 percent (9 percent by number) in the Middle East and North Africa, 15 percent(10 percent by number) in Sub-Saharan Africa, 12 percent (14 percent by number) in East Asia and Pacific, and 6 percent (10 percent by number) in South Asia. Even though Latin America and the Caribbean leads in absolute commitment volume, it has remained constant over the last five years. In contrast, South Asia, the Middle East and North Africa, and Sub-Saharan Africa experienced an upward trend during FY06–12 compared to the last five years. Growth in these two regions is mostly due to new investments in India and Pakistan. The top 5 countries hold about 48 percent of the entire PPP portfolio by volume (45 percent by volume).

[3] IFC Advisory Services started tracking activities reliably in 2006.

[4] More than 59 percent of the projects (51 percent by volume) are in LMICs. By region, about one-third of IFC Advisory Services in PPPs support the Sub-Saharan Africa Region (27 percent by funding and 21 percent by number). Although most of its portfolio is in the transport (38 percent by volume and 34 percent by number) and power (33 percent by volume and 29 percent by number), IFC's PPP Advisory Services target a variety of sectors, including health (about 12 percent by volume and numbers) and education (about 4 percent by volume and numbers), among other sectors, reflecting its diverse agenda and strategy within the business line.

[5] The majority of guarantee volume issued in support of PPPs (70 percent) can be found in MICs and is concentrated in non-IDA countries (51 percent). MIGA's PPP guarantees are concentrated in Sub-Saharan Africa and the Latin America and the Caribbean Regions, with 29 and 26 percent by volume (and 32 percent and 31 percent by number), respectively.

[6] This sample is statistically representative with confidence level at 99 percent and a confidence interval of +/–5.

[7] This amount represents the prorated value assigned to a PPP component.

[8] Fifty-one percent of PPP Lending can be found in lower LMICs. The World Bank also shows regional concentration in Sub-Saharan Africa and Latin America and the Caribbean with about 25 percent by PPP volume (33 percent and 27 percent by numbers, respectively).

[9] For IFC Advisory Services, few data are available beyond financial closure, hence it is difficult to judge the actual performance of PPPs that IFC has advised on. An evaluation of their role and contribution, however, is still possible and provided below.

[10] The scarcity of data on actual PPP results is corroborated by a recent large-scale systematic literature review, conducted by the Dutch Policy and Operations Evaluation Department (Ministry of Foreign Affairs of the Netherlands 2013). This study concluded that "[o]ne of the most striking outcomes of the systematic review is that the evidence on PPP performance is still rather sparse. Robust empirical analyses regarding the net effect of PPP (including both before-and-after analyses and compared to a counterfactual to either public or private program execution) are virtually absent."

[11] The only source of performance data (access, fiscal, efficiency, and so forth) for PPPs supported by IFC advisory are the six available post-implementation reports. This represents only a small sample of IFC advisory work and methodologies of these reports vary. Reports make an effort to record access (in five of the six cases) with relatively good results 80 percent. However, efficiency, quality and fiscal effects (which appear in more than 50 percent of the cases) achieved or at least partially achieved improvements in about 40 percent of the cases. In contrast to investments, financial soundness indicators are rarely recorded.

[12] Because of the limited amount of data available for the effects of PPPs on access, quality, efficiency, and pro-poor objectives, the overall IEG development outcome ratings of IFC's XPSRs and World Bank ICRs were taken as a proxy for conducting economic analyses.

[13] The same EIU scores were used as in Chapter 2.

[14] For this analysis the EIU's scoring system was taken as a reference. The EIU assesses the three regions— Latin America and the Caribbean, East Asia and Pacific, and Europe and Central Asia—according to country level maturity on a scale of 0 (nascent) to 100 (mature). http://www.eiu.com/public/thankyou_download .aspx?activity=download&campaignid=infrascope2012.

[15] Note for IFC PPP Advisory Services: this correlation was not possible to be established, as their portfolio has a significant share (>50 percent) in Africa for which the EIU does not publish maturity scores.

[16] $R^2 = 0.0548$; $y = 0.0117x + 3.1127$. The fact that World Bank projects correlate less with country maturity can be explained by the fact that about half of the projects that support PPP transactions also have an upstream policy reform

component (see Figure 3.1). The development outcome score of such projects is a compounded rating, measuring PPP performance and progress of policy reform. With policy reform being a major factor of delay, the overall rating gets pushed down, lowering the overall correlation.

[17] *Sponsor/partner quality*—This captures the sponsor's experience, financial capacity, commitment to the project, and governance/business reputation. If the sponsor is rated low in these dimensions, sponsor quality is deemed to be low. This is measured as of the time of project approval, based largely on assessment of project documentation and, where available, public information and field visits/interviews. IFC is delivering development impact through partners, typically private enterprises, and therefore their capacity, integrity, and commitment are an important factor of development impact. This factor is rated on a binary scale, with 1 as high risk/low quality and 0 as low risk/high quality.

[18] *Market risks*—This captures the project's underlying competitiveness in the market in which it is operating and any market distortions such as high tariff protection, degree of presence of state-owned enterprises in the sector, artificial monopoly positions and other distortions that typically result in low competitiveness. This is measured as of the time of approval. Clearly demonstrated market competitiveness improves a venture's ability to meet business adversity and survive in its early years so that it may reach its development potential. Economic rates of return and development impact in general tend to be lower in distorted market environments. Distortions drive a wedge between market and economic prices, and financial and economic returns of a project, resulting in a divergence between private and social returns. Distortions are normally unsustainable over the long term creating also financial risks if a particular enterprise benefits financially from market distortions. This factor is rated on a binary scale with 1 as high risk/low competitiveness and 0 otherwise.

[19] Based on the IICCR, a measure of the risk of default on sovereign obligations, which is used in combination with other indicators as a proxy for the quality of a country's business climate for investors. Its scale ranges from 0 (most risky) to 100 (least risky). For the purpose of IFC's strategy, countries with a rating of 30 or less are defined as high-risk; those with ratings of between 30 and 45 are defined medium risk, and those with ratings of 45 are low risk.

[20] Only 10 percent of IFC investments are located in Sub-Saharan Africa, a region not covered by the EIU score; hence the assessment is quite representative of IFC's resources allocation.

[21] Also the cluster study by IEG (2013a) on PPPs in Africa underscores the importance of a thorough due diligence process—including sponsor risk mitigation for PPP success.

[22] Similar to the PPP portfolio, the majority of IFC's transport investments (77 percent by volume) were in non-IDA countries.

[23] Of the 29 percent of investments that were undertaken during early stages of sector reform, 80 percent turned out to be sustained, compared to 83 percent of average transport investments.

[24] Note that emerging PPP countries are mainly composed of upper middle income (48 percent), followed by lower middle income (26 percent) and high income (23 percent).

[25] A recent study by the Infrastructure Consortium for Africa indicates that the administrative budget for project development facilities, as a percentage of committed capital, could be as high as 16 percent (Infrastructure Consortium for Africa 2012).

[26] Of which the majority (20) are in power, followed by water (3) and liquefied petroleum gas/liquefied natural gas facilities (2), with projects are spread across all regions.

[27] Project development also has a high failure rate, particularly in IDA countries. *InfraVentures* expected that about 40–45 percent of its projects would reach financial closure, which is comparable to the share of IFC Advisory Services projects that reach commercial closure (51 percent). But not only in terms of country risk are *InfraVentures'* projects comparable with those of IFC Advisory Services. Also the nature of PPP projects appears similar, as both target pioneering (or niche market) projects, mostly first-of-a-kind transactions in difficult environments, for example, rural water projects or wind and renewable projects.

[28] Over time, the share of projects reaching contract closure has fluctuated considerably between 30 and 100 percent since FY05, but without any discernible pattern.

[29] When looking at the maturity of the country's framework to handle PPPs, Chapter 2 showed that IFC PPP Advisory Services is relatively stronger represented in already "developed" countries than those that are "emerging." It should be added that 21 percent of IFC's Advisory Services were located in Sub-Saharan Africa, a region not covered by the EIU scoring.

[30] Note that unlike the analysis for IFC investments and MIGA guarantees, juxtaposing project ratings related to development effectiveness, output and outcomes achievement, and IFC's efficiency of IFC PPP Advisory Services with those of other business lines (investment climate, access to finance and sustainable business advisory) was not useful, as transaction-specific advice follows different patterns and delivery processes.

[31] Set for disbursement delays of 24 months or more for investment operations or 6 months or more for emergency operations.

[32] Set for an elapsed time between Board approval and effectiveness of more than nine months for investment, more than six months for adjustments, and more than three months for emergency reconstruction operations.

[33] At risk flag is calculated as the sum of 7 at risk flags for development policy loan projects, or the sum of all 12 at risk flags for all other projects.

[34] Set based on unsatisfactory rating for the procurement rating.

[35] Evidence of achievement of environmental or social objectives was found in only 50 percent of the cases. This corroborates the findings of the safeguards study evaluation.

[36] With the exception of IFC's Credit Risk Rating reports, which are available for investments in PPP, there is little to no information available beyond the point of financial closure. These credit risk rating reports are conceived to focus on credit risk monitoring and hence cannot be expected to systematically collect data on PPP performance on a broader basis. IFC's DOTS, although useful in some areas, does not fill this gap either. And for the World Bank and MIGA, no data are available at all beyond project closure or contract signing.

[37] Because of the limited amount of data available for the effects of PPPs on access, quality, efficiency, and pro-poor, the overall IEG development outcome ratings of IFC's XPSRs and World Bank ICRs were taken as a proxy for conducting economic analyses.

[38] The business model of IFC Advisory Services appears also more suited to venturing into countries with untested frameworks. In case of a failure of an IFC advisory project, IFC's balance sheet would not be affected (even though the success fee would not be earned), whereas in case of a failure of an IFC investment, IFC is exposed with the amount of the entire investment volume.

References

AICD. 2010. *Ghana's Infrastructure: A Continental Perspective, Africa Infrastructure Country Diagnostic*. Washington, DC: World Bank.

ESMAP (Energy Sector Management Assistance Program). 2005. *Ghana: Poverty and Social Impact Analysis of Electricity Tariffs*. Washington, DC: World Bank.

IEG (Independent Evaluation Group). 2012. *Improving Institutional Capability and Financial Viability to Sustain Transport: An Evaluation of World Bank Group Support Since 2002*. Washington, DC: World Bank.

———. 2013a. *Africa and Public Private Partnerships—A Cluster Review of IFC Investments and Advisory Services.* Washington, DC: World Bank.

———. 2013b. *Brazil Country Program Evaluation, FY 2004-11: Evaluation of the World Bank Group Program.* Washington, DC: World Bank.

———. 2013c. *Knowledge-Based Country Programs: An Evaluation of the World Bank Group Experience.* Washington, DC: World Bank.

IFC (International Finance Corporation). 2013. *Emerging Partnerships—Top 40 PPPs in Emerging Countries.* Washington, DC: World Bank.

Infrastructure Consortium for Africa. 2012. *Assessment of Project Preparation Facilities for Africa—A Diagnostic and Recommendations.* Cambridge Economic Policy Associates and Nodalis Conseil.

Ministry of Foreign Affairs of the Netherlands. 2013. *Public-Private Partnerships in Developing Countries—A Systematic Literature Review.* The Hague: Ministry of Foreign Affairs.

Palmer, Keith. 2013. "Making Private Sector Infrastructure Investment Happen in Africa." PowerPoint Presentation: http://www.infracoafrica.com/presentations.asp.

World Bank. 2013a. "Energizing Economic Growth in Ghana—Making the Power and Petroleum Sectors Rise to the Challenge." Energy Environment Review No. 79656, Washington, DC.

———. 2013b. *A Stronger, Connected Solutions World Bank Group.* Washington, DC: World Bank.

World Bank and WBI (World Bank Institute). 2013. "Implementing a Framework for Managing Fiscal Commitments from Public-Private Partnerships." Operational Note, Washington, DC.

5

Working as One World Bank Group

HIGHLIGHTS

- The World Bank Group's support to PPPs addresses issues along the entire delivery chain, which involves about 20 different entities within the Bank Group.

- World Bank Group internal coordination and sequencing of instruments is largely working well, but a more systematic country diagnostic for PPPs appears needed that can turn a corporate strategic intention into a country-driven PPP program.

- Among MDBs and donors, the World Bank Group has been acknowledged as a leader at the country level in advancing the PPP agenda—offering the most comprehensive "PPP solution package."

- Efforts to measure collaborative behavior, set out in the 2013 World Bank Group strategy, are a step toward collaboration, but additional incentives have to be built into the delivery chain for this to become effective.

- A dedicated PPP pipeline and project development facility is needed to close the upstream deal gap—one of the major challenges for the future. A Bank Group-wide policy on dealing with unsolicited proposals will need to complement these efforts.

The World Bank Group's support to PPPs addresses issues along the entire delivery chain, from upstream support for the enabling environment and pipeline development to downstream transactions and execution. Figure 5.1 maps the Bank Group's PPP portfolio against its organizational structure. This picture broadly reflects the division of labor intended by the relevant strategies, that is, the World Bank working with client governments on policy, capacity, and institutional issues upstream, and IFC and MIGA focusing on transactions. This mapping indicates, in principle, the split of labor, but tells little about actual behavior.

FIGURE 5.1 World Bank Group Entities Engaged in PPPs

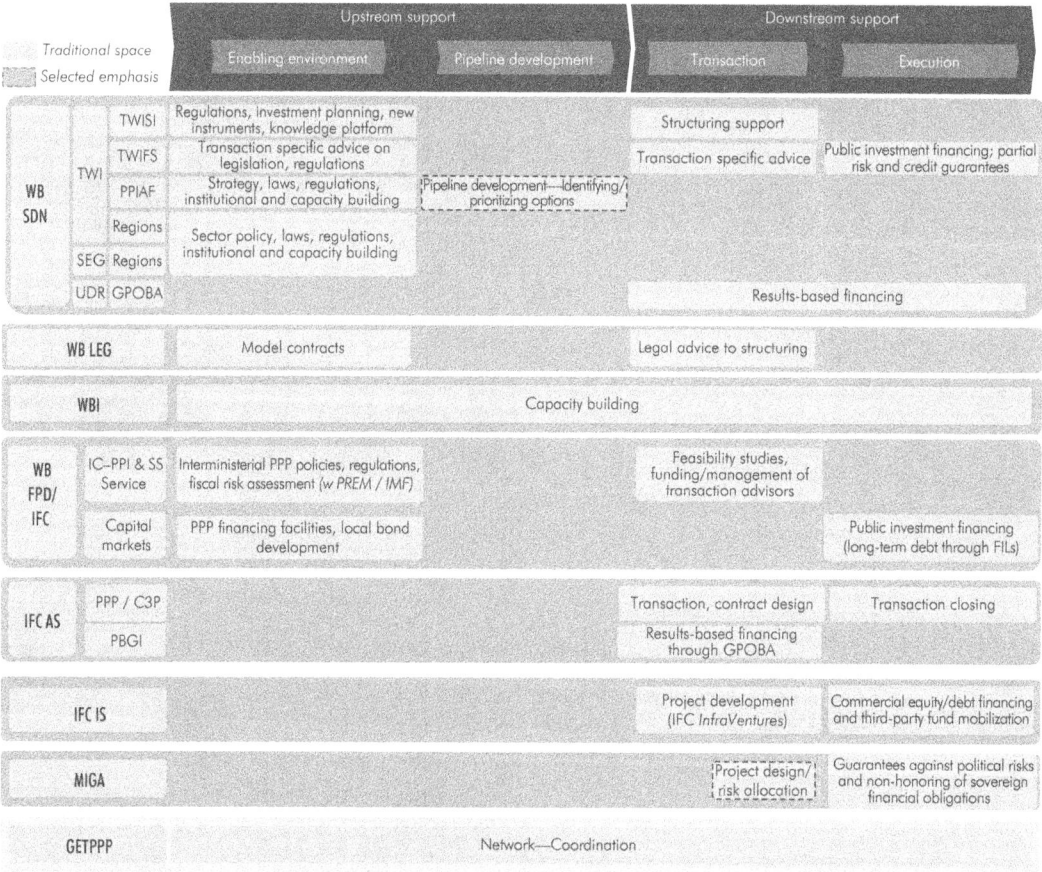

			Upstream support		Downstream support	
Traditional space / Selected emphasis			Enabling environment	Pipeline development	Transaction	Execution
WB SDN	TWI	TWISI	Regulations, investment planning, new instruments, knowledge platform		Structuring support	
		TWIFS	Transaction specific advice on legislation, regulations		Transaction specific advice	Public investment financing; partial risk and credit guarantees
		PPIAF	Strategy, laws, regulations, institutional and capacity building	Pipeline development—Identifying/ prioritizing options		
		Regions				
	SEG	Regions	Sector policy, laws, regulations, institutional and capacity building			
	UDR	GPOBA			Results-based financing	
WB LEG			Model contracts		Legal advice to structuring	
WBI			Capacity building			
WB FPD/ IFC	IC–PPI & SS Service		Interministerial PPP policies, regulations, fiscal risk assessment (w PREM / IMF)		Feasibility studies, funding/management of transaction advisors	
	Capital markets		PPP financing facilities, local bond development			Public investment financing (long-term debt through FILs)
IFC AS	PPP / C3P				Transaction, contract design	Transaction closing
	PBGI				Results-based financing through GPOBA	
IFC IS					Project development (IFC InfraVentures)	Commercial equity/debt financing and third-party fund mobilization
MIGA					Project design/ risk allocation	Guarantees against political risks and non-honoring of sovereign financial obligations
GETPPP			Network—Coordination			

SOURCE: IEG, based on World Bank 2012.

NOTE: AS = Advisory Services; C3P = IFC's Advisory Services in Public-Private Partnerships; FIL = Financial Intermediary loan; FPD = Financial and Private Sector Development; GETPPP = Global Expert Team PPPs; GPOBA = Global Partnership for Output Based Aid; IC–PPI & SS = Investment Climate – Private Participation in Infrastructure and Social Sector Adjustment; IS = Investment Services; LEG = World Bank Legal Department; PBGI = Performance-Based Grants Initiative; PPIAF = Public-Private Infrastructure Advisory Facility; PREM = Poverty Reduction and Economic Management; SDN = Sustainable Development Network; SEG = Sustainable Energy Department; TWI = Transport, Water, Information and Communications Technology; TWIFS = Financial Solutions Unit within TWI; TWISI = Infrastructure Policy Unit within TWI; UDR = Urban and Disaster Risk Management Department; WB = World Bank; WBI = World Bank Institute.

Collaboration across the Bank Group is of particular relevance to PPPs. Sequencing of upstream policy reform, assistance to pipeline development, project preparation and subsequent structuring and finance is essential, as shown in Chapters 2–4. When working along the PPP delivery chain, it is essential to transfer country-specific intelligence, for example, on sector reform aspects, in case one World Bank Group institution supports sector restructuring efforts and another plans to advise the government on structuring.

This chapter hence assesses the extent to which the various institutions have worked as "one World Bank Group." The analysis looks in particular for evidence that the various World Bank Group members have exploited their respective comparative advantage (given a country's need for them) and at synergy effects between upstream policy support and downstream transactions. Whereas the former need to necessarily be sector specific, care was taken that up- and downstream synergistic effects happened in the same sector and area of support. The assessment draws on evidence from the 40 country desk reviews with minimum World Bank Group PPP interventions (5) and insight from the 9 country case studies.

Leveraging of Synergies across One World Bank Group

The recently adopted World Bank Group strategy emphasizes the need to focus on working better as one World Bank Group. Strengthening the advantages of each agency will "contribute more to the group's value proposition by delivering on its mandates with respect to distinct client groups, reflecting its markets, products and competitors" (World Bank 2013). In fact, the Bank Group's unique position to provide support along the entire PPP cycle to both the public and private sector can be seen as one of the advantages over other bilateral agencies and other MDBs (see Chapter 6).

In about half of the countries reviewed (19 of 45) World Bank Group members leveraged their comparative advantage (Figure 5.2). In several of these cases either the World Bank or PPIAF entertained a policy dialogue with the respective country, which eventually resulted in a specific PPP where IFC provided transaction advice or finance. In a few cases, all three Bank Group entities were involved (see Box 5.1).

World Bank Group internal coordination and sequencing of instruments is largely working well, but a more explicit strategic role for PPPs may be required in LICs. IEG's nine in-depth country reviews provide confirmation. Joint CASs and Country Partnership Strategies generally set out relative responsibilities and strategies of the World Bank Group entities, which are well coordinated. Although it may sometimes be difficult to work exactly as set out in the CAS, the Bank Group entities seem to have used their tools in a complementary manner with little or no duplication.

FIGURE 5.2 Working as One World Bank Group—Evidence from Country Reviews

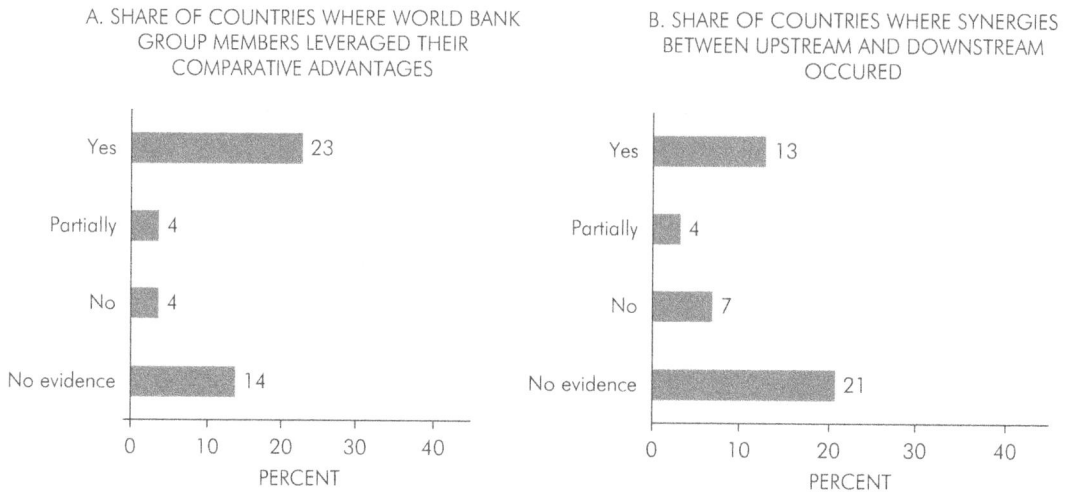

A. SHARE OF COUNTRIES WHERE WORLD BANK GROUP MEMBERS LEVERAGED THEIR COMPARATIVE ADVANTAGES

	PERCENT
Yes	23
Partially	4
No	4
No evidence	14

B. SHARE OF COUNTRIES WHERE SYNERGIES BETWEEN UPSTREAM AND DOWNSTREAM OCCURED

	PERCENT
Yes	13
Partially	4
No	7
No evidence	21

SOURCE: IEG.
NOTE: n=45.

There are several good examples of World Bank and IFC Advisory Services coordination, with the Bank working on upstream reform and IFC Advisory Services subsequently advising on transaction specific reform, for instance, in Brazil and Colombia, coordinating unbundling of rural power between the public and private sectors in the Philippines. In Guatemala, both IFC and MIGA PPP projects have built on upstream regulatory work undertaken by IBRD.

In several cases there was evidence of sequencing of upstream and downstream support. Results in 13 countries (of 45 reviewed) indicated effective sequencing between up- and downstream support; in 7 cases it did not happen. These results are sector specific, that is, they indicate that upstream policy support—for example, developing a regulatory framework—actually benefitted the sector, with downstream interventions following later. For examples, see Box 5.1.

The IEG cluster study of PPPs in Africa (IEG 2013) corroborates these synergies among World Bank policy or public expenditure management advice, sector reform efforts, and subsequent IFC investments. In the case of the *Vaalco Gabon Facility* in The Gabon, the World Bank had been providing support to the government in the form of loans and AAA to help the government design policies geared toward private sector growth. Following the reforms, IFC investments supported exploration activities by Vaalco, a junior oil and gas company, through loans and a reserve-based revolving credit facility. In Mozambique's Southern Africa Regional Gas investment, there was extensive World Bank support in areas like public expenditure management and privatization policies.

Cameroon—The World Bank and IFC coordinated efforts in the privatization of AES Sonel in early 2002 and later in 2006 for the 20-year concession agreement for distribution, transmission, and generation of electricity throughout Cameroon. The Kribi Gas Power Project is another example of IFC and IDA coordination: the project is a major infrastructure investment in Cameroon and would benefit from an IDA guarantee and IFC lending. The commercial bank lender group indicated that broad World Bank Group participation is also critical to mitigate the risks associated with the provision of long-term financing for a gas power project in Cameroon.

Kenya—PPIAF activities complemented some of the IFC and World Bank projects. For instance, the World Bank concession of the Northern Corridor was facilitated by a road concession study financed by PPIAF.

Lesotho—The replacement of QE-II Hospital is an example of how the resources of the World Bank Group were brought to bear to offer to the client the World Bank's public sector policy dialogue, coupled with IFC's advisory services, and to mobilize private sector resources for public ends.

Morocco—IFC Advisory Services and the World Bank are both involved in the development of the 500 megawatt Ouarzazate solar power plant through a PPP. IFC is the advisor of MASEN, the Moroccan Agency for Solar Energy, to provide, during the prequalification phase, general advice on design of the operation. The World Bank is assisting MASEN in financing its power purchasing agreement with the concessionaire company, by partially covering the incremental cost of Concentrated Solar Power over conventional technologies.

The Philippines—The MIGA/IFC joint collaboration in the financing of the North Luzon Expressway toll road demonstrated both deep and broad Bank Group support and boosted private investor confidence, which was at a low level after the financial crisis. After the Olangapo power system was pulled out of the Second Subic Bay Project (IBRD) because of political forces, IFC Advisory Services mounted a highly successful advisory effort to privatize the utility. PPIAF funds have been used by both the IBRD and IFC to fund specific studies, including drafting downstream documents. In the sectors concerned there have been no conflicts.

SOURCE: IEG ICR Reviews.

World Bank programs, especially those that are focused on governance in general and public expenditure management in particular, reduced the risk of underutilization of public revenue flows from extractive industry projects. In the case of GTI Dakar, IFC mitigated the credit risk of the state utility by taking backstop arrangements on large and well-paying customers and continued to work in parallel with the World Bank addressing sector and regulatory reforms.

Among its peer organizations, the World Bank Group has been acknowledged as a leader at the country level in advancing the respective PPP agenda, offering the most comprehensive "PPP solution package." The World Bank Group has had a broader role than the other development partners, covering both upstream and downstream activities, and is the acknowledged leader in terms of technical knowledge and innovation (see Chapter 6). Typically, other donors have provided upstream work (for example, the Inter-American Development Bank in Colombia) but have focused on public sector activities downstream, or alternatively they have worked on supporting downstream transactions (ADB in the Philippines and Agence Française de Développement Proparco in Vietnam and Senegal). On rare occasions PPIAF resources have been commissioned by other agencies (for example, ADB in the Philippines) to carry out upstream work, but generally such work has been undertaken by the Bank Group.

Some bilateral donors have provided resources for upstream advice and downstream project preparation, channeled through the Bank Group or other multilaterals, but they do not get involved directly (the U.K. Department for International Development and USAID in Ghana, AusAID in Vietnam and the Philippines), and others such as the Japan International Cooperation Agency have worked alongside the Bank Group (in Vietnam and the Philippines). Coordination has on the whole been satisfactory, with complementary roles adopted by agencies, but there have from time to time been differences in approaches. In China, ADB worked on regulatory reform in several sectors, and the World Bank Group supported national regulatory reform. Joint financing was undertaken in several projects, especially large ones, for example, a highway project in the Philippines.

Notwithstanding this, the Bank Group's overarching role in covering PPPs cannot be taken for granted. Run-of-the-mill transactions are increasingly being done without the need for World Bank assistance, and other agencies are getting involved in transaction advice, which was once the sole purview of IFC Advisory Services (as in the Philippines). The challenge for the Bank Group will be to focus on pioneering, innovative transactions.

There were also a few missed opportunities. The review identified also 4 cases (of in total 45 countries reviewed) with missed opportunities (Box 5.2). Evidence from the nine country cases studies indicated that in LICs, however, a more strategic response that explicitly defines

BOX 5.2 Missed Opportunities to Work as One World Bank Group

Nigeria—Infrastructure is an area where the Bank could have worked more closely with IFC to develop a shared approach to infrastructure development. Collaboration between the Bank and IFC has been limited largely to information sharing. The first Interim Strategy (2000) stated, "Joint Bank/IFC teams have been formed to undertake initial sector reviews in telecommunications, power, transport, and water." As these sector reviews are completed, a detailed agenda for sectoral reform and project support from the Bank on the public sector side will be defined, according to the Nigeria Country Assistance Evaluation (1998–2007). "If these groups were indeed formed, there is no evidence of any tangible products." In addition, both the Bank and IFC could have been more proactive by helping devise and implement tailor-made strategies for infrastructure privatization and offering a blend of Bank and IFC instruments to support privatization. Like the Bank, IFC also only recently placed an infrastructure specialist in the field.

Peru—There was limited leverage of the comparative advantages across Bank Group institutions. This is in part because PPIAF and Bank projects were not explicitly mentioned in the CASs. One Bank-PPIAF project was mentioned indirectly, which involved technical assistance to prepare the national ports law. Most of the IFC Investment Services projects (five of seven) were mentioned. With this PPP list it seems that the Bank Group did leverage its comparative advantages. However, it is worth noticing that the 2003–09 CPE says (IEG 2011, p. xviii), "Several areas stand out as examples of effective synergy between World Bank Group institutions."

Over the period, there was only one case of joint financial participation in a project among Bank Group institutions. However, engagement in several sectors reflected effective sequencing or complementarities among Bank Group instruments. For example, although IBRD helped establish appropriate regulatory environments and public oversight in the financial and extractive industry sectors in the 1990s, it was less actively engaged in these sectors over the review period. Instead, IFC took the lead by supporting private investment that helped further the Bank Group's objectives of helping stimulate growth; broadening participation in economic activities; and increasing attention to environment and social issues.

In another case, positive Bank Group synergy was seen between an IBRD project to formalize property ownership in urban areas and an IFC investment in a small and medium-sized bank that then increased its lending through use of the registered property as collateral. IFC's advisory services engagement in public sector capacity building at municipal levels reflected a supplemental, rather than duplicative, instrument available to the Bank Group in that the small initial scale of the interventions would likely have precluded IBRD engagement. From the CPE it is worth noting that within the Bank Group, the CASs reflected a relatively well-integrated Bank Group strategy, although there was less cooperation in its implementation.

continued on page 128

The two CASs produced by the Bank Group during the review period included constructive integration of IFC activities into a broader World Bank Group strategy. Although cooperation at the strategy development level was positive, less interaction and cooperation between the Bank and IFC at the operational level was apparent. Although the Bank and IFC are located in adjacent buildings in Lima, both IFC and Bank staff reported that they were often unaware of what projects the teams of the other institution working in the same sectors were undertaking. In some cases, such as IFC's engagement in municipal capacity development, closer Bank engagement might have helped enhance the program and its scaling up. In other cases, Bank staff reported concerns about the lack of IFC consultation with the Bank on proposed investments.

The lower degree of cooperation in implementation partly reflects differing organizational structures and incentives systems. In the Bank, the Country Management Unit is accountable for results achieved in the country, whereas in IFC, accountability for results is organized on regional and industry lines, implying that results may be achieved without the need to do business in any one particular country.

SOURCE: IEG.

roles for IFC and MIGA may be called for. In Ghana, although the preponderance of the effort has understandably been with IDA and PPIAF, a clearer role for the World Bank Group for assistance with specific PPPs could encourage broader Bank Group participation.

The shortfall in IFC Advisory Services leading to a financial transaction may also be viewed in the context of Bank Group-wide collaboration. The analysis of IFC Advisory Services in Chapter 4 revealed that more proactive dialogue with civil society stakeholders to build support and overcome political obstacles increased the probability of success. At the same time World Bank Group-wide collaboration made IFC Advisory Services transaction support more successful. It helped achieve political commitment and donor community consensus, accelerate policy and regulatory reform, and organize and coordinate among all the government institutions.

The fact that about half of IFC advisory services do not reach financial closure has to been seen in this context. This raises the question of whether the "hit rate" of IFC advisory service can be leveraged by more and closer Bank Group-wide collaboration. It may be unrealistic to expect that World Bank country teams have an existing reform program going on (with established networks) in all the sectors that IFC plans to advises on. However, forward strategic planning may increase the likelihood.

Going forward, working as "one World Bank Group" will become central. Accordingly, "collaboration across the group will be increased systematically, and planning and budgeting processes will be better coordinated at the corporate level. It will increase the number of joint projects, review its portfolio of products and services to improve synergies to eliminate overlaps and develop a metric for institutional collaboration" (World Bank 2013). In particular, the latter will—later on—allow the Bank Group to assess better the extent of actual group-wide collaboration. The intention to explore mechanisms to promote a stronger pipeline of joint infrastructure projects and the envisaged review of World Bank Group advisory services to governments (for example, transaction specific advice by World Bank through fee-based services and IFC's PPP Advisory Services) are essential for the PPP agenda; but most important, incentives must be in place for individual task managers and investment officers for them to collaborate.

Setting objectives and measuring collaborative behavior, as currently suggested by the strategy, sounds conceptually attractive, but will not increase collaboration per se. Task managers and investment officers will only collaborate if such collaboration adds value and allows them to achieve better results or at least the same results faster. Aligning practice areas through a "delivery lens" and integrating (including organizationally merging) currently separate units may be more effective than metrices that may be perceived as artificially superimposed.

The Case for PPP Country Diagnostics

How the World Bank Group engages in a specific country is currently decided on a case-by-case basis. Such a country-driven approach may be warranted because of the specific context and World Bank Group's engagement history; however, it can also be linked to recurrently identified challenges of turning the Bank Group's corporate PPP agenda into country-tailored programs.

The depth, width, and focus of the assessments of country parameters varied across the nine country case studies, making it difficult to compare the respective countries' PPP readiness with their peers. Knowing where countries stand with regard to their PPP readiness, however, could be useful in determining the most appropriate solution package, including who within the World Bank Group should take the lead, suggesting the adequate type of engagement and the most suitable instruments to be used. Stakeholder and government involvement exhibited also different degrees of thoroughness which, at times, led to inconsistent commitment by them. Valuable knowledge about a country's PPP readiness is currently stored at multiple locations. Retrieving Bank Group-commissioned reports that may be relevant to a country's PPP agenda then often relies on individuals, a process that can turn cumbersome because implementing a country's PPP agenda usually takes many years and task team leaders change over time. This deprives the Bank Group of the opportunity to build a knowledge platform on country-specific parameters as well as on lessons from its engagement.

Improving the focus of country programs through systematic country diagnostics will be particularly important for the PPP agenda. According to the 2013 strategy, "[W]hile today's country strategies are broadly aligned with the World Bank Group mission, it needs to provide clients with more coordinated and focused programs: activities and interventions need to be better prioritized according to their expected impact on the goals"; the Group needs to better reconcile country demands with strategic goals (World Bank 2013). This is particularly true for the PPP agenda, where the sequencing of policy reform work needs to be carefully synchronized with country parameters and further downstream work.

A country-level PPP diagnostic would assist in planning and implementing a one World Bank Group approach. Such a diagnostic could be useful in countries where at least a minimum prospect exists that a bankable pipeline of projects is likely to emerge. For cases where, for example, the countries' major challenges rest with rural roads and dysfunctional road funds for which PPPs will not offer a solution, engaging in a diagnostic process is, of course, not useful. Ideally, a PPP diagnostic forms an integral part of the Systematic Country Diagnostic currently under preparation—or at least they are linked to ensure integration in a broader country context.

To advance a PPP agenda it is important to recognize the need for a phased approach. Advising on dedicated PPP units in the absence of government commitment or instituting a complex regulatory regime in a country where institutions are prone to political interferences (which has stalled reform processes in several of the nine country case study countries) may not be effective; likewise, elaborating detailed fiduciary responsibilities for managing the PPP process may be of little use if key government officials lack a sound understanding of when to use PPPs strategically in their sectors. Figure 5.3 depicts a schematic framework that aims to identify the most critical constraints and opportunities to the PPP agenda, which will have to be supported by analytical methods and data. Such a diagnostic would allow the right mix of products and services along the various stages of a country's maturity to be determined as well as the appropriate entry point for the various Bank Group institutions, for example, for when IFC Advisory Services should start engaging in upfront stakeholder consultations and business development.

A PPP country diagnostic would have to consider country, sector, and project parameters. Country parameters—for example, government commitment or institutional readiness—form the foundation for any PPP framework. Next, sector parameters—for example, the robustness of the regulatory framework—are important, as they determine the financial viability of the sector—a crucial factor for private sector involvement. Then project parameters of commercial or technical feasibility of a specific PPP come into play. Often these three sets of parameters are tested in sequence, depending on the readiness of the country. Typically country

FIGURE 5.3 Systematic Country Diagnostic Framework for PPPs

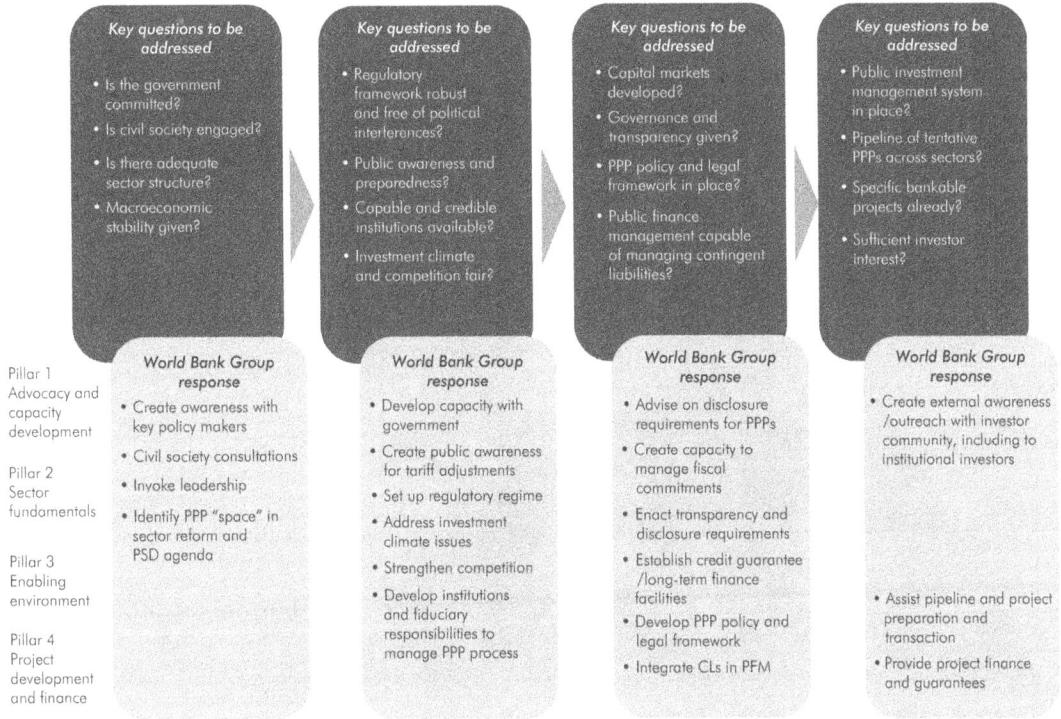

Key questions to be addressed	Key questions to be addressed	Key questions to be addressed	Key questions to be addressed
• Is the government committed? • Is civil society engaged? • Is there adequate sector structure? • Macroeconomic stability given?	• Regulatory framework robust and free of political interferences? • Public awareness and preparedness? • Capable and credible institutions available? • Investment climate and competition fair?	• Capital markets developed? • Governance and transparency given? • PPP policy and legal framework in place? • Public finance management capable of managing contingent liabilities?	• Public investment management system in place? • Pipeline of tentative PPPs across sectors? • Specific bankable projects already? • Sufficient investor interest?

	World Bank Group response	*World Bank Group response*	*World Bank Group response*	*World Bank Group response*
Pillar 1 Advocacy and capacity development	• Create awareness with key policy makers • Civil society consultations • Invoke leadership • Identify PPP "space" in sector reform and PSD agenda	• Develop capacity with government • Create public awareness for tariff adjustments • Set up regulatory regime • Address investment climate issues • Strengthen competition • Develop institutions and fiduciary responsibilities to manage PPP process	• Advise on disclosure requirements for PPPs • Create capacity to manage fiscal commitments • Enact transparency and disclosure requirements • Establish credit guarantee /long-term finance facilities • Develop PPP policy and legal framework • Integrate CLs in PFM	• Create external awareness /outreach with investor community, including to institutional investors • Assist pipeline and project preparation and transaction • Provide project finance and guarantees
Pillar 2 Sector fundamentals				
Pillar 3 Enabling environment				
Pillar 4 Project development and finance				

SOURCES: IEG; ADB 2012.
NOTE: CL = contingent liabilities; PFM = public financial management; PSD = public sector development.

parameters would be first, followed by sector parameters. Sector parameters would be assessed once country parameters are analyzed or in parallel, but before looking at project level parameters. Figure 5.4 delineates this hierarchy of country sector project parameters.

This framework could represent a platform for sharing knowledge as well as a guide for clarifying Bank Group-wide collaboration. For each stage of the assessment—and the corresponding country readiness—a specific expertise is required. For example, before transaction specialists start business development for specific deals, private sector development specialists could lead the diagnostic of the readiness of the country's public finance management and PPP institutional framework. Bank Group collaboration would benefit from clarifying which entity takes the lead at which stage.

Figure 5.4 describes the key requirements for each hierarchy level for the respective Bank Group entity involved, without indicating specific organizational labels. Eventually, Bank Group management would have to map these levels against the most suitable organizational entities emerging from the current ongoing restructuring. The indicated units could then take

FIGURE 5.4 Country–Sector–Project Parameters for PPPs

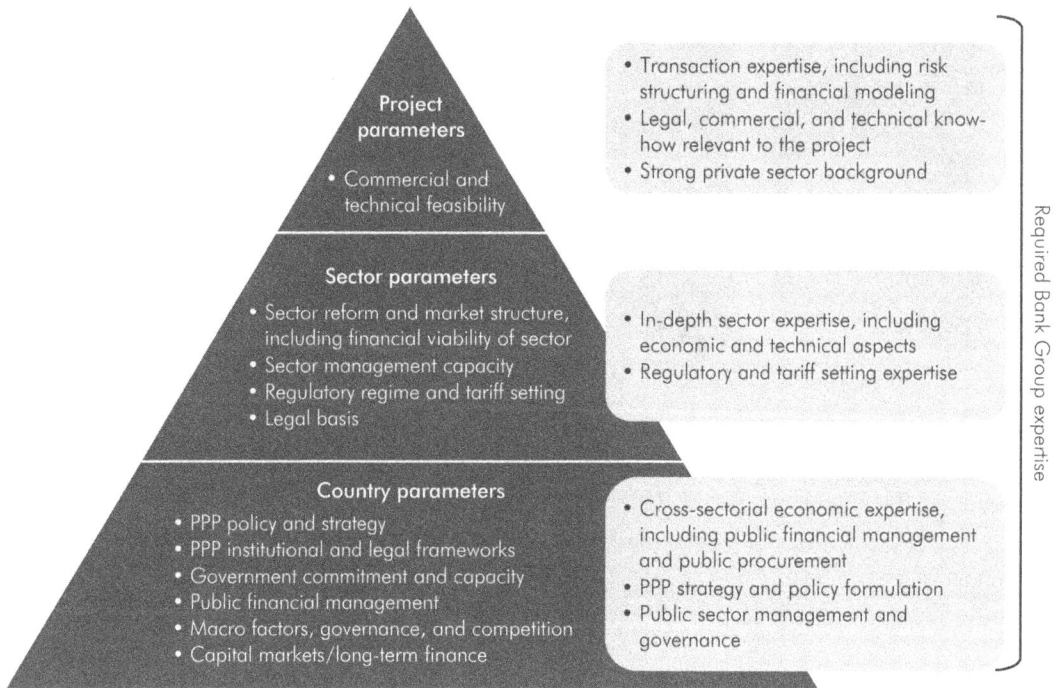

FIGURE 5.4 Country–Sector–Project Parameters for PPPs

Project parameters
- Commercial and technical feasibility

- Transaction expertise, including risk structuring and financial modeling
- Legal, commercial, and technical know-how relevant to the project
- Strong private sector background

Sector parameters
- Sector reform and market structure, including financial viability of sector
- Sector management capacity
- Regulatory regime and tariff setting
- Legal basis

- In-depth sector expertise, including economic and technical aspects
- Regulatory and tariff setting expertise

Country parameters
- PPP policy and strategy
- PPP institutional and legal frameworks
- Government commitment and capacity
- Public financial management
- Macro factors, governance, and competition
- Capital markets/long-term finance

- Cross-sectorial economic expertise, including public financial management and public procurement
- PPP strategy and policy formulation
- Public sector management and governance

Required Bank Group expertise

SOURCE: IEG.

the lead and function as a PPP champion on the Bank Group side, as a counterpart to the *country-level* PPP champion or unit.

In practical terms, this diagnostic can help determine who takes the lead in a more broad-based readiness assessment or a sector-specific analysis; eventually it can help determine the right time for IFC Advisory Services to start engaging in upfront stakeholder consultations and for IFC investments to launch into business development for specific PPP transactions, and ultimately help identify the point when commercial banks can serve the PPP sector adequately—the point at which the country can "graduate" from the World Bank Group's support.

A country diagnostic should place particular emphasis on advocacy, stakeholder consultation, and capacity building. The analysis of country strategies (see Chapter 2) revealed that political economy factors and questions of creating a broader PPP awareness were not systematically addressed in the 45 countries reviewed. At the same time, lack of awareness and government commitment and deficiencies in institutional capacity were the major obstacles for PPP success, as evidenced both in the portfolio review and country case studies. The emphasis on stakeholder assessment and on clarifying the Bank Group PPP response, mentioned earlier, are two key features of the suggested PPP country diagnostic that differentiates it from PPIAF's earlier efforts of preparing holistic Country Framework Reports (1999–2006).

Challenges and Opportunities for the Future

The current plan to institutionalize a PPP Cross-Cutting Solution Area offers a unique opportunity to strengthen the World Bank Group-wide PPP response. Although it is referred to in many conceptual and strategic notes, there is little guidance yet on how to implement a Group-wide PPP agenda or how to coordinate PPP solutions to support country teams (see Chapter 2). Despite this, the creation of a PPP Cross-Cutting Solution Area suggests the strategic importance being placed on this service delivery mechanism. Applying a consistent PPP diagnostic to tailor the Bank Group's response to countries—as outlined above—and managing a knowledge platform to ensure that evidence-based know-how on PPPs be accessible to internal and external policy makers and practitioners are areas that deserve increased attention. The PPP Cross-Cutting Solution Area could function as a host for most— if not all—of these activities and could facilitate coordination of the PPP agenda across the various entities involved.

The challenge will be to balance the roles of the PPP Cross-Cutting Solution Area and of the Global Practices. The ongoing change management process foresees the establishment of 14 Global Practices to manage the global technical expertise to deliver client solutions. PPPs matter for the work of several of these, including those related to water, transport, health, energy, or competitiveness. Furnishing the secretariat of the PPP Cross-Cutting Solution Area with sufficient authority to enable a consistent Bank Group-wide PPP response across these Global Practices and to draw on Bank Group-wide expert teams will be essential.

Another challenge for the future will be the development of bankable PPP projects. Generally, there is no lack of project opportunities or of finance (Palmer 2013). However, what seems to cause a gap of bankable PPP projects is the lack of capacity and skills. The lack of bankable PPP projects was found across all nine countries surveyed in this evaluation. Although in many countries tentative concepts for a PPP pipeline exist, governments have a hard time conducting solid prefeasibility studies to determine if these PPPs would be financially sound and under which conditions (and risk sharing arrangements) it would be advisable for them to go for a PPP solution.

A PPP Project Preparation Facility could help raise the needed funding. A concerted one World Bank Group approach is needed to close the upstream deal gap. The Bank Group has several tools in place to potentially address this issue, but traction is lacking to date. Figure 5.1 visualizes the various Bank Group entities engaged in the PPP agenda. Pipeline development, however, is underserved, a finding confirmed by the portfolio analysis in Chapters 3 and 4. *InfraVentures* was set up to help overcome the shortfall in bankable PPP projects in IDA countries, but to date it has not yet been able to take the bottlenecks out of pipeline development (see Chapter 4).

To close the upstream deal gap, the World Bank Group could consider raising funding for a facility dedicated to pipeline and project development. Such a facility could be overseen by the secretariat of the PPP Cross-Cutting Solution Area and work in partnership with the Bank Group's upstream and downstream work. IFC Advisory Services occasionally gets engaged in pipeline development, but as this sort of activity does not earn a success fee they would have to be funded through a mix of donor contributions and fees paid by the host government. Regardless of the design of the facility, close collaboration between IFC Advisory Services experts and World Bank sector experts will be essential. In parallel, IFC's investments—in partnership with MIGA—should intensify its business in emerging countries and to the extent feasible in nascent countries where the deal flow is less developed.

Unsolicited proposals often play a role in countries with an upstream deal gap. Rather than responding to an invitation to tender, unsolicited proposals are submitted by the private sector to undertake a PPP. Across the countries reviewed, unsolicited bids play an important role, in particular in countries where pipeline and project development are weak. For example, the government of Ghana faces unsolicited bids in the energy and transport sector. In Brazil unsolicited proposals are widespread across all sectors without having a formal framework to either reject or manage them. In Colombia, the newly approved PPP law covers unsolicited proposals for all (including non-traditional) PPP sectors, which is likely to trigger an increase in proposals.

Unsolicited proposals can mobilize private sector funds for project development but need to be handled in a transparent and competitive manner to benefit from the upside of them. However, countries need to have a framework in place to deal with them for various reasons: unsolicited bids (i) need to be linked to the public investment management system to ensure they address actual priorities; (ii) have to be handled in a transparent manner allowing competition; and (iii) have to follow a similar approval process as all other PPPs do, in particular when they involve fiscal commitments. Ensuring transparency and creating "competitive tension" is possible, for example, if the government or the winning bidder pay a "developer's fee," as is currently applied in Indonesia, or allowing for a Swiss challenge whereby an unsolicited approach is made open to a subsequent bidding process; if the party submitting the unsolicited bid is not successful, it has the option to match the winning bids, an approach currently used in the Philippines, Taiwan, and several states in India (WBI 2012).

To date, the Bank Group has not adopted a policy on how to address unsolicited proposals. In 2013, IFC advisory services issued guidelines on how to handle negotiated contracts for its PPP business line, expanding its product offerings; however, there is no Bank Group-wide practice yet. Ongoing Bank Group practice ranges from advising countries to reject unsolicited bids and solely rely on PPPs tendered to advising countries to designing a suitable framework for management them. Given their importance and the 2013 Bank Group strategy's emphasis on PPPs, there is a need to provide guidance on this issue to Bank Group staff engaged both in upstream as well as downstream work. The expanded product offering and resulting experience from IFC advisory services may offer useful lessons for the rest of the World Bank Group.

Working as one World Bank Group requires also watching out for interinstitutional operational conflicts of interest. In coordinating the range of financing instruments and services of the World Bank Group, it is essential that staff share information and experience and improve the quality of their advice and the investments/guarantees of their institutions. However, notwithstanding the potential benefits of improved coordination of services to clients, inter-institutional coordination and collaboration means that World Bank Group institutions face actual, potential, and/or perceived conflicts of interest in relation to their interrelated operational activities. In order to manage these conflicts of interest the World Bank Group system has evolved over time and the risks are currently managed by a dedicated interinstitutional mechanism (Box 5.3).

Conflicts of interest can occur between all Bank Group units that are engaged in the PPP agenda. Potential conflicts of interest across the World Bank Group can take on different types, that is, can occur between World Bank upstream policy advice, IFC advisory,

---

BOX 5.3 The World Bank Group's Mechanism to Manage Conflict of Interest

Currently the three World Bank Group institutions have a mechanism in place to identify and manage interinstitutional operational conflicts of interest. Responsibility for managing these conflicts rests with the respective Directors of the units of the institutions involved. The management structure includes a council, consisting of the three senior business people from MIGA, IFC, and the Bank, the three General Counsels, and the head of the Office of Ethics and Business Conduct. This council is ultimately responsible for Bank Group's approach in this area. In addition, each institution has a dedicated conflicts advisory function.

continued on page 136

FIGURE World Bank Group Conflict of Interest Structure

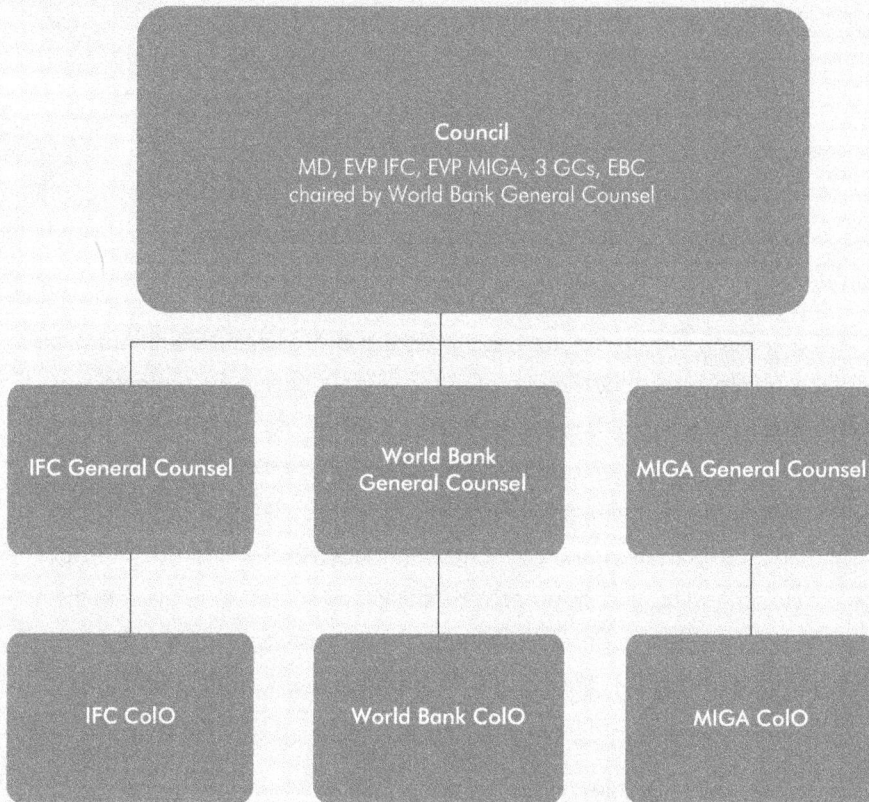

```
                        ┌─────────────────────────────┐
                        │          Council            │
                        │  MD, EVP IFC, EVP MIGA,      │
                        │       3 GCs, EBC             │
                        │  chaired by World Bank       │
                        │    General Counsel           │
                        └─────────────────────────────┘
                                     │
        ┌────────────────────────────┼────────────────────────────┐
        │                            │                            │
┌───────────────┐          ┌─────────────────┐          ┌─────────────────┐
│ IFC General   │          │  World Bank     │          │ MIGA General    │
│  Counsel      │          │ General Counsel │          │  Counsel        │
└───────────────┘          └─────────────────┘          └─────────────────┘
        │                            │                            │
┌───────────────┐          ┌─────────────────┐          ┌─────────────────┐
│   IFC ColO    │          │ World Bank ColO │          │   MIGA ColO     │
└───────────────┘          └─────────────────┘          └─────────────────┘
```

The council has published guidelines on conflict management. These set out the responsibilities, processes, and procedures for managing interinstitutional operational conflicts of interest between and among the different institutions of the World Bank Group. Where different World Bank Group units represent the interest of or have duties to different stakeholders, typical treatment would include identifying such conflicts; disclosure to the stakeholders; managing information flows to take account of confidentiality; and separate teams where required to appropriately represent the different interests. This management structure and process is complemented by training to staff.

SOURCE: World Bank Group Conflict of Interest Office.
NOTE: ColO = Conflict of Interest Office; EBC = Office of Ethics and Business Conduct; EVP = Executive Vice Presidency; MD = Managing Director.

IFC investment, and MIGA guarantees. For example, World Bank upstream advice on regulatory issues might be seen to be compromised to enhance the investment value of a subsequent IFC investment; but conflicts can also occur between two agencies engaged downstream. Table 5.1 summarizes the most important types of potential conflict of interest for a hypothetical PPP transaction.

The potential for conflict of interest is regularly identified through the tools and mechanisms of the Conflict of Interest Office(s) and the risks subsequently managed. According to the records of the Conflict of Interest Office, several cases were managed in the nine country case studies undertaken for this evaluation. In general, about 15 reported cases of potential conflict of interest are handled per year by the World Bank Group Conflict of Interest Office, most of which are in the infrastructure sector. In addition and more specifically to the potential of conflict of interest within IFC, about 20 referrals per year for potential conflict of interest cases have been brought to the attention of the IFC Conflict of Interest Office from the IFC PPP advisory staff.[1] Very few of these referrals ended up with an actual conflict of interest.

Going forward, the ongoing change management team needs to remain mindful of potential conflicts of interest issues in the PPP space. It is the Bank Group's strategic intention to work

TABLE 5.1 Examples of Potential Conflicts of Interest in a Typical PPP Transaction

Potential Conflict Between	Nature of Conflict
World Bank upstream work (technical assistance) and IFC advisory	World Bank's regulatory advice compromised to facilitate IFC investment
World Bank upstream work (technical assistance) and IFC investment	World Bank regulatory advice compromised to enhance IFC investment value
World Bank upstream work (technical assistance) and World Bank PRG/MIGA guarantee	Regulatory advice compromised to support World Bank PRG/MIGA guarantees
IFC Advisory and IFC Investment	Advisory is only trying to boost IFC investment value
World Bank/MIGA and IFC Investment	PRG compromised to support IFC investment
IFC advisory and World Bank PRG/MIGA	Transaction structure compromised to support PRG investments

SOURCE: World Bank Group Conflict of Interest Office.
NOTE: PRG = partial risk guarantee.

more closely along the entire PPP cycle, preparing tailor-made country solutions, supported by interdisciplinary teams, drawing on Bank Group resources. Though this is likely to improve the effectiveness of delivery, it may also "crystallize" or increase the risk of conflicts of interest as all players start working more closely. The change management team is therefore well advised to provide high priority to this issue when considering organizational adjustments. Subsequent regular reporting on how conflicts of interest are being managed in a transparent and visible manner will help create trust in the system.

Conclusion

Leveraging of the comparative advantages of the various World Bank Group institutions works quite well. In about half of the countries reviewed the World Bank Group members effectively coordinate and collaborate across policy reform aspects and PPP transactions, and in a few cases all three entities were involved. There is also evidence for proper sequencing of instruments across upstream and downstream support. Among its peer organizations, the World Bank Group has been acknowledged as offering the most comprehensive PPP solution package. However, there were also a few missed opportunities.

Working as one World Bank Group will become the norm, according to the 2013 strategy. The intention to explore mechanisms to promote a stronger pipeline of joint infrastructure projects and the envisaged review of World Bank Group advisory services to governments are essential for the PPP agenda; but most importantly, incentives must be in place for individual task managers and investment officers to collaborate. They will only collaborate if such collaboration adds value and allows them to achieve better results or at least the same results faster. Aligning practice areas through a "delivery lens" and integrating currently separate units may be more effective than any actions that may be perceived as being artificially superimposed.

Improving the focus of country programs through systematic country diagnostics will be particularly important for the PPP agenda. Country-level PPP diagnostics would assist planning and implementing a one World Bank Group approach. As any diagnostic is resources intense, it should be applied mainly to countries where at least a minimum prospect exists that a bankable pipeline of project will emerge. A PPP country diagnostic would have to consider country, sector, and project parameters as part of a phased approach and could represent a platform for sharing knowledge as well as clarify Bank Group-wide collaboration.

To this end, specific Bank Group entities should take the lead in this country-sector project diagnostic hierarchy. Advocacy and stakeholder consultation have thus far received too little attention and should therefore be emphasized. This diagnostic would facilitate assessing which role the various World Bank Group institutions should play given the country's level of maturity of handling PPPs. Thus, such an approach would help (i) ensure that the Bank Group institutions leverage their respective comparative advantages, (ii) tailor upstream support to country-level constraints, and (iii) determine who should take the lead in advancing the country's PPP agenda.

A concerted one World Bank Group approach is also needed to close the upstream deal gap—one of the major challenges for the future. Lack of funding and capacity causes a gap of bankable PPP projects across client countries. To close this gap, a dedicated PPP pipeline and project development facility would greatly help, this being an initiative that would demand a concerted effort by IFC, the World Bank, and MIGA.

Working as one World Bank Group also requires watching out for conflicts of interest. Going forward, as the restructuring process develops concepts for organizational adjustments to the various Bank Group PPP stakeholders, management is well advised to regularly consult with the World Bank Group conflict of interest specialists.

Given the importance of unsolicited bids, there is a need for a Bank Group-wide policy on how to handle them best. Unsolicited proposals often play a role in countries with an upstream deal gap. To benefit from the upside of unsolicited proposals, that is, funding of project preparation and innovation, countries need to have a framework in place to deal with them. Guidance to Bank Group staff engaged in both upstream as well as downstream work will be crucial going forward.

Note

[1] There are about 30 IFC PPP advisory mandates per year, but multiple referrals may be made per PPP project.

References

ADB (Asian Development Bank). 2012 *Public-Private Partnerships Operational Plan 2012-2020*. Manila: Asian Development Bank.

IEG (Independent Evaluation Group). 2011. *Assessing IFC's Poverty Focus and Results*. Washington, DC: World Bank.

———. 2013. *Africa and Public Private Partnerships—A Cluster Review of IFC Investments and Advisory Services*. Washington, DC: World Bank.

Palmer, Keith. 2013. "Making Private Sector Infrastructure Investment Happen in Africa." PowerPoint Presentation: http://www.infracoafrica.com/presentations.asp.

WBI (World Bank Institute). 2012. *Public-Private Partnerships Reference Guide*, Version 1.0. Washington, DC: World Bank Institute and Public Private Infrastructure Advisory Facility.

World Bank. 2012. "PPP Strategy for the FDP Network." Presentation, Washington, DC.

———. 2013. *A Stronger, Connected Solutions World Bank Group*. Washington, DC: World Bank.

6

The Experience of Other Multilateral Development Banks with Public-Private Partnerships

HIGHLIGHTS

• For most MDBs, PPPs are of great strategic relevance and several feature PPPs explicitly either in stand-alone strategy documents or as an integral part of sectoral/corporate strategies.

• Despite the strategic relevance of PPPs, it is difficult to judge the magnitude of support that PPPs have received by all MDBs—because of the lack of a consistent PPP definition or a system capturing the share of operational activities devoted to PPPs.

• Across the MDBs, three (ADB, AfDB, and the IDB) have PPP approaches that recognize the importance of upstream as well as downstream support, with the World Bank Group likely the group with the widest and deepest PPP offering.

• With regard to implementing these strategic plans, some MDBs have come up with specific roadmaps and dedicated matrix management structures.

• The interdependency of PPP success and an enabling environment emerge as common features for success.

• To improve access to finance, several MDBs are contemplating project financing facilities to catalyze financing for PPPs.

The World Bank Group is not alone in its efforts to promulgate the smart use of PPPs—all MDBs have work programs on PPPs as well, many of which are in World Bank Group client countries. This analysis benchmarks the strategic relevance of PPPs across MDBs, the nature of their PPP support, organizational and managerial solutions they use to deliver their respective PPPs, and their experience with implementing PPPs—which issues emerged and which lessons the World Bank Group can use. The analysis encompasses work by the ADB, the African Development Bank (AfDB), the Inter-American Development Bank (IDB), the European Bank for Reconstruction and Development (EBRD), and the European Investment Bank (EIB).

Asian Development Bank

PPPs have been an increasingly important element of the infrastructure support of the ADB over the last decade, but implementation has not been straightforward. During the period 1998–2004 ADB substantially increased the number and value of approved projects with intended PPPs. This number increased from six projects valued at nearly $0.4 billion in 1998 to 18 projects valued at $2.9 billion in 2008. However, not all these loans resulted in PPPs: there was on average one public sector project with an actual PPP component between 1998 and 2006, whereas in 2007 and 2008 there were four such projects each year.

Over the entire 1998–2008 period, 137 public sector loans were seen to have PPP elements amounting to $20 billion, which was roughly 20 percent of public sector loans. Ninety-three of these loans envisaged investment components that were PPPs (the rest had technical assistance components), but only 15 actually materialized. Several reasons accounted for this attrition, related to the projects (such as delayed compliance changes in design and financial and economic risks), public partners (lack of clear laws and policies, lack of institutional and financial capacity and lack of standard computer bidding procedures among others), and private partners (availability of interested private sector partners reluctance the private sector to assume risks and financial capacity). During the same period, there were 37 private sector projects with PPPs, amounting to $3 billion, again about 20 percent of private sector lending.

These earlier experiences with PPPs also indicated weaknesses in sustainability and economic impact of PPPs. In 2009 ADB's Independent Evaluation Department issued a Special Evaluation Study on PPPs concluding that although ADB's interventions were relevant to country strategies and effective in that they achieved intended outcomes, sustainability had been rated as less likely and economic impact and financial additionality were modest. Key recommendations of the report were (i) stronger linkages between PPP support and other ADB sector operations; (ii) improved assistance for new PPP modalities and related capacity development; and (iii) greater involvement in the transport and water sectors.

As of 2012, ADB had adopted a PPP operational plan and anchored its PPP agenda in its long-term Strategy 2020. Strategy 2020 identified private sector development and private sector operations as drivers of change in Asia and the Pacific, and PPPs are seen as an important instrument in this regard. The operational plan is based on four pillars: (i) advocacy and capacity development, (ii) enabling environment, (iii) project development, and (iv) project financing, and it sets out accountabilities for each pillar. It also has guidelines for the regional departments and Private Sector Operations Department to work together. PPPs have a formal definition; risks are identified in detail; and techniques for appraisal, value for money analysis, and monitoring are set out. Plans are also articulated for staffing requirements and staff awareness and training, and a PPP Community of Practice (CoP) has been established. The CoP will contribute to knowledge management and staff capacity development and review lessons from successful (and failed) transactions and share with staff.

Organizationally, a matrix structure is being set up for governance of PPPs, as called for under the operational plan. The goal is to integrate PPP activities across the institution. Responsibilities for planning (both from the Country Partnership Strategies and business plan perspectives), implementation, and monitoring have been defined across the regional departments, the Private Sector Operations Department, the community of practice, budgeting, evaluation, and other support areas. The aim is to be more strategic in PPP selection by carefully screening for PPP options early in the CPS cycle and deciding how it will be allocated between private and public financing, which in turn defines the organizational accountability for its preparation and implementation (regional department and/or operations department).

The four pillars of the organizational plan also help define the PPP instruments that ADB will offer. ADB's support to PPPs is somewhat narrower than the World Bank Group's, as it does not offer fee-based transaction advisory similar to IFC Advisory Services or PRI as MIGA does. ADB is currently working to strengthen its advisory capacity, including possibly some fee-based activity, although it appears unlikely it will extend to contracted transaction advice. One factor to note is that the operations department (the wing of ADB equivalent to IFC Investment Services) does more corporate loans than limited recourse loans tied to specific projects, as many international banks have pulled out of infrastructure lending, and corporate loans are more straightforward when dealing with domestic partners. The operational plan recognizes the need for project development facilities to spur project preparation for PPPs and guidelines for establishing such facilities at the country level are included therein. In addition, ADB is now exploring the possibility of setting up a regional Project Development Fund.

Since 2008 ADB has worked closely with WBI on capacity building in PPPs. ADB was also a partner in the preparation of the PPP reference guide (done by PPIAF with input from the World Bank, ADB, and IDB). It co-authored a flagship report with IDB and has worked on transactions together with the World Bank Group and the EBRD. It has cooperated with IFC Advisory Services on transaction advice (an appendix of the operational plan is devoted to the advisory services of IFC), although there can be some instances where the approach for the two entities differ.

Overall, ADB has taken the results of a 2009 evaluation to heart and rebuilt its processes and framework for PPPs on an institution-wide basis. In particular, it has defined PPPs as a process, constituted a CoP for it, and created a system of identifying potential operations early in the country strategy formulation process that also facilitates cooperation between the private and public sector arms of the institution. It is also looking at the possibility of creating a subregional project development facility to speed development of PPPs in the Association of Southeast Asian Nation countries.

European Bank for Reconstruction and Development

EBRD's mandate implicitly encourages PPPs support and—since its inception in the early 1990s—it has also been active in supporting PPPs. EBRD has a mandate to encourage economic and political transition in the former Soviet Union countries and the Eastern Bloc satellites through the development of market economies. Since the beginning of its operations in 1991, EBRD has been involved in creating the legal environment for private investment in its countries of operation, including concession laws. EBRD considers PPPs and concessions a powerful and efficient mechanism for the delivery of public services.

In 2001 EBRD adopted a concession policy, which describes its approach to selecting and approving concession-based projects. Some of the key requirements that this policy articulates are competitive procedures, fairness of contracts, and effective and balanced risk sharing between the public and private sectors.

Organizationally, EBRD's support for PPPs comes from primarily the Infrastructure Business Group, which consists of two departments, one working at the national level, primarily transport, and the other at the municipal level (municipal and environmental infrastructure – MEI). Transport infrastructure includes roads, ports, national railways, airports and logistics. MEI provides support for were urban transport, water and sewerage, district heating and solid waste management. EBRD has been involved in financing PPPs in the transport sector since 1993 and in MEI since 1996. Since 2002 (the start of the evaluation period of this study) EBRD has financed 19 private projects in the MEI sector, accounting for 25 percent of total EBRD MEI commitments, although some of these may not have been PPPs. In the transport sector, EBRD has financed a similar number of PPPs (12) since 2002, including several controversial PPPs. EBRD is also involved in the energy sector but has supported only two PPPs.

EBRD supports PPPs mainly through finance, with transaction advice or other technical assistance work largely absent—at least until recently. In EBRD's approach, country strategies are vehicles for transactions; a focus on project finance and World Bank-type AAA activities is generally absent. Policy dialogue is thus incidental to the transaction, and as such is generally quite narrow. Although there are no prior actions required, reforms that are necessary or desirable (such as changes in law) are added to the transaction. EBRD also recognizes that because the transactions are relatively small, seeking ambitious reforms through transactions is not realistic.

For the same reason, fiscal space issues are not evaluated as part of the transaction—the EBRD mission is more to change the nature of the sector than to look at PPPs as an instrument for fiscal savings. However, through its Legal Transition Programme, EBRD has benchmarked national concession legislation against international best practices and examined how these laws actually work. In addition, it has provided advisory services to several governments in their efforts to upgrade national PPP legislative and regulatory regimes.

Going forward, EBRD intends to broaden and deepen its technical assistance work, which could increase support to countries to reform or improve enabling environment for PPPs, but this will need to be balanced against its transaction-driven approach. EBRD does not have a specific PPP plan or roadmap, as its business is intrinsically demand driven.

EBRD works closely with the European Union (EU) and, at times, with IFC. EBRD has a close relationship with the EU, with funds from the latter sometimes being used in the context of financing transaction or to fund feasibility studies. EBRD also has worked with IFC in several instances to provide financing to projects, but none of them relates to PPPs.

Past experience with PPPs has been uneven with lack of demand for PPPs in the Europe and Central Asia Region. EBRD assessed 14 PPP projects in 2008 that it had financed in power and energy, municipal infrastructure, and transport over the previous decade and evaluated its achievement in attracting and maintaining private sector involvement and ensuring legal protection of the private partner and commitment of the public agency. The evaluation concluded that EBRD has had uneven success in PPP projects. EBRD's evaluation department is undertaking an assessment of PPP transactions; results of the study were expected in December 2013.

EBRD's experience is that reform at the municipal level is limited, and consequently there is not much scope for demand-driven transactions. Moreover, many municipalities continue to be driven by Soviet-era priorities and actions to make projects financially attractive to private sector participants (for example, increasing tariffs) are not palatable. The latest EIU Infrascope in 2013) also indicates severe shortages with government capacity and processes in EBRD's client countries.

Lessons from one PPP study concluded that the diversity of law, enabling environment, and public policy objectives among countries make it hard to simply transplant approaches between countries. EBRD commissioned a study to look at best practices for regional and fiscal policies and in particular the experience of Australia, Hungary, the Netherlands, Portugal, and the United Kingdom in contrast to Croatia, the Czech Republic, and Romania. Although the enabling environment was better developed, there was greater budgetary discipline, and the link between the local and national governing entities was better spelled out in the more advanced economies. The study concluded that each country used PPPs to advance its public policy and local objectives, and it was difficult to make a judgment that one system was better than another.

EBRD is perhaps unique among the MDBs on the extent to which downstream transactions figure in its support of PPPs. On the one hand, this is simpler and makes for focused, transaction-oriented design and implementation, but on the other hand, as some of its projects have demonstrated, rigorous planning in terms of cost-benefit, fiscal exposure, and well-understood roles for the public and private sector are important success factors for robust PPPs (and demonstrate ownership of the PPP process in the host government).

Inter-American Development Bank

The ninth of capital increase of the IDB ($70 billion, the largest in its history), completed in 2010, set a strategic goal of development through private sector strategies, including PPPs. The IDB-9 framework increased the limit of non-sovereign guaranteed (NSG) operations to 20 percent (from 10 percent) on an interim basis until formal new limits could be put in place; it asked that guidelines for NSG lending to public, municipal, and semipublic institutions be reviewed to facilitate PPPs and to foster joint ventures. However, although the IDB has taken most of the formal steps required under the capital increase (private sector development strategy, business plan for NSGs), a 2012 independent evaluation noted that the organization still lacked a workable roadmap. In particular, some fundamental questions—such as how to best align private and public-sector interests and how its comparative advantages could be used to maximize how the benefits of more open and competent markets—remained unanswered.

Organizationally, the IDB handles PPPs primarily through two units: its private sector infrastructure unit and its public sector infrastructure unit. The latter works on upstream interventions and provides some downstream public sector support; the former is responsible for supporting the private sector. In addition to upstream support, the public sector unit can also provide, through several project development facilities, support for project preparation. Project preparation funding for is provided either for non-reimbursable technical assistance or for project preparation with contingent recovery to the sponsors (if the IDB eventually participates, there is no recovery).

Apart from these two units, where most of the IDB's PPP work is carried out, there are two other entities that together make up the IDB group. The Multilateral Investment Fund—a multidonor trust fund—provides assistance on upstream regulatory framework and capacity development, including for design, execution, and management of PPPs. This Fund is funded by 39 donors, comprising IDB borrowers and others. It was the counterpart in IDB that worked on the EIU Infrascope on PPPs in Latin America. Its model remains unique among MDBs in its ability to provide a mix of grants, debt, and equity targeted at very-early-stage enterprise development, often in the poorest populations, but is relatively small (annual commitments of about $100 million). To complete the picture the Inter-American Investment Corporation is also a part of the IDB group and provides financing for small and medium enterprises (annual operations about $300 million).

There is no formal PPP management framework for the IDB group, and coordination is informal. Much of the sectoral expertise is located in the public sector infrastructure unit, which supports projects being done through the private sector unit. In addition, there are biweekly meetings between the Multilateral Investment Fund and the public sector unit. However, there is considerable overlap and lack of coordination among the units that are involved in PPPs and the private sector windows. Currently IDB management is considering a reorganization of the units involved in private sector development—the options appear to be a "merge out" model that separates private sector operations from public sector operations more formally but bring all the windows together, or alternatively a "merge in" model that binds them all together in one organization.

Although there is no formal classification of PPPs, roughly 20 percent of IDBs' $12 billion in 2012 lending went to PPPs. Mostly all of the public sector lending ($1.5 billion) was in PPPs and another $600–700 million of lending was devoted to PPPs downstream. For large projects, both public and private sector units provide financing, as was done recently for the $4billion San Paulo beltway, in which the IDB provided $500 million shared roughly equally between the units.

IDB's lending instruments relevant to PPPs are primarily investment loans, sometimes complemented by B-loans. Reform activities are sometimes carried out under policy-based loans. Performance-based instruments are in theory available, but have not been utilized. Although public sector guarantees are authorized in the IDB's Articles, there have been only two instances to date: in Brazil and Guyana. More recently a proposal for contingent lending was introduced, but this was linked to natural disasters and financial shocks rather than to guarantee public sector risks. Finally, equity instruments are not utilized the IDB, and it has been suggested that they should be introduced.

Upstream work carried out by IDB (within the sovereign lending group, the Multilateral Investment Fund, and Inter-American Investment Corporation) is focused on financial markets, development of firms, small and medium enterprises, and sector reform at national and state levels. Notably, a significant portion of this lending was to financial markets, reflecting the importance of developing domestic finance in the primarily middle-income client base of the IDB. IDB also encourages peer learning between its client countries through frequent seminars and meetings. It has also, in this context, partnered with the ADB, recognizing the potential for learning between the MICs of Latin America and Asia. Downstream participation in projects is primarily by in the form of loans, mostly NSG. Although the private sector unit is involved in both upstream and downstream work, conflicts have not been identified in the 2012 evaluation report.

One striking parameter for the IDB is that it is primarily focused on MICs, where domestic and foreign sources of capital are generally available. For perspective, IFC and IDA work in most of the of the world's approximately 65 countries with per capita incomes below $1,205; IDB's regional focus means that Haiti and Nicaragua are the only client countries to fall below this threshold. Accordingly, its greatest leverage for PPPs would be to work on issues that will catalyze finance, rather than provide finance itself, and thus work on capital markets (as it is doing) and upstream support for institutional and regulatory reform would seem to be the most important.

African Development Bank

PPPs are an integral part of the AfDB's Private Sector Development Strategy 2013–17, engaging the bank both upstream and downstream. This new strategy calls on the AfDB to support initiatives that improve the institutional and operational frameworks for PPPs; including strengthening the analytical capacity for their selection, evaluation and monitoring, as well as transaction-level project preparation. It foresees the identification and preparation of integrated or complementary sovereign and nonsovereign operations, including PPP opportunities in collaboration with sector departments.

The importance of infrastructure for Africa is widely recognized: infrastructure has been identified as a key priority under the African Union's Strategic Plan for 2009–12, and the Programme for Infrastructure Development in Africa was approved by the African heads of state in January 2012, calling for new models of partnership among business, government, and donors to implement the 51 Priority Action Plan infrastructure projects already identified.

Private sector operations of the AfDB have averaged about 18–20 percent of overall lending in the past few years, amounting to about $1.1 billion in 2012. Of this, about $75 million was via the private sector window. Only some of these operations were PPPs. There were several projects in water supply and sanitation energy and transport that have been completed over the past several years. PPPs in the energy sector include geothermal, hydro, and wind power generation. In transport, PPP projects include toll roads, railways, airports, container terminals, and ports, and in the water sector projects have been for both water supply and wastewater treatment. Instruments provided by AfDB in support of PPPs include investment loans, private sector loans and equity, and partial risk guarantees. In addition, AfDB has provided technical advice for management contracts (in the water sector) and advisory services for some transactions.

Organizationally, several departments have responsibilities for PPPs but there is no focal point. The line departments that support infrastructure (energy, water, transport) work both upstream and downstream on PPPs. The Private Sector Operations Department works on private sector development, as well as equity and loan participations directly with the private sector. The Governance, Finance, and Economic Management Department works on upstream public sector management, including accounting for financial exposure. The Regional Integration and Trade Department acts as the secretariat for the Infrastructure Consortium of Africa, as well as being the point of contact with other Africa-based institutions, such as the United Nations Economic Commission of Africa and the African Union and their infrastructure units. To date, most of the PPP operations have emerged from the operations department.

AfDB proposes developing project financing facilities to support PPPs for infrastructure in Africa. In July 2013, AfDB management presented to its board the concept note for the Africa 50 fund (named for the $50 billion infrastructure gap the continent faces). The Africa 50 fund is a response to requests from the African heads of state to create a mechanism to finance critical infrastructure. It is envisaged that the fund will have two components: project development and project finance. It is to be financed with $10 billion in equity and $40 billion in lending, and the initial aim is to raise $3 billion in equity.

Although AfDB's activity has only recently begun to pick up, it is viewed by African nations and the donor community as a focal point for infrastructure financing on the continent. Accordingly, it has become very involved in addressing the issue of the critical infrastructure needs in Africa and devising approaches to catalyze finance.

European Investment Bank

The EIB, owned by the 28 members of the EU, is the biggest project finance lender in the world. EIB support for PPPs is derived from the significant and increasing use of this approach in its member countries. It structures its own participation in a way that optimizes the ability of the public sector to meet EU public policy objectives. As is to be expected, roughly 90 percent of its activities are undertaken within the EU, and the remaining 10 percent are distributed among countries that are parties to framework agreements in several geographical areas. These are the ACP countries (Africa, Caribbean, and Pacific), the Maghreb, Asia and Latin America, Enlargement countries, EU neighbors, and central Asia. The EIB also hosts the European PPP Expertise Center, a knowledge and advisory services partnership of its member countries to compile and share PPP practices primarily within the EU.

EIB has provided financing to a high number of PPPs, mainly in transport and in the EU's poorer countries. The EIB supported 160 PPP projects in 18 countries in the EU (and Turkey), amounting to over €35 billion in the period 1990–2012. While the United Kingdom accounted for 28 percent, EIB concentrates its efforts on poorer member states; in 2005, 93 percent of its signed loans were granted within the enlarged EU, with a large part benefiting from guarantees from member states or public institutions. Transport projects accounted for the majority of projects, with 80 percent of total by investment volume. Though the bulk of EIB's PPP activity is in the EU member countries, the bank also works outside the EU.

EIB's definition of PPPs is broad. The EU and the EIB count private construction of public facilities as PPPs (for example, build-transfer of hospitals)—and these are not always consistent, so direct comparisons of volumes with other institutions must be done cautiously.

EIB is very attentive to credit tests and is known for its conservative approach to the quality of projects. The EIB's operating guidelines require that the maximum at-risk capital per transaction is €300 million; amounts over that need to be guaranteed, usually by an export credit agency or bank. The guidelines also require that its financing is to be used solely for greenfield (that is, new) investments. Even when the overall project involves rehabilitation, the component of the project financed by the EIB must be new and additional. It also has strict eligibility criteria—for example, defense or correctional facilities are ineligible. PPPs financed by the EIB are for project finance and overwhelmingly for senior debt. There are instances where EIB has funded mezzanine finance, and it can also finance equity through equity funds. The EIB can also provide guarantees to other senior debt providers, but this is infrequent. Priority is accorded to projects with European significance, such as trans-European networks.

In non-EU member countries, the EIB provides advisory services. The European PPP Expertise Centre (EPEC) has extended advisory services and project preparation resources beyond its EU membership. Currently the European PPP Expertise Center is working in five North African/ Middle East countries to provide peer learning similar to its activities in the EU (such as closed door public sector only groups to encourage information sharing and joint learning); it also supports a couple of fairly modest project preparation facilities—one in conjunction with IFC and the Islamic Development Bank, and another in conjunction with the EBRD and KfW. In the past, a similar peer learning activity was also supported in the Southern Africa Development Community countries, but this has ended. Although the European PPP Expertise Center has received requests for continuation of that program, the focus currently is on Europe. It is unlikely that any programs will be expanded or new ones initiated in the foreseeable future.

The EIB also directly funds PPP projects in several developing countries, mostly in the African, Caribbean, and Pacific area. These are primarily in the energy sector (Uganda, Cape Verde, and Cameroon) but also include other sectors, such as transport and agribusiness. In other regions there has been some activity (for example, a wind farm in Jordan), but these are not systematically classified. Eight projects amounting to roughly €2.5 billion were supported by the EIB between 2004 and 2012, with its own contribution totaling €410 million. Six were energy projects in Africa and the other two were transport projects in the Caribbean.

The EIB, in conjunction with the European Community, has recently introduced a new pilot to broaden sources of finance in anticipation of the huge investment needs in infrastructure in its member countries through 2020. The Project Bond Initiative aims to attract institutional investors to the capital market financing of projects by enhancing the credit quality of project bonds issued by private companies. Under the Initiative, the EIB (with grant cofinancing from the European Community) will provide eligible infrastructure projects with credit enhancement in the form of a subordinated instrument—either a loan or contingent facility—to support senior project bonds issued by the project company, in order to improve their credit rating.

The first operation funded by the pilot is currently being structured, and the plan is to integrate the PBI into the EU's multiannual financing framework 2014–20. This initiative, though obviously not directly relevant to the World Bank or its client countries, is not dissimilar to similar initiatives being launched by the ADB and the AfDB to create subregional project development facilities to jump-start early project preparation and provide options for credit enhancement to make projects more bankable. The fact that the EIB and EU are embarking on this initiative against the backdrop of highly developed capital markets in Europe underscores the importance for such financing facilities to catalyze project finance.

Conclusions

Although each of the MDBs approaches PPPs in ways best suited to its client countries and their institutional objectives, some common themes emerge. For most MDBs, PPPs are of great relevance, and several feature PPPs explicitly either in stand-alone strategy documents or as integral part of sectoral/corporate strategies. Despite the strategic relevance of PPPs, it is difficult to judge the magnitude of support that PPPs have received collectively by MDBs—because of the lack of a consistent PPP definition and system to capture the share of operational activities devoted to PPPs.

With regard to implementing these strategic plans, some have come up with specific roadmaps and matrix management structures. In particular, the ADB undertook an evaluation of PPPs that has triggered a rethinking of the institution's approach to PPPs and has moved to make the process more strategic and less opportunistic. Its operational plan for PPPs turns strategy in implementation more readily. The four pillars of its operational plan also help define the PPP instruments that ADB will offer.

Similarly, the AfDB developed an operational framework for PPPs in conjunction with its private sector development strategy, where PPPs figure prominently. At the same time, several of the other MDBs are currently executing or are planning evaluations of PPPs. It will be instructive to see how the different institutions learn from each other.

Across the MDBs, three (ADB, AfDB, and the IDB) have PPP approaches that recognize the importance of upstream as well as downstream support. This contrasts with the approach by EBRD, which focuses mostly on downstream transactions. The EIB is different again in that the bulk of its transactions are in the EU, which has fairly well-developed institutional frameworks and thus focuses on finance and stimulating peer learning between its member countries. Compared to its peers, the World Bank Group offers the widest and deepest set of services and products, a conclusion corroborated by IEG's nine country missions.

Organizationally, a best practice for managing PPPs has yet to emerge. MDBs take different approaches to delivering their PPP response, from rather central approach of one unit managing the PPP agenda to an explicit matrix approach, such as in the ADB or the World Bank Group.

The interdependency of PPPs' success and an enabling environment emerge as common success factors. The work of all MDBs either acknowledges the significance of or directly supports the creation of an enabling environment, including policy and sector reform.

With regard to improving access to finance, MDBs' financing in developing countries is usually undertaken in conjunction with other development banks. Several MDBs are contemplating project financing facilities to catalyze financing for PPPs. Some of this is being triggered by the staggering needs for infrastructure many regions face.

7

Conclusions and Recommendations

Conclusions
STRATEGIC RELEVANCE

PPPs are of high strategic relevance to the World Bank Group. The recently adopted World Bank Group strategy *A Stronger, Connected, Solutions World Bank Group* (World Bank 2013) expresses the firm intention to "increasingly promote public-private partnerships," given its ability to work with both public and private sector client. PPPs are also envisaged as a Cross-cutting Solution Area working in coordination with the 14 Global Practices. Prior to this, scaling up PPPs was emphasized in the infrastructure strategy update, *Transformation through Infrastructure: Infrastructure Update FY12–15*, and in 2002 the Private Sector Development Strategy elevated private participation in infrastructure—and with it PPPs—for the first time to the strategic level, after the Asian crisis of 1997–98 revealed the underlying weaknesses of many private participation in infrastructure projects. In addition, PPPs are also widely reflected in several other World Bank Group conceptual and strategic notes.

However, there has been little guidance on how the World Bank Group intends and plans to translate its strategic intentions into operational country programs. It is not clear how those 20 Bank Group entities that are currently engaged in the PPP response will collaborate and how corporate ambitions are turned into country programs. The currently envisaged PPP Cross-Cutting Solution Area will have to be equipped with sufficient authority to be able to advance the PPP agenda across the World Bank Group.

Going forward, spelling out the solution area's role in relation to the 14 Global Practices and its capacity on knowledge sharing will be important.

Strategic resources deployment was in sync with the countries' needs but did not sufficiently push the limits when it comes to IFC's financing PPPs in frontier areas. The World Bank Group's resources have been deployed in countries where they are most needed, that is, synchronized with their respective level of maturity of handling PPPs. The World Bank and PPIAF's upstream work focuses in particular on "nascent" countries, that is, those that are about to embark on the process of establishing PPP frameworks. Hence World Bank and PPIAF support goes where it seems particularly relevant. Similarly, MIGA has been able to emphasize those "nascent" and "emerging" countries when issuing guarantees.

By contrast, the IFC's financial support reached often already "developed" PPP countries. It is understandable that IFC investments flow into such "developed" countries as sound enabling environments are conducive to PPP success The extent of IFC's business in developed countries, however, is higher than what the market allocation would suggest, indicating that IFC could shift some of its support to "emerging" countries, that is, countries with less established PPP frameworks or a more limited track record of handling PPPs. Such a shift would not be to the detriment of development outcomes, as results indicate.

At the country level, World Bank Group support for PPPs was relevant to client countries inasmuch as it supported clear development priorities. Typically, the Country Partnership Strategies and CASs embedded PPPs in sector reform programs. The most common PPP constraints addressed are governance issues, regulatory failure, and inadequate sector structure. Country strategies, however, tend to less systematically address other important PPP constrains, such as capability of governments to take a strategic decision on PPPs based on Value for Money assessments, or to assess fiscal implications associated with PPPs; political economy factors and issues of the government's commitment to the PPP agenda are almost entirely ignored. Looking at country level relevance from a "dynamic" perspective over the period evaluated (FY02–12), the World Bank Group was responsive to client countries' needs and changing priorities.

WORLD BANK GROUP SUPPORT FOR POLICY REFORM AND INSTITUTION BUILDING

PPPs require an enabling environment for their preparation and successful execution. This evaluation hence assessed how well the World Bank Group has assisted client countries in creating an enabling environment so that these countries can engage in PPPs. Such upstream policy support for PPPs is provided by four World Bank Group entities: PPIAF, the World Bank, WBI, and some IFC Advisory Services.

Most of World Bank upstream support for PPPs was delivered through broad-based sector reform efforts. Such efforts typically aim at increasing the financial viability of the sector, restructuring sector-relevant institutions, increasing sector management capacity, improve the regulatory regime and create a space for private sector participation. Sector reform efforts were, however, the most difficult to achieve. Despite the World Bank's leverage and country presence, success on sector reform was only evident in 55 percent of World Bank loans—an important finding given that proper sector reform is often a necessary condition for implementing PPPs successfully. Sector reform efforts were particularly prominent in the water and energy sectors, indicating the heavy reliance of PPPs in reform in these areas. Sector reform failed often because of complexity and political implications; project design and unrealistic timing on the side of the World Bank were factors contributing to failure as well. The choice of lending instrument is another essential factor in advancing the PPP agenda and need to be made contingent of the country's readiness.

Relatively narrow interventions, for example, efforts to build institutional frameworks for PPPs, worked the best. Building the legal and institutional frameworks for PPPs and capacity building were found the next most frequently addressed enabling factors. These relatively narrow interventions worked the best. Similarly, building consensus or regulatory commissions succeeds more often.

Contingent liabilities for governments that emerge from PPPs are rarely fully quantified at project level, although World Bank Group projects tend to give attention to ensuring adequate risk sharing at the project structuring. Recent efforts to systematize and introduce a framework are under way.

The most frequent factors influencing the extent to which policy reforms were successful were strong government commitment to sector reform and the availability of a capable government champion to promote the PPP agenda. Active involvement of local staff likewise contributed to success of policy reform. Privatization of state-owned enterprises has been a strong precursor to encouraging the PPP process, as it enhances competition and usually is accompanied by regulatory reform.

Addressing regulatory failure has been key to World Bank Group upstream support so PPPs could gain a foothold, in particular in the energy and water sectors. In addition to sector reform, a PPP-specific enabling environment including a minimum of an institutional framework, processes, and roles helped the PPP agenda take off. Whether a dedicated "PPP unit" at the country level is needed remains to be seen; identifying a "PPP champion," however, may facilitate inter-ministerial coordination in any case. The design of PPP component(s), if and how they are embedded in a World Bank lending operation with complementary knowledge products, matters and suggests the PPIAF resources should be used more strategically.

On the side of country governments, a lack of skills and resources for the preparation of a PPP pipeline and bankable PPP projects is a serious limitation across all World Bank-supported countries. For subnational PPPs to become successful, capacity, regulations, and incentives need to be in place and embedded in a clear accountability system.

DID PPPS DELIVER?

PPPs are largely successful in achieving their development outcomes. According to the development outcome rating of project evaluations, PPPs are successful in more than two-thirds of cases across IFC investments, MIGA, and the World Bank. The 187 IFC-supported PPPs show particularly high development outcome ratings, with 83 percent rated satisfactory or better. This high rate of success should not, however, lead to the conclusion that all PPPs necessarily perform well. IFC is selective with regard to where it conducts business; that is, it concentrates on countries that already have more proven frameworks to handle PPP; its due diligence screens out sponsors of lower quality and mitigates projects risks through smart structuring. IFC also plays an active role in supervision. These success factors may lack in cases without IFC engagement.

To shed more light on important aspects of public service delivery—for instance, access, pro-poor aspects, and quality of service delivery—PPPs need to be measured in a more multifaceted manner. But such data are rare. The existing monitoring and evaluation systems primarily build on a PPPs business performance. Project-level evaluations, IDGs and DOTS measure mainly the operational aspects of a PPP that are relevant to cash flow, such as the number of people that obtained access to infrastructure.

Therefore, data are available for only about half of projects for one dimension; there is not a single project with data available for all of the above-mentioned dimensions. Fewest data are available on pro-poor and fiscal effects; access has the most data available. In view of the Bank Group's central goal of fighting poverty—reaffirmed by the new 2013 strategy's dual goal of ending extreme poverty and promoting shared prosperity, and in light of the intent to increasingly pursue PPPs—there is an urgent need to introduce a more systematic way of monitoring PPPs. Such a system should not only capture better the end-user aspects of PPPs, but should also monitor PPP performance beyond the early years of operational maturity, as envisaged by the post-completion monitoring system, currently under implementation by IFC advisory. Existing systems, such as IDGs or DOTS would have to be strengthened—and possibly expanded to the World Bank—to better assess the breadth of PPP effects.

Improving access was generally achieved. When data were available, financial, efficiency, and quality improvements could also be confirmed for the majority of cases, but data on efficiency and quality were scarce. A statistically nonrepresentative but in-depth assessment of 22 PPPs conducted as part of the nine country cases studies indicates good results along all dimensions, except for efficiency where results were mixed. It cannot, however, be assessed how far PPPs benefited the poor, as large data gaps exist. Confirmation that access did improve for the poor was only recorded in about 10 percent of cases. Beyond reaching the poor through improved access to infrastructure, a review of broader benefits showed that such effects, for example employments effects, occurred in 42 percent of World Bank PPPs, in 39 percent of IFC investments and in 20 percent for MIGA's guarantees.

Country readiness drives PPP success. Development outcome ratings of PPP projects tend to be better in countries with a higher level of readiness in handling PPPs. As a general rule, the presence of a strong regulatory framework was necessary for projects to succeed in the water and power sectors, but in the transport sector (ports airports roads) project-level parameters on pricing and oversight, along with the legal framework governing PPPs, seemed adequate. Hence cross-sector approaches as envisaged by the World Bank Group 2013 strategy would have to be synchronized with and rooted in reform efforts of individual sector. In addition to country readiness, PPPs need a sound business case and a competent sponsor to be successful.

IFC investment added value to PPPs during due diligence and implementation, in addition to providing finance and catalyzing other financiers. IFC-supported PPPs tend to be less risky than other infrastructure investments because of the thorough due diligence. This thoroughness is also reflected in the high work quality ratings for IFC investments in PPPs. As a consequence, IFC-supported PPPs exhibit consistently higher development outcome ratings than other infrastructure investments – and significantly higher ratings than the rest of the portfolio. Risk is also adequately priced into IFC's PPP deals – resulting in an even higher-than-average business success and investment outcome. IFC-supported PPPs are often located in countries with already well-established enabling environments, and less in emerging countries. Supporting more PPPs in emerging countries will not decrease their success rate: in fact 86 and 88 percent of PPPs are successful in developed and emerging PPP countries, respectively. Even nascent countries exhibit a success rate of 50 percent.

IFC could afford taking more "smart risk," as envisaged by the 2013 strategy. This could help support more PPPs in countries that need IFC's support the most, that is, those that are building up their PPP frameworks and have a limited track record of implementing PPPs. Such investments would set an important demonstration effect and show that private participation is possible even in less tested regulatory regimes.

The focus of IFC Advisory Services is to bring PPP transactions to commercial and financial closure. Although almost all transaction cases (97 percent) reviewed delivered the specific advice for the first phase of the process (up to the decision to open a bidding process), about half resulted in an award of a contract, a prerequisite for creating a successful PPP. Among projects that led to commercial closure, the largest success factors are government commitment and IFC's role. IFC's value added is also demonstrated by its ability to adjust and balance government objectives with the needs of a bankable transaction, which would interest the private sector.

IFC advisory lacks some of the long-term and close relations, in-depth policy dialogue, and financial leverage that the World Bank would normally have with governments which may also explain this pattern; and so can the fact that IFC advisory operates a lot in LMICs and Sub-Saharan Africa, where one could expect relatively untested PPP frameworks. IFC advisory's experience in these countries could therefore inform IFC investments on the country's and market's readiness and help leading their investment more into emerging—and even nascent—countries. More upfront work should be undertaken, including a more proactive dialogue with key stakeholders and the civil society. Determining the appropriate entry point for IFC Advisory Services could be facilitated by a Bank Group-wide country diagnostic for PPPs.

MIGA guarantees helped effectively increase investors' confidence and improve their capacity to raise capital, lower their financing costs, and mediate disputes with government. MIGA's effectiveness and underwriting quality for PPP projects is on a par with the quality of underwriting of other MIGA projects. As with all World Bank Group PPP transactions, regulatory failure and political economy factors were drivers of success and failure. MIGA's political risk insurance offered coverage for specific risks and was effective in helping establishing a track record of PPPs in countries that need support the most, that is, those that are in the process of building up their PPP frameworks. MIGA-supported PPPs have been more strategically relevant than their other infrastructure projects, corroborating their important role in nascent and emerging PPP countries. Strengthening MIGA's role in World Bank Group-wide efforts and benefiting from its role appears to be the way forward when bringing PPPs to more nascent and emerging countries.

For the World Bank, 62 percent of its supported PPP downstream transactions were successful. This means that, measured by their overall development outcomes, PPPs are quite successful, but significantly less successful than IFC's investments in PPPs, of which 83 percent are rated satisfactory. But the World Bank takes on significantly more country risk. Countries in which the World Bank engages tend to have worse IICCRs and a higher share of them are nascent countries (19 percent, compared to 6 percent for IFC investments). Furthermore, PPP projects are markedly more difficult to implement than normal infrastructure projects.

They are often restructured, delayed, or flagged for procurement issues. This stems from the rather complex nature of PPP projects, half of which combine upstream policy work and downstream transaction support. Leading factors of failure are overly complex project design and an unrealistic timeframe to start with, that is a timeframe that forces reform measures into a World Bank project cycle, instead of acknowledging the complexity and political nature of such processes.

As with IFC and MIGA, government commitment plays an important role. Adhering to E&S safeguards also contributed to slow implementation to the extent that it sometime clouded the appreciations of project benefits. But implementing these safeguards was important and delivered public benefits.

Bank Group–supported transactions often created a market for PPPs through their demonstration effects and, at times, helped shape the regulatory environment. Demonstration and replication effects of individual PPPs may be at times equally important as the actual transaction. Bank Group engagements led to subsequent follow-up investments in PPPs by other. Frequently Bank Group–supported PPP transactions also helped shape the regulatory environment, often facilitated by close Bank Group-wide collaboration and stakeholder involvement.

WORKING AS ONE WORLD BANK GROUP

The World Bank Group's support to PPPs addresses issues along the entire delivery chain, from upstream support for the enabling environment and pipeline development to downstream transactions and execution. It touches on about 20 different entities of the World Bank Group. Collaboration across these entities is crucial for proper sequencing and leveraging of the relative comparative advantage each institution holds.

Leveraging the comparative advantages of the various World Bank Group institutions works quite well. In about half the countries IEG reviewed, the World Bank Group institutions effectively coordinate and collaborate across policy reform aspects and PPP transactions; in a few cases even three institutions were involved. There is also evidence for proper sequencing of instruments across upstream and downstream support. Among its peer organizations, the World Bank Group has been acknowledged as offering the most comprehensive PPP solution package. However, there were also a few missed opportunities.

Going forward, working as one World Bank Group will become the norm, according to the 2013 strategy. The intention to explore mechanisms to promote a stronger pipeline of joint infrastructure projects and the envisaged review of World Bank Group advisory services to governments are essential for the PPP agenda; most importantly, incentives must be in place for individual task managers and investment officers to collaborate. They only collaborate if such collaboration adds value and allows them to achieve better results or at least the same results faster. Introducing a metrics to measure collaborative behavior, as suggested by the latest Bank Group strategy, is likely perceived as artificially superimposed and will not necessarily increase collaboration. Aligning practice areas through a "delivery lens" and integrating currently separate units may be more effective.

Improving the focus of country programs through systematic country diagnostics will be particularly important for the PPP agenda. A country-level PPP diagnostic would assist planning and implementing a one World Bank Group approach. As any diagnostic is resource intensive, it should be applied mainly to countries where at least a minimum prospect exists that a bankable pipeline of project will emerge.

A PPP-specific country diagnostic would have to consider country, sector, and project parameters as part of a phased approach and could represent a platform for sharing knowledge as well as clarify Bank Group-wide collaboration. To this end, specific Bank Group entities should take the lead in this country-sector project diagnostic hierarchy. Advocacy and stakeholder consultation have thus far received little attention and therefore need to be emphasized. This diagnostic would facilitate assessing which role the various World Bank Group institutions should play, given a country's level of maturity of handling PPPs. Thus, it would help (i) ensure that the Bank Group institutions leverage their respective comparative advantages, (ii) tailor upstream support to country level constraints, and (iii) determine who should take the lead in advancing the country's PPP agenda.

A concerted one World Bank Group approach is needed to close the upstream deal gap. A dedicated PPP pipeline and project development facility appears beneficial, given the lack of funding and skills for this important part of the PPP cycle. An effective and efficient operation of such a facility would demand close partnership among all three World Bank Group institutions.

Working as one World Bank Group requires also watching out for conflicts of interest. As the change management process moves forward and the three institutions intensify their collaboration on PPPs, management is advised to place a high priority on having in place a sound system for the identification and mitigation of potential conflict of interests in PPPs.

Given the importance of unsolicited bids, there is a need for a Bank Group wide policy on how to handle them best. Unsolicited proposals often play a role in countries with an upstream deal gap. To benefit from the upside of unsolicited proposals, that is, funding of project preparation and innovation, countries need to have a framework in place to deal with them. Guidance to Bank Group staff engaged in both upstream and downstream work will be crucial going forward.

For most MDBs PPPs are of great relevance and several figure PPPs explicitly either in stand-alone strategy documents or as integral part of sectoral/corporate strategies. In implementing these strategic plans, some MDBs have come up with specific roadmaps and matrix management structures. In particular, the ADB undertook an evaluation of PPPs that has triggered a rethinking of the institution's approach to PPPs and in particular has moved to make the process more strategic and less opportunistic. Its operational plan for PPPs turns strategy into implementation more readily. The four pillars of its operational plan also help define the PPP instruments that it will offer. Similarly, the AfDB set up an operational framework for PPPs in conjunction with its private sector development strategy where PPPs figure prominently.

Across the MDBs, the ADB, the AfDB, and the IDB have PPP approaches that recognize the importance of upstream as well as downstream support. Compared to its peers, the World Bank Group likely offers the widest and deepest set of services and products, a conclusion corroborated also by IEG's nine country missions.

Recommendations

The following recommendations are intended to strengthen the implementation of the PPP-relevant aspects of the latest World Bank Group strategy. Ultimately, PPP interventions should deliver the maximum value to client countries and private sector partners, which requires that the PPP agenda of the Bank Group build on better country diagnostics, be pursued in a more strategic manner, and leverage the comparative advantages of all Bank Group institutions and trust funds involved in the PPP response. The recommendations are clustered into two groups: strategic and organizational and operational recommendations.

STRATEGIC AND ORGANIZATIONAL RECOMMENDATIONS

Recommendation 1: IFC Investment Services should identify avenues that would allow IFC to invest increasingly in PPPs located in countries and markets that do not yet have a well-developed enabling environment, while keeping its mandate of achieving high development outcomes and remaining financially self-sustaining.

Recommendation 2: IFC PPP Advisory Services should rethink its client engagement management with a view to ensuring broad stakeholder consultation up front and maintaining or even improving government commitment to PPP transactions, in collaboration with relevant World Bank Group staff.

Recommendation 3: Once the new PPP Cross-Cutting Solution Area has been established, it should translate the World Bank Group's strategic intentions with regard to PPPs into an operational framework, covering aspects of organization and processes, resources, knowledge management, and monitoring and evaluation. This framework should (i) define the role of the PPP Cross-cutting Solution Area and its interactions with other relevant Bank Group stakeholders, (ii) facilitate the identification of country-tailored solutions based on country diagnostics, and (iii) foresee a Bank Group-wide PPP knowledge management platform.

Recommendation 4: The World Bank Group should systematically integrate efforts to assist governments in (i) making strategic decisions with regard to the level and nature of private sector participation in infrastructure and social service provision and (ii) assessing fiscal implications, including any fiscal liabilities associated with PPPs.

Recommendation 5: The World Bank Group should provide authoritative guidance to its staff on how to handle unsolicited PPP proposals, both in its upstream and downstream work. Given the importance of unsolicited bids, in particular in countries with an upstream deal gap, there is a need for a Bank Group-wide policy on how to handle them best, so that countries can benefit from the upside of unsolicited proposals—that is, funding of project preparation and innovation—while at the same time safeguarding public interests and integrity.

Recommendation 6: The World Bank Group should define principles for the monitoring of PPPs over the long run, that is, beyond operational maturity (IFC/MIGA) and projects closure (World Bank), to capture all vital performance aspects of PPPs, including—where relevant—user aspects.

Reference

World Bank. 2013. *A Stronger, Connected Solutions World Bank Group.* Washington, DC: World Bank.

Appendix A
Methodology Used to Identify Public-Private Partnership Projects

PPP targeted World Bank projects are not coded as such. Hence IEG had to conceive a methodology to identify a universe of PPP World Bank Group projects for this evaluation. Added complications were that there is no World Bank Group wide officially endorsed definition of PPP; secondly, PPP-relevant elements may at times be a referred to at the component or subcomponent level of World Bank projects that required that the identification of PPP projects considered the entire Project Appraisal Documents.

The identification of PPP projects built on the evaluation's definition of PPP. Once a tentative list of PPP projects had been created they were screened individually against this definition at the entry stage of the evaluation and a second time when conducting the portfolio analysis.

For World Bank PPP projects, IEG built on the methodology developed by World Bank management that they had used to identify PPP projects for their latest infrastructure strategy update. Based on this methodology, IEG developed an information technology-supported database search and, with the help of it, identified PPP targeted projects amid all approved World Bank projects exited FY02–12, using Project Appraisal Documents.

In total, 26 search strings/key words were used for this information technology–supported methodology were: (DBO | DBFO | OMM) | private sector participation | concession | concessionaire | management and operating | construction and operation | lease | developer finance | operations and maintenance | operations, maintenance | rehabilitate, operate | rehabilitate-operate-transfer | operations-maintenance | Public-Private partnership | Public private partnership | Private public partnership | Public-private partnerships | Public/Private partnership | Build-operate-transfer | Build operate transfer | Build, operate, and transfer | Build own operate | Build-own-operate | Build, own, operate.

To ensure robustness, the outcome of the methodology was tested against World Bank's own results. IEG's results, that is, the tentative list of World Bank PPP projects identified by the above methodology, were compared against the World Bank PPP projects that management had prepared themselves for the infrastructure strategy update for FY09–11. IEG's method proved robust, as the overlap of project identified by World Bank management and IEG was greater than 90 percent.

To ensure additional accuracy of the thus generated pool of PPP projects to be evaluated, World Bank management reviewed the projects. The final list of PPP projects was than share with World Bank Group management who circulated it to relevant sectors and regions. This review resulted in 14 projects being added to a total of 478 already identified projects.

IFC and MIGA projects the identification of PPP projects was relatively straightforward as the respective PPP was the object of investment and as such easily identifiable. In both cases, PPP projects were identified by a manual review of relevant projects, and IFC (Investment and Advisory Services) and MIGA management confirmed the accuracy of the PPP projects subject to this evaluation.

Appendix B
Public-Private Partnership Indicators

	Water and Sanitation	Toll Roads	Ports	Airports	Rail
Access 1	Number or water connections	Increase in traffic	Volume of goods shipped through the port	Landing frequency	Quantity of freight (ton-km/year):
Access2	Number of sewerage connection	n.a.	Cost of moving goods through the port	Passenger frequency	n.a.
Quality 1	Clean water availability (99% potable)	Performance Standards are met (maintenance, road safety, signage)—Performance-based contract only	n.a.	International Air Transport Association (IATA) rating (A–D)	n.a.
Quality 2	Water pressure in pipes	n.a.	n.a.	n.a.	n.a.
Efficiency 1	Waste water treated per connection	Vehicle operating costs	Ship productivity (time taken to service ships)	Tax load per Passenger	Derailments per ton-km/year

continued on page 166

	Water and Sanitation	Toll Roads	Ports	Airports	Rail
Efficiency 2	Percentage of uncollected bills Share of technical losses	Reduction in travel time	Efficiency of port operations (loading/unloading charges per container, cost of moving goods to the port)	Other efficiency indicator	n.a.
Financial 1	Financial statements, EBIDA	Revenue: target vs. actual	Financial statements, EBIDA	Financial statements, EBIDA	Financial statements, EBIDA
Financial 2	n.a.	Long-term sustainability of fees is assured—Performance-based contract only	n.a.	n.a.	n.a.
Fiscal 1	Level of contingent undertakings, transfers, subsidies	Level of contingent undertakings, transfers, subsidies	Level of contingent undertakings, transfers, subsidies	Level of contingent undertakings, transfers, subsidies	Level of government subsidies, contingent undertakings
Poor 1	Increase in connections in poor areas:	Bus share of traffic	Development of economic zones	n.a.	Passenger traffic

	Urban Transport	Energy Generation	Energy Distribution	Health
Access 1	Increased in the number of public transport passengers:	Added capacity (megawatts)	Net increase in connections	Number/increase of inpatients treated per year, occupancy rate of hospital beds, outpatients treated
Access2	n.a.	Other Access Indicator	Other Access Indicator	Number/increase of services, for example, X-rays, medicine/vaccine distributed to the public by year
Quality 1	On time, cleanliness	Other quality indicator 1	Reliability—hours of service, load shedding	Government payments linked to performance indicators?
Quality 2	n.a.	Other quality indicator 2	Other quality indicator	Were quality targets met?
Efficiency 1	On-time service	Output/worker	Connections/worker	Operating capacity, government payment as reimbursement, capitation, diagnosis related
Efficiency 2	n.a.	Other Efficiency Indicator	Percentage of Uncollected bills Transmission losses	Patient waiting time for procedures, investments in equipment and long term maintenance
Financial 1	Bus company profitable, or has transparent levels of subsidy	Financial statements, EBIDA	Financial statements, EBIDA	Existence of national insurance plan

continued on page 168

	Urban Transport	Energy Generation	Energy Distribution	Health
Fiscal 1	Level of contingent undertakings, subsidies	Level of contingent undertakings, subsidies	Level of contingent undertakings, subsidies	Fiscal effects on public expenditures, savings
Poor 1	Model Share Increase (buses vs. private cars)	n.a.	Increase in connections in poor areas	Increase access to health services to poor
Poor 2	Pro-poor accessibility (cost)	n.a.	n.a.	Access to medication to poor

NOTE: EBIDA = earnings before interest, depreciation, and amortization; n.a. = not applicable.

Appendix C
Country Case Study Methodology

Guiding Principles

Country cases follow a multiple country case study design, that is, focus on three regional clusters each with three sets of PPP projects with distinct features. In total nine country case studies were selected on a purposive basis with a view to generating three sets of case studies in Latin America and the Caribbean and East Asia and Pacific, the two most active regions in applying PPPs, and Sub-Saharan Africa, with one of the lowest PPP activity levels and high cancellation rates. This allowed learning from both the "common case" as well as the "critical case." Each set contains one country where the World Bank Group provided mainly upstream support to study its effects on the country's PPP agenda and/or subsequent PPP transactions; one country where the World Bank was active mainly downstream; and one country where the World Bank was active both upstream and downstream to study the added value of continuous engagement and the effects of direct support to PPPs. See Table C.1 for countries covered by all nine case studies. Drawing lessons within and across these regions, in particular across these "horizontal" cases yielded more valid and robust lessons.

The purpose of country case studies is to enrich the learning agenda of the evaluation and to fill certain gaps. More specifically, country cases are conducted to …

- Answer questions of **"how" and "why,"** that is, to obtain the necessary contextual information and insights to identify drivers of success and failure; we **do not aim to tell a "rating story"** based on country cases.

- Address the question of whether PPP projects produced desired outcomes as a result of specific **sectoral factors** or as a result of overall **governance/framework/country factors** that could be transferred across sectors and may be country specific.

- Collect information on if and how **Bank Group upstream work** was used by the governments/countries for subsequent PPP transactions—whether supported by the Bank Group or not.

TABLE C.1 Countries Covered by Case Studies

	LAC	EAP	SSA
Upstream countries	Guatemala	Vietnam	Ghana
Continuous engagement countries	Colombia	Philippines	Uganda
Downstream countries	Brazil (based on CPE)	China	Senegal

NOTE: CPE = country program evaluation; EAP = East Asia and Pacific Region; LAC = Latin America and the Caribbean Region; SSA = Sub-Saharan Africa Region.

- For downstream work, to assess **PPP sustainability in the longer term**, including the need to renegotiate PPP during their lifespan.

- Address issues of **complementarity and synergies** which may not be evident from country or project level documents.

Country case studies covered the entire World Bank Group PPP portfolio, as identified by the project team. These PPP interventions were recorded in the portfolio analysis database by the team and the case study author was advised to make use of this information when answering the evaluation questions, preferably when preparing for the mission as well as when drafting the case study report. During the actual field visit to the country, the incumbent evaluated these Bank Group PPP interventions in greater detail and answered the evaluation questions (see next section) through interviews with relevant counterparts, government officials, beneficiaries, investors, industry associations, civil society organizations, academia, and other suitable stakeholders, complemented by data gathering and site visits. If because of size not all interventions could be reviewed in detail, a sample was chosen purposively—in coordination with the task team leader—so that the selected sample …

1. Mirrored the overall portfolio composition in terms of Bank Group entities engaged and in terms of types of interventions, even if the sample size for each intervention type was likely not statistically representative.

2. Allowed for a rich learning experience with regard to the country's PPP agenda.

3. In case IFC Advisory Services or MIGA projects could be assessed in the country even in an "upstream country," they had to be assessed, as outcome information is scare in the portfolio review. Each author coordinated the selection of the PPP projects with the team and task team leader and documented the selection up front in the country case study.

Depending on the type of the country the focus of the case study was on the relevant type of support, that is, for upstream countries on World Bank Group upstream support, for continuous engagement countries on the entire spectrum of Bank Group support (up and downstream), for downstream countries more Bank Group support to actual PPP transaction. This, however, did not preclude an assessment of some upstream work even in a downstream country or conversely, of some downstream work in an upstream country. In general, the evaluation focused on Bank Group interventions that have already been delivered, for example, closed World Bank projects, completed PPIAF/WBI activities, and/or operationally matured IFC/MIGA investments.

Template for Country Case Study[1]
SECTION I: THE COUNTRY EXPERIENCE AND PPP AGENDA, FY02–12

- Recent relevant political economy developments

- Relevant macroeconomic developments FY02–12

- Overview of the country's experience with implementing its PPP agenda.

SECTION II: WORLD BANK GROUP ROLE AND RELEVANCE

- How did the role of PPPs evolve in World Bank Group country strategies (CAS, ISN)?

- Did the World Bank Group's PPP interventions address development priorities in that country; that is, were they relevant?

- How did the World Bank Group engagement operationally in the country's PPP agenda (add table, if needed), did this engagement change over time (for example, see a shift in the mix of tools or a shift from upstream to more transaction oriented work) and if so why? Was the Bank Group responsive in case priorities changes or emerged?

  - What's the role of the World Bank Group in the country's PPP agenda and vis-à-vis other major donors/MDBs? Was the Bank Group more active upstream or downstream vis-à-vis the other players? Did the Bank Group provide a comprehensive solution package, including up and downstream work?

  - How was coordination of World Bank Group work with other major players in the PPP agenda of that country, for example, other MDBs, DFID, USAID, other national agencies, the United Nations?

To be able to answer questions in Sections 3–5, the country's PPP-related projects needed to be assessed first one by one. The portfolio analysis and the field visits provided the necessary information, with the field visits providing a more up-to-date and more detailed information. Then the findings of the portfolio analysis were considered together with the information collected during the field visits when answering the below questions at an aggregate level.

- Has the World Bank Group provided strategic advice to client countries in making informed decisions about the nature and level of private sector involvement in sector reform, the choice between public investment versus PPP, and type of PPP? Is there evidence that this advice taken on board and knowledge actually delivered? Are there examples of well conducted *Value for Money* analysis, due diligence applying the *Public Sector Comparator* Model, and so forth?

- To what extent have World Bank Group interventions[3] and project components that targeted the enabling environment for PPPs achieved *their stated objectives;*[4] that is, have PPP units taken up their jobs, are the regulators functional, are PPP laws actually used to process PPP transactions, and so forth?

  - What were the factors enabling or preventing the achievement of these objectives?

  - What can we learn from cases where the implementation of upstream measures was particularly successful or failed?

  - Has the World Bank Group enhanced the public sector's capability to assess and account for contingent liability and recurring expenditures related to PPPs?

  - In how far did country parameters (for example governance issues, enabling environment income level, absorption capacity, investment climate, and so forth) or sector parameters (for example lack of cost recovery, size of market) drive the role and effectiveness of PPPs?

- Has the World Bank Group's upstream support achieved its *long term outcomes*, that is, helped countries to execute PPP transactions?[5] How useful did recipients perceive World Bank Group upstream support when implementing subsequent actual PPP transactions?

  - Subsequently, did those PPPs improve access to infrastructure and social services through subsequent PPPs, regardless of World Bank Group involvement in the actual PPP transaction? How did these PPPs work out; that is, is there evidence that these PPPs contributed to improve and inclusive access, quality of service delivery, and increased efficiency? If so, why and why not? Was failure due to shortcomings in upstream work?

Note: When assessing World Bank Group–supported projects, rely on your assessment of it under Section IV.

- Is there evidence that PPPs have leveraged scarce public sector resources through private sector funds?[6] Is there evidence that PPPs deliver their services in a sustained manner? What can we learn from successful or failed PPP transactions?

SECTION IV: EFFECTIVENESS OF DOWNSTREAM SUPPORT

- Have PPPs that benefited from World Bank Group downstream support (IFC Advisory Services, IFC Investment Services, World Bank lending or non-lending or MIGA) contributed to improved access to infrastructure and social services?

  - Have PPPs actually contributed to improved and inclusive access, quality of service delivery, and increased efficiency?

  - Did these PPPs leverage public sector resources through private sector funds? If not, what prevented private investors to contribute?

  - Have these PPPs provided sustained services over time, that is, beyond project closure/operational maturity?

  - Assess what drove success or failure during preparation, bidding and finance. In cases of fully operational PPPs, what factors enabled/impaired sustainability/longevity? In case applicable, what were the reasons for MIGA projects being cancelled?

  - How far did country parameters (for example the enabling environment, the country's income level, absorption capacity, investment climate, and so forth) or sector parameters (for example, lack of cost recovery, size of market, and so forth) drive the success of these PPPs?

  - Can any effects beyond the immediate projects scope, for example, at broader sector level or country level, be observed?

SECTION V: WORK QUALITY AND COORDINATION

- What were the roles of the different World Bank Group entities in the country's up and downstream work, how was their work quality and what their added value or shortcomings?

  - Were there unique roles of IFC Advisory Services and World Bank (AAA, fee-based services, and so forth) with regard to advising on transactions, including pipeline management, project preparation, bidding and finance? What did the client appreciate most about their work, what the least? What went right and wrong, and why? Please provide specific examples of where coordination was lacking and what was the result of this in other words, what would have happened with better coordination? Please refrain from referring to a general lack of coordination.

- What did the client appreciate most about the role and contribution of IFC Investment Services, MIGA and World Bank loans with regard to financing PPP transactions? What should be improved?

- At the country level, has World Bank Group's PPP agenda been adequately coordinated?

  - Has the World Bank Group leveraged synergies and exploited the comparative advantages of its various public and private sector arms and its products? Can coordination and collaboration be found at the level of specific projects? If not, have efforts been coordinated at regional sectoral or strategic level?

  - What can we learn from successful or failed World Bank Group coordination across the various units contributing to the PPP agenda?

  - According to the World Bank CD, the IFC Head and their key staff, has the Bank Group been able to deliver a country specific PPP solution?

  - With the World Bank and IFC Advisory Services being involved upstream and IFC Investment Services downstream, has the management of conflicts of interest been a potential or real issue? If so, how was it handled?

- From a country perspective, is there a need to adjust the World Bank Group's organizational structures, processes, and incentives to better enable a coordinated and effective delivery of PPP targeted activities?

  - From the World Bank Group field offices perspective, client, financier or counterpart perspective, is the current organizational set-up, allocation of skills and resources, and functions across the World Bank Group with regard to implementing the PPP agenda, and its embedded incentives systems and standards conducive to an efficient and effective PPP response?

- Looking at both, upstream and downstream work, to what extent was corruption an issue along the entire value chain of a PPP, that is, from pipeline development, setting of specific technical standards, project selection preparation, bidding, and finance?

  - Is there any evidence that corruption led to dropping of projects? Is there any evidence that the lack of competition had an effect on the risk allocation?

  - How well is the country positioned to address systemic corruption risk? What did the World Bank Group do about addressing corruption at the systemic as well as project level?

Notes

[1] Build the analysis on the available portfolio analysis level I and II data, that is, on available data on operational trends in terms of volumes and nature of World Bank Group engagement and its results.

[2] Country case studies cover "active projects" during FY02–12, that is, including those approved before FY02 but closed after FY02.

[3] Mainly PPIAF, WBI, and World Bank lending and non-lending, but if applicable, also IFC Advisory Services.

[4] For example, in the Project Assessment Document, Board Documents, Underwriting Document, and so forth.

[5] If the country engaged in subsequent PPP transaction, try to establish the usefulness of the World Bank Group's upstream work. To this end, link the upstream work components (PPIAF, WBI, and World Bank) to entities (and their capacities) that later on executed PPP transactions and report on the perceived/reported usefulness of World Bank Group prior support.

[6] Leveraging refers to direct leveraging through World Bank Group guarantee and insurance products (partial risk and credit guarantees, PRI, and so forth) and mobilization of private finance through public financing. The evaluation also takes stock of ongoing efforts of the way the World Bank Group accounts guarantees overall.

Appendix D
Methodology for Assessing Sponsor and Market Risk in IFC Investments

Sponsor Risk: Based on experience, commitment, capacity, and reputation

High risk: Either (i) the sponsor is rated high risk in at least one subindicator and medium risk or high risk in at least one other subindicator; or (ii) if sponsor's prior performance in an IFC project, or general business reputation, reflects performance unreliability.

Low risk: The sponsor is not rated high risk in any subindicator and is rated medium risk in not more than one subindicator.

Medium risk: All other cases.
(BINARY ANALYSIS: high risk versus low risk [inclusive of medium])

TABLE D.1 Sponsor Quality Subindicators

Sponsor Risk Indicator[a]	High Risk	Medium Risk	Low Risk
1. Specific experience in project's business line (production and market)	Less than 5 years	All other cases (not high or low risk)	10 or more years
2. Commitment to the project and strategic importance of project to sponsor	Less than 25% equity stake; or project of low strategic value to sponsor	All other cases (not high or low risk)	At least 51% equity stake; no collateral profit-taking "above the bottom line"; or project of high strategic value to sponsor

continued on page 178

Sponsor Risk Indicator[a]	High Risk	Medium Risk	Low Risk
3. Financial capacity relative to obligations or commitments to support the project	Source of equity or internal cash generation (existing operations) or net worth less than 2 times actual and contingent financial obligations to support the project	All other cases (not high or low risk)	Source of equity or internal cash generation (existing operations) or net worth more than 4 times actual and contingent financial obligations to support the project
4. Business reputation & commitment to good governance and EHS sustainability; prior performance in IFC projects[b]	Opposite of low risk, or predominant absence of the listed low risk factors	All other cases (not high or low risk)	Good performance in prior IFC projects (if any) over at least 5 years from IFC commitments.. Long and/or several business ties with multi-nationals; long membership and responsible roles in business associations; directorships in other, especially listed, companies; absence of material legal problems. For sponsors of existing companies: good record of compliance with government regulations; good accounting & management information systems; reputable external auditors; and so forth.

a. The main source of data for these ratings is the appraisal documents only in the case of mature projects (that is, projects with XPSRs). Sponsor ratings for new projects approved from FY00–03 may use additional data as indicated in the next note.
b. Some important data sources for rating sponsors, particularly business reputation, not available in the appraisal documents but reasonably obtainable during any project appraisal are: at least three good references, preferably from IFC clients, local banks, international creditors, or World Bank Group staff; and ratings from local credit agencies (if available). Sponsors who may be involved with illegal activities are extremely high risk and will be rated over-all as high risk automatically under this rating system. IFC does not knowingly deal with such sponsors because of reputation risks to IFC, although IFC could inadvertently have supported such sponsors in the past.

Market Risk: Captures the project's underlying competitiveness in the market in which it is operating, and any market distortions that typically result in low competitiveness.

State-owned enterprises active in the market? (market share >=20% = high risk)
Inherent competitiveness not demonstrated
      (Indicate the source of competitiveness)
Price assumption optimistic?
      Price (G)/Margin (E) assumption used in base case:
          Historical price (G)/margin (E)
Excessive reliance of cash generation?
      (a) C.G. as % of project cost
      (b) Cash in project as % of discretionary CF

In the case of PPP, market risk analysis involves contractual arrangements that can control market risk (that is, offtake agreements and so forth, that minimize revenue volatility) = low risk.

Bibliography

Akash, Deep. 2009. "Developing an Enabling Environment for Public Private Partnerships." Presentation at the Public Private Partnerships Seminar, Dubai, April 13 Kennedy School Harvard University.

Akitoby, Bernardin, Richard Hemming, and Gerd Schwartz. 2007. "Public Investment and Public-Private Partnerships." IMF *Economic Issues* 40.

Araújo, Sónia, and Douglas Sutherland. 2010. "Public-Private Partnerships and Investment in Infrastructure." OECD Economics Department Working Papers No. 803, Paris.

Beato, Vives. 1996. "Private-Sector Participation in Infrastructure: Risk, Fiscal, and Efficiency Issues-in Public-Private Arrangements for the Provision of Services." *Infrastructure,* 1 (3): 3–14.

Beckett, Mehalah, Susannah Drazin, David Finlay, Hannah Kingsley-Smith, Nathan Martin, Rachel Neathey, James Robertson, and Mark Wynniatt. 2009. *Performance of PFI Construction: A Review by the Private Finance Practice.* London: National Audit Office, The Stationery Office Limited.

Burger, Philippe, Justin Tyson, Izabela Karpowicz, and Maria Delgado Coelho. 2009. "The Effects of the Financial Crisis on Public-Private Partnerships." IMF Working Paper, WP/ 09/144.

Colverson, Samuel, and Oshani Perera. 2012. "Harnessing the Power of Public-Private Partnerships: The Role of Hybrid Financing Strategies in Sustainable Development." Policy Brief. Winnipeg, Canada: International Institute for Sustainable Development.

Delmon, Gassner, Kacaniku, and Baghat. 2010. "Overview of Public Private Partnerships (PPPs) in Infrastructure in Developing Countries." Background Note for the G20 Seoul Meeting, November 2010.

Duffield, C.F. 2008. *Report on the Performance of PPP Projects in Australia when Compared with a Representative Sample of Traditionally Procured Infrastructure Projects.* National PPP Forum-Benchmarking Study Phase II, Melbourne University, Melbourne Engineering Research Institute.

Eggers, William D., and Tom Startup. 2006. *Closing the Infrastructure Gap: The Role of Public-Private Partnerships.* Deloitte Research Study, Deloitte. http://www.deloitte.com/view/en_US/us/Industries/US-federal-government/2ea59a17c900e110VgnVCM100000ba42f00aRCRD.htm

EIB (European Investment Bank). 2005. *Evaluation of PPP Projects Financed by the EIB.* Luxembourg: Operations Evaluation, European Investment Bank.

European PPP Expertise Centre. 2010. *A Guide to Guidance Sourcebook for PPPs in TEN-Transport.* Luxembourg: European Investment Bank.

———. 2011. *The Non-Financial Benefits of PPPs: An Overview of Concepts and Methodology.* Luxembourg: European Investment Bank.

Farquharson, Edward, Clemencia Torres de Mästle, and E.R. Yescombe, with Javier Encinas. 2011. *How to Engage with the Private Sector in Public-Private Partnerships in Emerging Markets.* Washington, DC: World Bank and PPIAF.

Finlay, David, Kevin Browne, Marisa Chambers, and Colin Ratcliffe. 2003. *PFI: Construction Performance.* London: National Audit Office, Stationery Office Limited.

Fischer, R. 2011. "The Promise and Peril of Public-Private Partnerships: Lessons from the Chilean Experience." International Growth Centre Working Paper 1/0483 June 2011.

Foster, Vivien, and **Cecilia Briceño-Garmendia (eds.)** 2010. *Africa's Infrastructure: A Time for Transformation.* Washington, DC: World Bank and Agence Française de Développement.

Fourth High-Level Forum on Aid Effectiveness. 2011. *Busan Partnership for Effective Development Cooperation,* Busan, Republic of Korea, November 29–December 1.

Fussell, **Heather,** and **Charley Beresford.** 2009. *Public-Private Partnerships: Understanding the Challenge.* New York: Columbia Institute Center for Civic Governance.

Gantsho, **Mandla S.V.** 2010. "The Role and Pitfalls of Private Sector Involvement in Infrastructure." Paper presented at the Sixth Annual Collaborative Africa Budget Report Initiative Seminar: Open Budgets and Good Governance, Mauritius.

Guasch, **J. Luis.** 2004. *Granting and Renegotiating Infrastructure Concessions: Doing It Right.* Washington, DC: World Bank Institute.

IFC (International Finance Corporation). 2011. "Healthcare and PPPs." *Handshake: International Finance Corporation's Quarterly Journal on PPPs.* Issue 3.

Kragelund, **Peter.** 2010. "The Potential Role of Non-Traditional Donors' Aid in Africa." Issue Paper No. 11, InternationalCenter for Trade and Sustainable Development, Geneva.

———. 2012. "The Revival of Non-Traditional State Actors' Interests in Africa: Does it Matter for Policy Autonomy?" *Development Policy Review,* 30 (6): 703–18.

Mumssen, **Yogita, Lars Johannes,** and **Geeta Kumar.** 2010. *Output-Based Aid—Lessons Learned and Best Practice.* Directions in Development. Washington, DC: World Bank.

OECD (Organisation for Economic Co-operation and Development). 2009. "Conclusions—Network Meeting on Knowledge Transfer in Donor Organization Programs with the Private Sector, Public-Private Partnerships." Meeting with Established and New Donors, Vienna, June 8–9.

Peterson, **George E.** 2009. *Unlocking Land Values to Finance Urban Infrastructure.* Washington, DC: World Bank.

Sfakianakis, **E.,** and **M. van de Laar.** 2012. "Assessing Contingent Liabilities in Public-Private Partnerships (PPPs)." UNU-MERIT Working Paper Series 2012-030, Maastricht Economic and Social Research Institute on Innovation and Technology.

Taz, **Chaponda.** 2010. "Financing Infrastructure in Africa." Presentation, 2nd Africa PPP Conference, December 1–2.

UNECE (United Nations Economic Commission for Europe). 2008. *Guidebook on Promoting Good Governance in Public-Private Partnerships.* New York: United Nations.

World Bank. 2002. *Private Sector Development Strategy—Directions for the World Bank Group.* Washington, DC: World Bank.

———. 2012. *Transformation through Infrastructure: Infrastructure Update FY2012–2015.* Washington, DC: World Bank.

www.ingramcontent.com/pod-product-compliance
Lightning Source LLC
Chambersburg PA
CBHW082354270326
41935CB00013B/1617